ELLAND ROAD

e:males

by Dave.Shack @ Ononon.co.uk

The Parrs Wood Press
Manchester

FIRST PUBLISHED 2003

THE PARRS WOOD PRESS
St Wilfrid's Enterprise Centre
Royce Road, Manchester, M15 5BJ
www.parrswoodpress.com

© **Dave.Shack @ Ononon.co.uk** 2003

Cover design by LeeWalker@Grafix-fx.co.uk

ISBN: 1 903158 51 6

Printed and bound in Italy

Dedications

For 'Uncle' Brian -
whose tickets first took me to Elland Road.

For Len (Grandad) & Peggy (Nan)
- you'd have both been proud.

Acknowledgements

For all Leeds fans far & wide - be proud, be broad-shouldered & believe that one day we'll be back. Until that day keep marching. On on on...

To my Mum (Joyce), Dad (Tony) & brothers Richard & Craig, we may all be miles apart but we're still strong, close & united by this one great United. Also to Gran, Car, Lucy, Barbs, Andrew & Glynnis & Clare (welcome!)

To my Leeds Fan friends - Adam Woodgate (who inadvertently started this book!), Croz, Stuart & Family in Dubai, Eddie, Fraser, Mick & Shane Devine, Richard Adams, Shelley, Graham & the 'Raptors, Carol "Scam, Scam" Adams, Jim Rowlands, Radio Rhys, Olivia Hendrie, Tom Lascelles, Dave Mather, Mark Plunkett, Lyndsey at Elland Road, Duff Battye, Shonadh F, Big Andy, Ewen Pearson, Lisa & Darren Boston, Scouse, Wally, Eden Blackman, Robert Horsfall, Tim Delaney, Dave Steele, David Lascelles, Peter Bunch, Simon Hurd, Gavin Reeve, Joanna Jones' Anthony, Grainne's Darren, Guilherme's son Joao Pedro, Ben H, Patrick (AY), Steve Levitt, Paul Carr, Chalky, Steve Humphreys, Digger Barnes, Terry Edison, Brian Harris, John Reynolds, Tony Harlow, Pete Thompson, Tim Booth, Lee Farrar & all the Mavericks, 'Finchy', Andy Goodison, the Telford Bros, Peter Mc, 'Aunt' Molly, Jo Mc & Phil (Leeds, QPR, Fulham?) Hardy. The list goes on, on, on...

To the people who made this book possible - to my Agent, David Luxton @ Luxton Harris Ltd (There's more coming...just wait!), To Andy & the crew @ The Parrs Wood Press (Man U Fans can spot a good book even if it slags them off...), Nick (Chelsea scum I.T King!) Dann, Justin Slee (Main Photo), Nick (Boycee)@ Cool Breeze for the addresses & web site, Lee Walker for making my modern/retro (?) sleeve vision come true & Jackie, Lisa, Sarah, Laura, Rob and Craig @ The UK Centre for Events Management.

Thanks to all the professionals that encouraged me despite saying 'no' to the book, but never the format: Bill Scott-Kerr (Leeds Fan!), Stuart Slater, Gail Rebuck, Peter Burrell, Robert Dodds, Jake Lingwood, Christopher Little & Bill Campbell.

To the Monkeys - my golfing buddies who keep me sane & level headed ... and especially to Rich$ - the greatest Tottenham fan in the world and my best friend. Spurs Get!

Finally, to my wife, Nicki - who puts up with the sulks, the long drives, late returns, inaudible radio signals, last minute foreign travel, dodgy LUFC clothes and everything that football fans inflict on their nearest & dearest.

Nicki, you need to know that there is one thing you cannot change in life - your football team. For me there's two things... and I'd change Leeds before I changed you.

Dave Shack, July 9th 2003

Elland Road E:males
First XI: Season 2002-03

Andy@Whitetoreply.co.uk - Andy Lawson has been a Kop season ticket holder for 5 years & a Leeds fan for life. On the edge of dis-illusionment (O'Leary going was almost too much for him!) his typical Yorkshire stoicism sees him clutching a half-empty, not half-full, pint of Strongbow. Still based in Leeds, Andy has a unique place in this motley crew of ex-pats - he can get home from a match in 20 minutes!

Chris@Captaindom.co.uk Moylesy - the self-proclaimed saviour of Radio 1FM is a dyed in the wool Leeds fan who juggles a Radio & TV career with zipping up the M1 in his sexy 2-seater. A permanent fixture in the players' lounge & the bar at Leeds' Malmaison on match days. His on air rants are now legendary & provide welcome respite for Leeds fans the country wide.

Chris@Noredscum.co.uk - Tammsy (or beer boy to his closest friends) was public schooled in Harrogate, but graduated from the Elland Road stands. His humour, anger & hatred of all things emanating from the Comedy Tent are legendary. He's a music PR by trade, but rarely sugar coats anything when he's talking about Leeds.

Dorian@ThePeacocks.co.uk - can often be found in Shack's office at BMG Records discussing all things Leeds. Cup draws, afternoon Euro matches & LUFC web flashes all seem to coincide with 'high level strategy meetings' behind that same closed door. A seasoned traveller with & without LUFC, Dorian has lived in Spain & is in the process of a move to South Africa.

Russ@VivaLeedspana.esp is an ardent Leeds cockney and as befits this stereotype he now lives in Spain!. He & Shack met on April 26th '92 via a mutual friend. They were chased by a gang of Sheffield thugs that day, but the only injury they sustained was a broken tooth from Leicester Forest Services doughnut. Unable to buy a bottle of Champagne that night in Swiss Cottage they wrote a letter to the Government proposing a reform of the licensing laws & are still awaiting a reply...

Jeremy@Donsgloryears.co.uk Recently named in the Top 50 most influential Music industry players, Jeremy Lascelles, his brothers, father, nephews & now son are staunch Leeds fans. Refusing to let worldwide travel get in the way (and not getting the same abuse for his Elland Rd absence that Shack suffers!), Jeremy always seems to know what's happening at Elland Road and, more importantly, has an opinion on it.

DavidHarveysmonkey@aol.com is a top draw media player as well as a Leeds devotee & 'insider'. Anonymous for his insights, but refreshingly honest and applying less spin than either Ian Harte or the Leeds media machine, he is invaluable in his observations for the rest of the e:males to debate..

Dave.Shack@Ononon.co.uk See inside back cover

Firhad@Eltelasia.ma & then Firhad@FareastReid.ma is our Malaysia-based Leeds lover. Another work colleague of Shack's, they met in 1993 in Penang where Firhad received a worn Leeds shirt & a pin badge he still wears to this day. He may be 6500 miles away, but don't feel sorry for him, he sees more Leeds matches on TV than we do!

Nelly@whitellie-phant.co.uk is another 'insider' but much more a fan. Nelly has clocked up more miles following Leeds (& that includes the reserves & the youth team!!) than anyone I know. His knowledge of the M1 and international travel routes is second only to that of LUFC and there is no truth in the rumour that he is the spitting image of Jason Wilcox.

Rob@the-unforgiven.com is the acclaimed co-author of The Unforgiven, one of the best books ever written about Revie's Leeds. He joined Elland Road e:males during the Xmas transfer window on a free...and immediately made an impact by mentioning Joy Division as a soundtrack to Leeds' season!

CONTENTS

Introduction

They say that everybody has got at least one good book in them. I actually think I 've got more than that, but it has taken a kind of 'cheat' route to get that first one out.

I say 'cheat' because, at worst, this book is merely a collection of e:mails telling the story of Leeds United's either gruesome or glorious first season under new boss Terry 'El Tel' Venables. At best it is a unique, modern twist on a successfully tried & tested soccer book format that, whilst fiercely partisan, has (hopefully) a much wider appeal to football fans far and wide - and people who might just want to see what a whole book of e:mails looks like which isn't an instruction manual with a pre-fix like 'Any dummy can do this...'

Everyone gleans inspiration from somewhere & my particular catalyst was Neil Jeffries & Fraser Marr's 1997 Mainstream publication - "Love Hurts - Motorways, Madness & Leeds United". I was the occasional companion in his Canterbury Tales style pilgrimages to Elland Road under the sobriquet The Biggest Yorkshireman In London. With this immortality ensured, my first book was always going to be about Leeds United. It is.

A second, equally influential, book helped shape the genesis of this ambition. It provided the vehicle to make this book different from all the other football books - the book was M@tt Beaumont's (sic) fictional masterpiece "e".

For bringing this book &, therefore, this format to my attention I have to thank one of my worldwide work colleagues, then Senior VP, Asia Pacific & now CMO, Global Marketing (what a difference a season makes!) Mr Tim Prescott. I remember sitting in an Australian nightclub bar, beer in hand, bemoaning our e:mail culture. He told me I had to read this book "e" and that he would send me a copy. He did & my wife Nicki & I fought to finish it first. It was one of the best pieces of fiction I've ever read and in such a cool format. Yes, you guessed it, it was all e:mails.

Eight months later, after yet another long-haul business trip gave me sleeping problems, I finally sat upright in bed Eureka-style and felt that I had it (no, not a nudge from Mrs Shack!), but the exact twist I wanted to make this book something special in the linear passage of Leeds United books. If David O'Leary's Leeds United On Trial was a watershed for the club, then so too was this. The difference being that they wouldn't notice. Yes, I could see it - Leeds United would be the first club to embrace the technology of the new millennium, we would have beaten all comers to this brave new (book writing) world. Leeds 1 Rest of World (especially Man Utd) 0. Yeeeesssss!!!!!

To me the vernacular of e:mail is perfect to convey the passion that is football. Never mind the diction - you can express yourself so perfectly with CAPS, a whole line of exclamation marks !!!!!!!!!!!!!!!!!!!!!!!!!!!!!!!!!!!, bold, italics and now even emoticons:☺☹

We're at our most lucid, humorous, terse, flirtatious (although not in this book) & poignant best when conversing via e:mail. We're brave, audacious, witty, acerbic & concise. We're also long-winded, pompous, insincere and lazy. Welcome to this book where I *resemble* all of the above. In fact, it's not just me - it's a whole (almost) First Eleven of us. In fact, 'author' of this book is probably pushing it a bit - I'm more an editor, certainly a creator, but I haven't written it all.

It's a team effort - and what a team. If only Leeds could rely on such motivated, committed & creative geniuses then there would be no time to write a book, we'd all be out celebrating. The lion's share of the work has been done in a variety of styles, syntax & subjectivity that I could only have dreamed of when I picked the motley crew of Leeds fans to correspond with over a season. Expect typos, mis-spellings, non-sequeters. Expect not just split infinitives, but also split lines!

Spell check? Ha! Imagine using that to make Olly Dacourt into Carol Smiley's side-kick - Olivier Décor? What about star striker Mark Viduka becoming every Manager's nightmare as Mark Vodka? And I daredn't even type in Candsell-Sheriff to see what appears!

This is a communicative format that has been embraced so completely into football culture - from Five Live's 6.06 show taking more & more e:mail content, ditto Talksport and all the TV footy shows ever increasing their prevalence. Check out some of the message boards on football websites to see an army of word-smiths who certainly negate the claim that this country is losing its literary hegemony - it isn't, it's just going into cyber-space.

Join me and them in cyber-space and, who knows, you could be in a sequel!

On,on,on.

Dave.Shack@Ononon.co.uk
Chiswick, West London. Eve of 2002-2003 Season .

Elland Road E:males

File   Edit   View   Insert   Format   Tools   Message   Help

Match   Live   Press   Cup   Euro   Don't Spell
                                                                                                                ABC
Send   Report   Gooal!   Match   Undo   Check   Speculation   Match   Match   Check

Subject

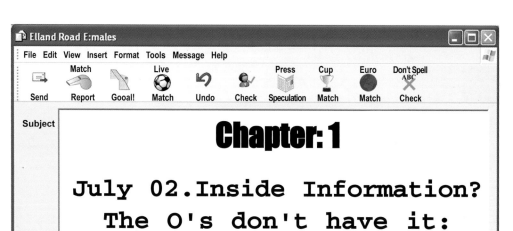

Chapter: 1

July 02.Inside Information?
The O's don't have it:
It's ELL and Tel!

Impact   18   B *I* U A

PREFACE:

And this is how it all started. O'Leary has gone & speculation is rife about his replacement. Cue a seemingly innocuous e:mail from a radio station pal up north which set forth the formation & then mailing of the 10 man 'team' referred to as **TheWhites, all 02/03 user group**. It was kind of spur of the moment to group these guys together, but it soon became as robust as if it were planned for a season or so. A couple of 'insiders' have to remain protected, but the rest of the guys are Leeds fans from around the globe - some work colleagues, some old pals & some music industry professionals. There may be some additions (come the transfer window in January!) but for now it's all we've got & it should provide the diversity that true fans often find & respect.

1

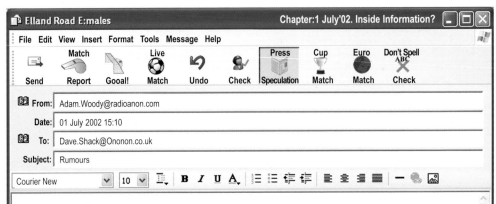

-----Original Message-----
From: Adam.Woody@radioanon.com
Sent: 01 July 2002 15:10
To: Dave.Shack@Ononon.co.uk
Subject: Rumours

Dave
I've heard there will be an announcement on the Leeds manager
within the next 48 hours.
Aparently William Hill have closed the book on taking bets on
Martin O'Neill...I wonder who it will be?

ADAM

-----Original Message-----
From: Dave.Shack@Ononon.co.uk
Sent: 01 July 2002 17:21
To: Adam@radioanon.com
Subject: RE: Rumours

pls be O'Neil. Pls, pls pls & not some third rate dick head

-----Original Message-----
From: Adam@radioanon.com
Sent: 02 July 2002 08:58
To: Dave.Shack@Ononon.co.uk
Subject: RE: Rumours

We're hearing there will be an announcement tomorrow, the
newsteam are awaiting confirmation...but we strongly believe
Ridsdale was in London on Friday to meet O'Neill. I know he
was in London, because I was on the same plane as him Friday
morning from Leeds Bradford.
We'll see...fingers crossed

2

Verdana | 10 | B *I* U A | ☰ ☰ ☲ ☲ | ☰ ☰ ☰ ☰ | — 🌑 🖼

-----**Original Message**-----
From : Dave Shack@Ononon.co.uk
Sent: Friday 5th July 2002
To: the Whites, all 02/03 group
Subject: A Tale of two O's - Leary & Neil.

Lads, an old radio mate tells me it's all on for O'Neil. PR (Ridsdale) was in London meeting him (my mate was on the flight & has an in!). He says William Hill has closed the book on him & his radio news-team are all ready for the story. Wicked! Great for us, unlucky for Old Trafford... hey! one of his first games will be against Rangers!! Fate or what?

-----Original Message-----
From: chris@Noredscum.co.uk
Sent: 5th July 2002 18:36
To: Dave.Shack@Ononon.co.uk
Subject: Re: A Tale of two O's - Leary & Neil.

Well, are these the same sources that said we'd have him last time?

He'd be a great acquisition if we can get him but I'm get terrible feelings of deja-vu.

Ridsdale could teach Alistair Campbell a few things about spin - is it true that he is making all the schools that he looks after use the Leeds Utd key stage schools books?

Its a shame O Leary's gone but perhaps now we can have a manager who knows that you can actually bring on substitutes.

-----Original Message-----
From: Jeremy@Donsgloryyears.com
Sent: 5th July 2002 11:17
To: Dave.Shack@Ononon.co.uk
Subject: RE: A Tale of two O's - Leary & Neil.

O'Neill's got to be the right choice. I wasn't so sure last time around in 98 (making the most of meagre resources at Leicester did not necessarily mean he could handle a bigger club with bigger players), but his success at Celtic has dispelled my doubts, and shown that above all he is a winner.

Century Gothic ▾ 10 ▾ 𝕴▾ **B** *I* U A̲ ▾ ☰ ☷ ⫶⫶ ⫶⫶ ☰ ☱ ☲ ☰ — 🖉 🖾

-----Original Message-----
From: Nelly@ theWhiteEllie-phant.co.uk
Sent: 5th July 2002 11:20
To: Dave.Shack@Ononon.co.uk
Subject: A Tale of two O's - Leary & Neil.

Shacky,
Could be... he's certainly not been allowed to splash the cash up ther.
Ridsdale must look like a Fairy Godmother to him in comparison with the
Bhoys' chairman. I'm a bit woreried about his thousdand yard stare, though.
Watch him interviews on TV, his eyes just go off in to the distance. Possible
horror movie material.

Nelly

-----Original Message-----
From: Andy@Whitetoreply.co.uk
Sent: 5th July 2002 21:11
To: Dave.Shack@Ononon.co.uk
Subject: Re: A Tale of two O's - Leary & Neil.

Dear Shack
Oh no, the ink's only just dry on my application to renew the old season ticket
(something I deliberated long and hard over this time around), and we have no
manager. O'Neil being in the frame is a good choice, but he would have to develop a
better sense of humour if in charge of Leeds. By this I don't mean because Leeds
are a joke, but we all know how much stick Allan Hanson gives us. Did you see how
touchy O'Neil was with Hanson's comments during the World Cup?
To be honest, I can't see it happening. I think that Martin still has a chance to prove
something with Celtic. Being dominant in Scotland is one thing, but proving it on the
International stage is another, and he has the team and the chance to prove it in
this years European Champions league. Also, I see him as a pretty honourable guy
who will stick by his commitments. However, should he come, it wouldn't be a bad
thing and I think it would be of benefit to us. Let's face it we certainly don't want BK
stepping up. Maybe Eddie G, but not BK, oh no, "Burger" that.
Sweeping wider afield, the only other person I would like to see would be Mick
McCarthy. Aha you might say if you were Alan Partridge, but it's not just that anyone
who gets the better of a spoiled brat like Roy Keane is top dog in my book, no no. I
think he is a great man manager, does well with adequate resources, and presents
himself well in the media spotlight.
Who else is being touted? Well there's El Tel, the man from hell, he uses words of
one Syla-bell. Please god not him. I can't stand a season of "The lads done good".
I'll keep the old fingers crossed and talk to you later. Cheers, Andy

Arial   10   B *I* U A | ≣ ≣ ⁇ ⁇ | ≣ ≣ ≣ ≣ | — 🌐 🖼

-----Original Message-----
From: chris@CaptainDom@.co.uk
Sent: 5th July 2002 18:34
To: Dave.Shack@Ononon.co.uk
Subject: Re: A Tale of two O's - Leary & Neil.

Is he related to Charlie O'Neal the model. I bloody hope so. We could do with a manager with a fit model daughter!

Moylesy

-----Original Message-----
From : Dave.Shack@Ononon.co.uk
Sent: Monday 8th July 2002
To: the Whites, all 02/03 group
Subject: Ell & Tel! (geddit?)

Well, sod my radio source - God only knows what they're broadcasting now? So here I am in the South of France, resting my broken ankle (don't ask) and spending more time in front of Sky Sports News than I am in the sun. (Yeah, Nicki's really bloody impressed, not!). I can't believe it. I'm shocked & I'm doing my best to come to terms with it. My step-brother Richard phoned to tell me & I told him it was a wind up & to piss off!

What's killing me is that I called Russ last week in Spain & wound him up that it was T.V & he nearly started crying. From one cockney talking about another he was gutted. Shit, I feel responsible...if only I hadn't done the wind up...

----Original Message-----
From: russ@vivaleedspana.sp
Sent: 08th July 2002 10:13
To: Dave.Shack@Ononon.co.uk
Subject: Re: -Ell & Tel! (geddit?)

BOLLOCKS!!! that's your fault shagger, thats what happens when you do stupid wind up's on your mates THEY COME TRUE!!!.
I thought O'Neil would come this time simply because of the media interest created, i just hope now that the club leave it along and never go after him again, he's made us look a bunch of wankers.
as for el tel, well he's the best of the bunch thats been left, tremendous

motivator, but i don't think he's the one, to be able to take us all the way to the title.
Fa Cup this season at best
rtb

-----Original Message-----
From: chris@Captaindom.co.uk
Sent: 8th July 2002 11:34
To: Dave.Shack@Ononon.co.uk
Subject: Re: Ell and Tel! (geddit?)

Get what?
El Tel !! My mate !!I only interviewd him the other week. If he'd have told me I could've made some cash!!

Was it a choice to pick him or were ITV Sport selling off their pundits? Suppose it's better then ending up with Gazza!!
Just imagine "The new manager of Leeds United .... Des Lynham"
Fucking ell .. tel!

Moylesy

-----Original Message-----
From: Wathen, Dorian, thePeacocks.co.uk
Sent: 8th July 2002 11:36
To: Shack, Dave, Ononon
Subject: RE: A Tale of two O's - Leary & Neil.

we're all going Ell Tel Crazy ... I don't think so.
Surely a stop-gap until someone sensible comes along without a second hand car dealership.
A few dodgy results and surely he'll walk (back to the Premiership panel with his mate Des)... hoping I'm proved to be talking bollocks.

-----Original Message-----
From: chris@noredscum.com
Sent: 8th July 2002 11:44
To: Dave.Shack@Ononon.co.uk
Subject: Re: ELL and Tel (geddit?!!)

Well you could have knocked me down with a feather (or should that be a Rolex?) - I've been asked by several people what I feel about El Tel - to be honest I've not come to a decision.

Courier New ▾ | 10 ▾ | B _I_ U A, | ≣ ≣ 拜 拜 | ≣ ≣ ≣ ≣ | — 🐌 🖼

He has the knack of bringing the best out of average players -
he may not have won a major title for a while but he knows
the game and lets face it he has tons of charisma (something O
Leary was sadly lacking in) and should get people talking
about for the right reasons. As a long time England travelling
supporter El Tel will always bring back fond memories lets
hope we get some silverware to go with it.
It was good to see that toellandback.com broke the story on
Friday none of the tabloids even mentioned it until Monday -
but then they all had it as an exclusive.

-----Original Message-----
From: Nelly@ theWhiteEllie-phant.co.uk
Sent: 08 July 2002 12:36
To: Dave.Shack@Ononon.co.uk
Subject: Re: Ell & Tel! (geddit?)

Just goes to show that even the best inside sources are unreliable. I got a
really hot tip it was McLaren from a very respected national newspaper.We
should have listened to Ridsdale - Venbales was the only name he ever
mentioned... It should be good, we've got the best squad we've ever had -
better (becasue it's bigger) than Revie's even, and yet O'Leary couldn't turn a
top-of-the-table team into anything other than a UEFA Cup qualifier.
We need a proven coach who can kick them all up the backside, let's hope
El Tel (Ell' Tel!) has got his size tens ready.

Shack

-----Original Message-----
From: Andy@whitetoreply.co.uk
Sent: 8th July 2002 18:18
To: Dave.Shack@Ononon.co.uk
Subject: Ell & Tel! (geddit?)

Oh Jesus. El Tel. No, what a nightmare. All my worst fears realised in that
appointment. The anti-christ of the footballing world is upon us and we must do his
bidding. Woe unto the whites.
It may just be me (and I'm sure it isn't), but does he give anyone else a feeling of
an impending slide down the ranks. Surely anything he is likely to be associated with
doing that turns out as a success will be because of others at Leeds, and anything
that turns out bad will be blamed on others.
Hey, I just don't like or trust the guy. However, if he is to have one redeeming
feature in my eyes, I hope it is that he proves me wrong. Time will tell us!
Yours in prayer mode

Times New Roman ▾ | 10 ▾ | ▤▾ **B** *I* U A̲ | ☰ ☷ ⫤ ⫥ | ▤ ▤ ▤ ▤ | — 🌐 🖼

-----Original Message-----
From: mailto:Jeremy@Donsgloryyears.co.uk
Sent: 8th July 2002 19:00
To: Dave.Shack@Ononon.co.uk
Subject: Ell & Tel! (geddit?)

Wouldn't have been my first choice. Too shady a past, and too many skeletons in the closet if the press are to be believed. And as for his singing aspirations....

On the other hand, we all know he is (or at least was) a top quality coach - players seem to love him and want to play for him. You'd hope this would put paid to the idea of Rio leaving, and would also expect him to get the best out of Harry again.

Trying to persuade myself it's a good appointment and do think it could work brilliantly, but please no jobs for all his old cronies. My greatest fear is waking up in the morning to read the headline "Leeds sign Dennis Wise", and please God, no Terry Fenwick!

Incidentally, am I the only person who thinks he is total crap as a TV pundit? Most of his so-called expert analysis is incomprehensible gibberish. If you don't believe me, try writing down on paper the actual words he uses next time he is on a TV panel. Perhaps we could start a competition for his most inane, grammatically twisted utterances.

-----Original Message-----
From: Firhad, Mohd, Eltelasia.ma
Sent: 09 July 2002 08:18
To: Shack, Dave, Ononon
Subject: Ell & Tel! (geddit?)

Got a mail form my boss Clive Gardiner (gosh MU supporter)...........El tel is with us?! Thats good news to me. Admired his work on Baraca and England.. Leeds need a new perspective on things. May blend a new found flow within the team. Adding some continental flair with the gritty determination and skills exhibited the last 3-4 years and exploiting our potentiual to the max. Titles in the shelfs. We need it badly. O'Leary is indeed good but last year his substitution exploitation remains a lot to be desired. maintaining an 11 when a new player may add up new alternative to changing the flow of the game. Sorry guys, think El tel will be alright !!!!!!!!

El tel will rule OK in Elland Road. Hope you noticed my private web address! Eltelasia.ma - that's how confident I am for him.

Firhad

8

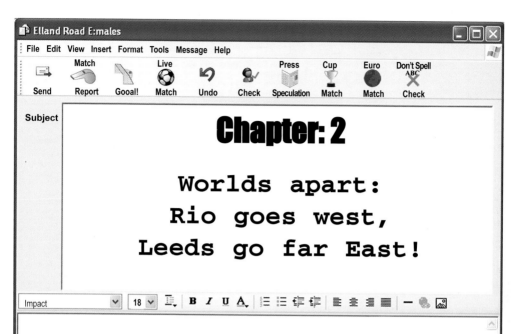

Chapter: 2

Worlds apart:
Rio goes west,
Leeds go far East!

PREFACE:

So, Ell Tel is installed at the helm of the good ship Leeds Utd & despite a mixed but overall optimistic reaction from all around the club, some dark clouds loom on the horizon. The boss makes it clear he's not for turning on the Rio situation - he stays! But, very soon, money talks & one of the finest players is leaving. That's bad enough, but when the proposed suitor is Man Utd, Ell Tel soon finds out the hard way about Yorkshire passion & loyalty. The Team go to Asia, but Big Nige, Batts &, of course, Rio stay behind...

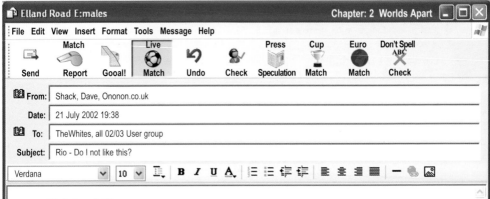

File   Edit   View   Insert   Format   Tools   Message   Help

Match			Live			Press	Cup	Euro	Don't Spell
Send	Report	Gooal!	Match	Undo	Check	Speculation	Match	Match	Check

From: Shack, Dave, Ononon.co.uk

Date: 21 July 2002 19:38

To: TheWhites, all 02/03 User group

Subject: Rio - Do I not like this?

Verdana   10   B   I   U   A

-----Original Message-----
From: Shack, Dave, Ononon.co.uk
Sent: 21 July 2002 19:38
To: TheWhites, all 02/03 group
Subject: Rio - Do I not like this?

Lads,

So the worst kept secret in football is out. Rio's off to t'other side o't Pennines. Ever since Fergie told Beckham & all the other Rag England lads to spend as much World Cup time working on our impressionable young lamb, this has had an air of dark inevitability about it. Despite El Tel giving us some (vain) hope of keeping him there's been more smoke around this deal than there was in the whole of the UK on November 5th last year. What's killer is that it's them. God it hurt when Eric did it -I remember seeing a piece on the news back in Yorkshire where some poor baker in Leeds had to chuck a whole basket of Cantona Croissants on the day Eric became a traitor. This actually, doesn't feel half as bad as that does it? Now, I know we've had a few off them - but Lee Sharpe hasn't exactly restored the balance has he? He only played one great game for us in a pre-season friendly in Ireland from what I remember. The rest was a waste of space - like a bloody Fergie Trojan horse.
Well, at least we got a pile of cash (although they should have paid every last bloody penny now!) and we might be able to plug some of our gaps with it.You know what? Writing this has made me realize that worse could have happened - imagine selling Harry to them or someone like Smithy (not that he'd ever do this, because he knows)- they would be 10 times worse. Shame Spider (O'Leary) & Co. made him so good, and made him skipper - but maybe it'll be the making of Woody. Hopefully Lucas has another year in him & with Dom we might be O.K. in the middle. Cover for Hartey & Mills is so blindingly obvious though it's frightening...and I don't like being frightened.

Courier New | 10 | B *I* U A | lists | align | —

-----Original Message-----
From: chris@noredscum.co.uk
Sent: 22 July 2002 18:34
To: Dave.Shack@Ononon.co.uk
Subject: Re: Rio - Do I not like this?

Rio is an absolute twat - end of story - this is an email
that I sent to his bigfanof.com website - personally I don't
think I swore enough...

*Well for a start I bet this email doesn't appear on your
website.*
*Thanks for being so loyal to a club that put you in to the
world footballing limelight.*
*To make it worse you are considering a move to Manchester
United - you know how Leeds fans feel about that club. Why are
you doing it - Champions League? Why not go to Real Madrid?
Bayern Munich? Liverpool? Arsenal?*
*All these teams have already qualified - but no you want to
go to Man U - oh how we would laugh at you if they didn't
even qualify.!*
We even make you captain and how do you repay us?
*You typify everything that is wrong with football - you make
an absolute fortune every week and then still want more - do
you have no idea how ordinary football fans' lives revolve
around how good your performance every Saturday is? Which lets
face it last season was hardly amazing.*
I hope you are happy with the decision you make
*Get the hell away from our club as quickly as possible you
lowlife!*

-----Original Message-----
From: chris@Captdom.co.uk
Sent: 22 July 2002 18:34
To: Dave.Shack@Ononon.co.uk
Subject: Re: Rio - Do I not like this?

Can just see the looks on the merchandise man's face at elland road!! Imagine that
conversation:

"Rio's gonna go?
You're joking?
He's promoting the new fucking strip!
There's posters of him all over the bastard shop!

Arial   10   B *I* U A

There's a special chapter about him on the end of season DVD for Christs sake!!
I can't believe that greedy bastard is gonna lose us shit loads of cash ... where's the
loyalty!!?

Oh well, we didn't need him anyway. I mean, it's not like he scored in the world cup
or anything is it!

Moylesy

-----Original Message-----
From: nelly@ whitellie-phant.co.uk
Sent: 22 July 2002 11:00
To: Dave.Shack@Ononon.co.uk
Subject: Re: Rio - Do I Not like this?

Sod Rio, if he doesn't want to play, I don't want him to stay. Bloody shame
though, innit? Plus - here's the best way to look at the whole deal: because
we thought we'd lose Woody we invested in the world's best defender for 18
months. Then, our biggest rivals give us £12 million quid. We're back in the
black - and get another England international centre-back in the squad on a
free!

-----Original Message-----
From: mailto:Jeremy@Donsgloryears.co.uk
Sent: 24 July 2002 19:25
To: Dave.Shack@Ononon.co.uk
Subject: Re: Rio - Do I Not like this?

It's at times like these that I seriously question why we invest so much of our time and energy
in worshipping the players who play for our team.
Many people I know who deal directly with professional football tell me that all players are
whores and mercenaries - it's hard to disagree. Where is the loyalty that we, the fans, show
those players? Would that there were more of the ilk of Gary Kelly; you seriously believe that
he would happily serve out his entire career at Elland Road, and I hope we give him the
opportunity to do that.

So, Mr. Ferdinand - what is there to say? I'm only going to repeat what I am sure every Leeds
fan will be saying here: we took an enormous gamble on a player that was clearly talented but
distinctly flawed less than two years ago. We gave him the opportunity to play on the
international stage, and to play in a system not designed to cover up his shortcomings (I'm
talking about West Ham's 3 central defenders), and help turn him into a true world-class player.
Not only that, but we make him captain of the club as well. And how does he repay us? By
engineering a situation to make sure not just that he leaves but he goes to our most hated rivals.

Times New Roman | 10 | B *I* U A | ≡ ≡ ≡ ≡ | ≡ ≡ ≡ ≡ | — 🌐 🖼

What a fucking act of treachery! What is the purpose of having contracts when you can walk out of one 18 months into a 5 year deal? He was on astronomical money anyway (and would certainly have got big rises from us over time) - I mean how much more fucking money do you need? And don't try to tell me that Ferguson didn't make sure that all the Man U players (including the England captain) tapped him up big time during the World Cup. What I can't believe is Rio's parting comment, that he's sure all Leeds fans would understand why he wanted to leave.

Yeah, sure, I can just see the banners unfurl at Elland Road on Sept 14 when the Scum come to town saying "Yes, Rio we really understand"!

-----Original Message-----
From: Andy@Whitetoreply.co.uk
Sent: 2nd August 2002 18:30
To: Dave.Shack@Ononon.co.uk
Subject: Not just Rio but Bowyer too...

The sagas of this pair just go to prove my point that loyalty is a word seldom found in the Top Flight footballer's vocabulary. "Money talks - and unless it's sorted I won't play I'll walk" may be a bastardised version of a Leo Sayer (??) song, but it certainly sums up their attitudes. Both of them have been treated well by Leeds and their names immortalised in songs from the cop.

Maybe Bowyer thinks that a fresh start is needed elsewhere, particularly with the civil case still weighing heavy on his shoulders, but Ridsdale seems to want him to stay and so did the fans. Me? Well yes I do too. For whatever else might flaw his character, he is still very talented and of great influence in our midfield.

As to Ferdinand, well I can't believe after the great treatment he has had at Leeds, 18 months later he's off to Man U. Jesie Creesie, how much does he want. Does he not understand the Leeds ManU thing? If this is how he wants to repay us then may he rot in hell on the lowest level of the Abyss being buggered by demons.

Andy "WhitetoReply" Laws

-----Original Message-----
From: Shack, Dave, Ononon.co.uk
Sent: 2nd August 2002 19:38
To: Andy@whitetoreply.co.uk
Subject: Curly hair or not curly hair?

Mate, try again with Leo Sayer. Think jewelry, think Jazz singer, think my mum loved him...?

13

Tahoma | 10 | B I U A

-----Original Message-----
From: Andy@whitetoreply.co.uk
Sent: 3rd August 2002 18:04
To: Dave Shack @ Ononon.co.uk
Subject: Curly hair or not curly hair...

I was very worried about the Leo Sayer bit anyway so I checked with my aged colleagues today and we think it should be Neil Diamond. Sorry.

-----Original Message-----
From: Shack, Dave, Ononon.co.uk
Sent: 3rd August 2002 19:38
To: Andy@Whitetoreply.co.uk
Subject: Re: Curly hair or not curly hair...

Well done mate - remember: "Money talks - but it don't sing & dance & it don't walk. 'Long as I can have you here with me, I'd much rather be...Forever in Blue Jeans, babe...."

Neil Diamond, "Forever In Blue Jeans"

-----Original Message-----
From: Andy@Whitetoreply.co.uk
Sent: 3rd August 2002 18:13
To: Dave Shack
Subject: Re: Curly hair or not curly hair...

I knew I could rely on you, being in the musak industry and all that!!

-----Original Message-----
From: Shack, Dave, Ononon.co.uk
Sent: 11 August 2002 13:32
To: TheWhites, all 02/03 User group
Subject: Rio - K.O! Oh the Lord moves in mysterious ways...

All the prayers, the voodoo Corinthian figure curse, the collective indignation of him leaving for them could all be solved if the reports in the Mail, Express & News Of The Screws are to believed. Rio's ankle has at best been twisted in a bungled & seemingly innocuous ballet dance with his own keeper Roy Carroll (where's baldy?) & Boca Jnrs striker Marcelo Delgado. 23 minutes in (Batty's squad number strikes again!) & he's off the pitch looking 'disconsolate'. A scan is booked for when the swelling goes down but if it's ligaments it could be 6 weeks out - and that could

14

Verdana   10   **B** *I* U A̲ | ☰ ☰ ☰ ☰ | ▬ ▦

mean the Leeds game. O sweet justice...
Signing Paul Okon? - if he's related to Paul Oakenfield we might be in
luck! Bet radioaire will be happy if he is. But another midfielder? - bet
Seth Johnson is feeling well loved at the moment.

On, On On...

-----Original Message-----
From: Andy@Whitetoreply.co.uk
Sent: 12 August 2002 21:19
To: Dave Shack
Subject: Re: Rio - K.O! Oh the Lord moves in mysterious ways...

"Ha ha ha ha ha ha ha ha ha ha ha ha ha ha ha ha ha ha. Now that's what I call
sweet music to my ears. I know they have a short career, but those at the top are
mainly money grabbing gits with little loyalty to the fans and clubs who give them a
big break. A little break in return is not enough punishment as far as I'm concerned,
and Man U deserve all the bad luck they can get. Hey I'm not bitter, but mine's a
pint to celebrate"
 Cheers bud. Be in touch soon. Andy

-----Original Message-----
From: Russ@Vivaleedspana.spa
Sent: 13 August 2002 09:31
To: Dave.Shack@Ononon.co.uk
Subject: Re: Rio - K.O! Oh the Lord moves in mysterious ways...

Yeh well there's nothing to excite at the moment with those too sighnings & sod
rio I aint talking about that wanker after what he done to us. Captain? - wanker.
It will be good to get under way on saturday to stop the bullshit talking and see
what some of our highly paid under acheivers can really do!!!!

Later. r t b

-----Original Message-----
From: chris@noredscum.co.uk
Sent: 12 August 2002 18:10
To: Dave.Shack@Ononon.co.uk
Subject: Re: Rio - K.O! Oh the Lord moves in mysterious ways...

Lets hope his nursing staff have been watching Kathy Bates in
Misery!! In fact I'm going to borrow the girlfriends nurses
outfit (don't ask!) and go and show him how disappointed I am

Courier New ▾ | 10 ▾ | **B** *I* U A | ≡ ≡ ≡ ≡ | ≡ ≡ ≡ ≡ | — 🔗 🖼

with his loyalty. Couldn't happen to a nicer guy - what's the
betting he suffers a resurgence of this injury immediately
before 14th September?

There may be a god after all

-----Original Message-----
From: Shack, Dave, Ononon.co.uk
Sent: 1st August 2002 13:32
To: TheWhites, all 02/03 User group
Subject: Far East not Farsley whites?

Lads, apart from Firhad & my Oz work colleague , Dicko - see his note
below- anyone got any contacts out there to ask about the matches? Are
we going there more for strategic than stamina & practice reasons?. The
games in Melbourne, Bangkok & China have,no doubt, done more for
football shirt bootleggers than BA airmiles recently did for Trevor Sinclair .
Whatever, the games (always described as against tough local opposition
- Hmm, Green Tea Town, or whatever they were called - and those giants
of South American football, Coca-Cola, sorry Como-Como should provide
us Leeds fans back home with a welcome distraction to the Rio saga
If not, at least there's a man (almost) on the spot: exiled Brit, Ian
Dickson who works for my record label, BMG in Sydney. A Birmingham
City Fan, he naturally hates Leeds. But here's what he said:

-----Original Message-----
From: Shack, Dave, Ononon, London
Sent: 01 August 2002 10:34
To: Dickson, Ian, BCFC-Australia
Subject: Mighty Whites Down under!

Dicko,
G'day mate! Well, we've beaten Green Tea Town, half the squad have
probably been round >to the Kewell household for a Barbie & we're about
to play the only team currently in Oz that isn't sponsored by booze :(hey
& that includes us!) Bring on Coca-Cola FC!! Mate, I hope you can get
your Brummie arse there this week & grab me a programme.
Cheers pastie, Shack.

-----Original Message-----
From: Dickson, Ian, BCFC-Australia
Sent: 02 August 2002 02:34
To: Shack, Dave, Ononon, London
Subject: FW: Kewell Wonder goal!

Georgia   10   B *I* U A

Shacky
Didn`t make it to Melbourne but saw the game, great goal, Aussies crowing about it,
him being a local boy and all that.
Talk soon. Dicko

-----Original Message-----
From: Shack, Dave, Ononon, London
Sent: 03 August 2002 01:34
To: Dickson, Ian, BCFC-Australia
Subject: Re: FW: Mighty Whites Down under!

Dicko,
Leeds give your UK soccer-starved arse a chance to see some real talent &
you stay at home drinking West Coast Cooler & eating pies with mushy
peas already inside 'em. If only you could get over your Birmingham
bigotry & the fact that you can't stand anywhere near a brick-wall since
1970 something...
Great goal? It looked like a bloody deflection to me! Great shimmies for
sure, but it wasn't quite reminiscent of the one vs your old enemies Villa
was it?
Oh well, can't wait for Aug 31st when we make you wish you were still in
Div 1 praying for a penalty to go in at the playoffs every May...
Shacky

-----Original Message-----
From: Dickson, Ian, BCFC-Australia
Sent: 03 August 2002 02:04
To: Shack, Dave, Ononon, London
Subject: FW: Kewell Wonder goal!

Mate,
F*ck off & we will never, ever release one of your company's poxy records here.
Zulus have your photo... so good luck on August 31st if you dare!
Dicko

-----Original Message-----
From: Shack, Dave, Ononon.com
Sent: Tuesday, August 06, 2002 7:48 PM
To: Firhad, Mohd, Eltelasia.ma
Subject: RE: Pre-season friendlies

don't suppose you got to Bangkok did you? Were there any good reports
out there about Leeds?

---Original Message-----
From: Firhad, Mohd, Eltelasia.ma
Sent: 07 August 2002 03:27
To: Shack, Dave, Ononon.co.uk
Subject: FW: Pre-season friendlies - -

Good report but Alan Smiths flare up was highlighted but it was fair as they say that he was roughed up as well. I miss that match. Damn......sorry to let you down as first correspondent of the book. Still am very Leeds for you guys.

-----Original Message-----
From: Shack, Dave Ononon.co.uk
Sent: 07 August 2002 16:58
To: Fields, Robert Gersforever.net
Subject: Mighty Whites come for Revenge

Dear Sweaty,
You can run but you can't hide...if it wasn't for my broken ankle I'd be up there with you administering a football lesson. We stuffed Celtic in pre-season before so you're next. You can't keep living on '92 forever - and you can't say that either Hately or Robertson did us any favours in the Premiership.
Get me a programme & give our Irish lads a break.

-----Original Message-----
From: Fields, Rob, Gersforever.com
Sent: 07August 2002 17:00
To: Shack, Dave, Ononon.co.uk
Subject: Out of Office AutoReply: Mighty whites come for revenge!

I will be working away from the office for 2 weeks from August 5th. I will be contactable by mobile & will collect these e:mails daily. Please do not call during the Rangers vs Leeds game as my language may cause offence. Oh, 1992 - what a year! Hately & McCoist God bless You.

Kind regards,
Robert
P.S. Shack I know you'll e:mail me.

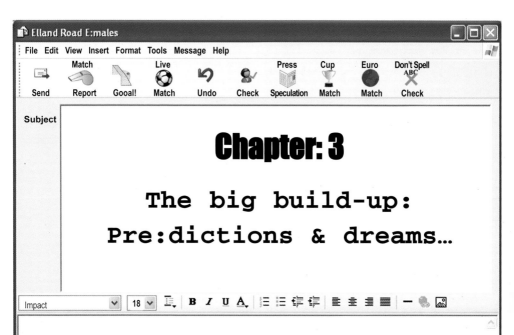

File   Edit   View   Insert   Format   Tools   Message   Help

| Match | Live | | Press | Cup | Euro | Don't Spell |
| Send | Report | Gooal! | Match | Undo | Check | Speculation | Match | Match | Check |

Subject

Chapter: 3

The big build-up: Pre:dictions & dreams...

Impact | 18 | B *I* U A | ☰ ☰ ☰ ☰ | ☰ ☰ ☰ ☰ | —

PREFACE:

After a pretty average pre-season, after showing a net debit on the playing squad left, the season is amongst us and like all great pundits - we all have to nail our colours (white with yellow & blue trim!) to the mast. Rule: If in doubt - let the heart rule the mind & let those age old football prejudices come flooding out...

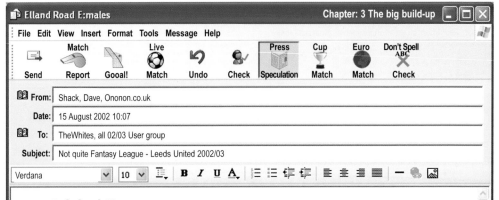

-----Original Message-----
From: Shack, Dave, Ononon.co.uk
Sent: 15 August 2002 10:07
To: TheWhites, all 02/03 User group
Subject: Not quite Fantasy League - Leeds United 2002/03

O.K. - here's the chance to record, for posterity, your predictions for the coming season. You've seen the friendlies, read the papers, now it's time to get stuck in. As a guide I'll give you mine, but just delete & replace my opinions with yours.

1. Top 3 - Arse, Scum. Leeds
2. FA Cup - Leeds
3. Golden Boot - Van Miss-a lot (Scum)
4.First Manager to go: (Cheer Up) Peter Reid
5. First major Leeds player to go: Nigel Martin
6. Score vs City: 3-1 Leeds
7.Leeds Top Scorer: Viduka
8. Player Of The Season: Kewell
9. Team vs Man City:

Martin
 Mills, Radebe, Matteo, Harte
Bowyer, Dacourt, Kewell,Bakke
Viduka, Keane

10(i)Best Case Scenario (Season): Leeds are not far off the pace all season with lots of goals coming from midfield. Robbo keeps swapping starts with Big Nige to become the #1 next season. We beat Man U early on & Rio get's sent off. Fergie goes mad & has Roy Keane lecture him. Rio laughs at him & they fight in the Red Cafe infront of a school party visiting from Surrey. In Europe we have an easy run to the final where we play Scum (having just beaten them in the Worthington Cup Final) and beat

Verdana   10   B *I* U A |

them again (they of course, dropped out of the Champions League early after the above bust up & subsequent sale of Rio to Barcelona). We finish Runners up to Arsenal in the league & have an FA Cup Final against them in which Alan Smith scores with a diving near post header. 1-0. Bowyer re-signs for 5 years & plays for England with Woody. Tel get's Manager of the year & retires to allow Martin O'Neil to say, "get stuffed Celtic & Man United - I always did want the Leeds job, but Ridsdale said I wasn't quite ready for it yet."

10(ii)Worst: Bowyer, Nige, Hartey, Dacourt & Keaneo leave before August 31st for not a lot of money. Woody & Dom get injured in training & Viduka & Dubes have to play in the centre of defence. In the Uefa Cup we lose in the first round to FC Zalaegerszeg, the team that Man Utd beat 15-0 after having lost the first leg 0-1. Birmingham City beat us twice & wreck our ground so we have to play at Valley Parade for the rest of the season. Fortunately this clears the way for Wetherall to make a sneaky return in defence without anyone noticing and we finish just above the drop zone. El Tel writes a soap opera about the Club with Sheree Kewell as the lead. Eric Cantona makes his TV acting debut as her love interest & because of some bizarre equity rules we have to swap all our players for the muppets on Sky's Dream Team - which pretty much buggers us for the following decade. The Soap Opera will be called not Eldorado, but TelBravado - which we all believed when he arrived at the club.

-----Original Message-----
From: Firhad, Mohd, Eltelasia.ma
Sent: 15 August 2002 10:34
To: Shack, Dave @Ononon.co.uk
Subject: Not quite Fantasy League - Leeds United 2002/03

Here's mine..........Long Live Leeds !!!!!!!!!!!

1. Top 3 - Leeds, Arse, Liver
2. FA Cup - Leeds
3. Golden Boot -Viduka
4.First Manager to go: (Cheer Up) Peter Reid
5. First major Leeds player to go: Nigel Martin
6. Score vs City: 2-0 Leeds
7.Leeds Top Scorer: Viduka
8. Player Of The Season: Kewell

10. Team vs Man City:

Batang   10   **B** *I* U A

Martin
 Mills, Woodgate, Matteo, Harte
Bowyer, Dacourt, Kewell,Bakke
Viduka, Keane

Best Case Scenario (Season):
Leeds are all set for the title on the word go !!!!!! M. City bites the
bullet in a flash.El tel worked miracles with Middlesboro with scarce
talent but with Leeds its only fine tuning a well oiled machine.
Underestimated to win the league, El tels weave his magic circa 80's Barca
and Leeds triumph on the first attempt. Scum sets forth to vent their
venom on Leeds but we hang on and beat em' out right and Rio, oh Rio! He's
all down and close to tears. The Leeds fans chanting "Now y'know Rio...El
tel Rules OK !!!!!!!!!".Keano looks on and Wetherall says "You ain't got
me".......Haaland says "serves you right" and Ireland moves on minus
Keano.
In the UEFA we go all the way to the finals and a treble in sight with the
League Cup in hand.El Tel is indeed the messiah and O Neill has to wait
another year for the transition. Robbo will now be ready to take
over.........

Worst:
Viduka dries up.........Rob Keano should have been sold. Smithy gets a
shot at Lennox lewis world title after another skirmish with Scums' Keano.
El Tel tries to work up the team after a 10 match no win slump. Tells
Bryan Kidd to back off and gets the team geared up for a Spanish training.
Employs a matador and each player will run as fast as they can to nod at
the red cloth. Instantly the magic works. Leed overcome the slump and lose
out in the Quarters of The FA Cup. El tels' instant success in Barca is
now revealed. El tel writes a book on soccer mental strenght -" The
Matador and The Peacocks".

Firhad

-----Original Message-----
From: chris@noredscum.co.uk
Sent: 15 August 2002 11:26
To: Dave.Shack@Ononon.co.uk
Subject: Re: Not quite Fantasy League - Leeds United 2002/03

1. Top 3 - Arse, Scouse Twats, Scum
2. FA Cup - Leeds
3. Golden Boot - Van Horse Face (Scum)
4.First Manager to go: Tigana (Fulham)

22

Courier New   10   **B** *I* <u>U</u> **A**   ≡ ≡ ≡ ≡   ≡ ≡ ≡ ≡   — 🔗 🖼

```
5. First major Leeds player to go: Village (Martyn)
6. Score vs City: 2 - 0 (Viduka, Smithy)
7.Leeds Top Scorer: God (Fowler)
8. Player Of The Season: Smithy
10. Team vs Man City:

Robinson
 Mills, Woody, Matteo, Harte
Bowyer, Dacourt, Kewell,Bakke
Viduka, Smithy
```

Best Case Scenario (Season): Scum don't even qualify for Champions League and get knocked out by one of the Inter Toto qualifiers in the first round of the UEFA cup.
We win a trio of cups (FA, Worthnothing and UEFA) and qualify for Champs league. Ridsdale actually learns to keep his mouth shut for more than 10 minutes. Bowyer signs a five year deal and goes on along with Smithy, God and Robinson to be England first choice players. Chelsea go bankrupt and Jimmy Floyd Piggybank has to go back on the bins.

Worst: Munich win something. El Tel and Ridsdale release a gangster rap charity record "Show me ya Rolex" which goes to number one for 20 weeks. Bowyer and Kewell leave to play for the Scum.

-----Original Message-----
From: Jeremy@Donsgloryears.co.uk
Sent: 15 August 2002 12:07
To: TheWhites,all 02/03 User group
Subject: Not quite Fantasy League - Leeds United 2002/03

O.K. - here's the chance to record, for posterity, your predictions for the coming season. You've seen the friendlies, read the papers, now it's time to get stuck in. As a guide I'll give you mine, but just delete & replace my opinions with yours.

1. Top 3 - Arse, Scum. Liverpool
2. FA Cup - Leeds
3. Golden Boot - Duberry (own goals!)
4.First Manager to go: (Cheer Up) Peter Reid
5. First major Leeds player to go: Robbie Keano
6. Score vs City: 2-0 Leeds
7.Leeds Top Scorer: Viduka
8. Player Of The Season: Kewell

9. Team vs Man City:

Robinson
 Mills, Woody Matteo, Harte
Bowyer, Barmby Kewell,Bakke
Viduka, Smith

Best Case: Ridsdale wins the lottery & Venables makes billions in an offshore investment finally coming good. They bank roll Leeds all the way, buying back Rio for a decent (ie half) price, refuse to sell any other players and we win the treble.

Worst Case: Venables is revealed as the redundant, has-been manager he is who spends more time on TV talking gobbledy gook than at Thorpe Arch.

The PLC have to flog the whole First XI and we build a team around Barmby, Sicknote, Okon & Gazza that just manages to stave off relegation by beating Tottenham on the last day of the season…

-----Original Message-----
From: Wathen, Dorian, The Peacocks
Sent: 15 August 2002 15:08
To: Shack, Dave, On,on,on.
Cc: Firhad,Mohd
Subject: RE: Not quite Fantasy League - Leeds United 2002/03

Top 3 - Arsenal/Leeds/Man U
FA Cup - Liverpool - we do rubbish in the cup.
Golden Boot - Judas (JFH)
First Managerial Casualty - Ranieri (Reid is too obvious) DOL joins Chelsea as manager ...
First Major Leeds player to leave - Kells
Score vs City - 2-1
Top Leeds Scorer - Viduka
Player of Season - Harry - no doubts. This is his season.
Team vs Man City:

Robinson, Mills, Harte, Dacourt, Matteo, Radebe, Bowyer, Bakke, Kewell, Viduka, Smith.

Best case - Arsenal & Man U match starts with 22 man on-pitch brawl - all players are suspended for the duration of the season and are deducted 20 points each thus leaving the path clear for the title.
Kewell scores 20 goals in inspirational season but thoughts of a transfer to Real Madrid disappear as he gets crocked in 90th minute of UEFA cup final after

Century Gothic   10   **B** *I* <u>U</u> **A**,   ≣ ≣ ≣ ≣ | ≣ ≣ ≣ ≣ | — 🌐 🖾

scoring winning hatrick - out for 3 months.

Worst - Arsenal and Man U are 20 points clear by Xmas and we're out of all the cups, prompting mass player exodus and Terry Chemicals turns to drink & drugs as reported in a News of The World exclusive.

-----Original Message-----
From: DavidHarveysmonkey@aol.com
Sent: 15 August 2002 18:51
To: Dave.Shack@Ononon.co.uk
Subject: Re: Not quite Fantasy League - Leeds United 2002/03

1. Top 3 - Newcastle, Man U, Arsenal
2. FA Cup - Leeds
3. Golden Boot - Beattie
4.First Manager to go: (Cheer Up) Peter Reid
5. First major Leeds player to go: Dacourt
6. Score vs City: 3-0 Leeds
7.Leeds Top Scorer: Viduka
8. Player Of The Season: Kewell
9. Team vs Man City:

Martin
 Mills, Radebe, Matteo, Harte
Bowyer, Barmby, Kewell,Bakke
Viduka, Smith
Best: we win everything except the Champions League, all the big players re-sign for years &
Batty is player of the season having scored a goal every other game
Worst: we win bugger all, we lose all our best players & batty gets frozen out by Venables. Oh &
Man U win a treble with us beating Arsenal & Newcastle right at the run-in…

-----Original Message-----
From: russ@Vivaleedspana.esp
Sent: 16 August 2002 09:51
To: dave.shack@Ononon.co.uk
Subject: Fwd: LEEDS UTD WINNING THE TITLE - FANTASY!

oy calm down san (as Dom would say) anyone would think it was cross that sent that e-mail!
Ok e're we go:
>
>1. Top 3 - Arse, Us, Scousers

Comic Sans MS   ∨   10 ∨   ≣,   **B** *I* U A,   ≣ ≣ ≢ ≢   ≣ ≣ ≣ ≣   — 🌐 🖼

>2. FA Cup - Leeds
>3. Golden Boot - Terry On Re(how due say that French letters name)
>4.First Manager to go: (Cheer Up) Peter Reid
>5. First major Leeds player to go: Ian art art art
>6. Score vs City: 4-1 Leeds
>7.Leeds Top Scorer: Fowler
8. Player Of The Season: Woodgate
>10. Team vs Man City:
>
>Robinson
> Mills, Radebe, Matteo, Harte
>Bowyer, Dacourt, Kewell,Bakke
>Viduka, Keane
 > Is that ok or did you want me to fill in the best and worst case scenarios?
good luck sat
I thought your e-mail was fabxxxxxxxxxxxxxxxx

-----Original Message-----
From: Chris@Captdom.co.uk
Sent: 16 August 2002 18:47
To: Dave.Shack@On on on
Subject: Re: Not quite Fantasy League - Leeds United 2002/03

Before you read mine, and I have to stress this AGAIN. I know as much about
football as Stevie Wonder knows about doing jigsaws. That said .. here we go:
1. Top 3 - Arse, LEEDS, Man u
2. FA Cup - Leeds
3. Golden Boot - dunno
4.First Manager to go: go where .. on holiday?
5. First major Leeds player to go: Trevor Cherry
6. Score vs City: 2-1 Leeds
7.Leeds Top Scorer: Kewell (wishing)
8. Player Of The Season: Smith
10. Team vs Man City: same as yours!
and where was number 9 shacky you daft twat!!
Best Case Scenario (Season): Leeds fly to the top and battle it out with Man City and
Arsenal all season beating them both to win the title. Manchester United are
BANNED from the premiership for selling illegal dodgy videos from the back of
Ferguson's car at the local car boot. Rio decides it's all too much, leaves footbal and
opens a wine bar called Rio's. Chelsea sell 5 players becasue Ken Bates' missus
wants a new conservatory. Alan Smith starts dating Kylie and she becomes a regular
at Elland Rd.

Worst: Risdale turns out to be a robot from the red planet and swaps all the first team with ex-bradford players. Sir Alex shags Kylie and Rio becomes mayor of Manchester. Alan Smith turns gay and starts a relationship with Robbo. Robbo doesn't save ONE goal. cos he's too busy looking at Al's arse!!
Told you I know F**K all about the game X

-----Original Message-----
From: Andy@whitetoreply.co.uk
Sent: 16 August 2002 22:32
To: Dave Shack
Subject: Re: Not quite Fantasy League - Leeds United 2002/03
Here's my predictions:

1. Top 3 - Arse, Leeds and Liverpool
2. FA Cup - Newcastle
3. Golden Boot - Owen
4.First Manager to go: Peter Reid
5. First major Leeds player to go: Nigel Martin
6. Score vs City: 2-1 Leeds
7.Leeds Top Scorer: Keane
8. Player Of The Season: Smith
9. Is this a free one?????
10. Team vs Man City:

Martin
Mills, Radebe, Matteo, Harte
Bowyer, Barmby, Kewell,Bakke
Viduka, Smith
Subs that will be used: Dacourt, Keane and Batty
Best case Scenario: WE win everything after El Tel resigns early and is replaced by Eddie Gray. Scum get relegated by Easter and Leeds announce a free pint to each season ticket holder for each game. Alternatively I would settle for one piece of silverware.
Worst: We win bugger all & Terry stays with us 'cos we can't afford to pay him off. We start playing Europe's "The Final Countdown" before home games... Jeez that's bad...

Enjoy L.A. Andy

-----Original Message-----
From: nelly@whitellie-phant.co.uk
Sent: 16 August 2002 14:14
To: Dave.Shack@Ononon.co.uk

Century Gothic   10   **B** *I* U A

Subject: Re: FW: Not quite Fantasy League - Leeds United 2002/03

1. Top 3 - Arsenal, Man United, Leeds
2. FA Cup - Arsenal
3. Golden Boot - Thierry Henry
4. First Manager to go: Peter Reid
5. First major Leeds player to go: Nigel Martyn
6. Score vs City: 1-0 Leeds
7. Leeds Top Scorer: Viduka
8. Player Of The Season: Kewell
10. Team vs Man City:
Robinson, Mills, Radebe, Matteo, Harte, Bowyer, Bakke, Barmby, Kewell, Viduka, Smith

Best Case Scenario (Season):
O'Leary's' squad plus Venables' nous = Championship

Worst:
Another bloody season without silverware.

-----Original Message-----
From: Shack, Dave, On on on
Sent: 16 August 2002 16:51
To: TheWhites, all 02/03 User group
Subject: LUFC Season 2002-3

Lads,

Could we be more excited? Shame about Woody, maybe a shame about Nige? But great for Lucas to be back. We all seem to feel there's a win there for us tomorrow so let's hope there is.

I'm away to L.A. tomorrow on business but my mobile works -so any updates would be gratefully received for when I land.

Enjoy it wherever you may be tomorrow & somebody pls tape me The Premiership (or Firhad, the whole match if you've got it!).

Marching on...on...on

-----Original Message-----
From: Nelly@whitellie-phant.co.uk
Sent: 16 August 2002 17:40
To: Dave.Shack@ononon.co.uk

Century Gothic | 10 | B *I* U A

Subject: Re: LUFC Season 2002-3

Actually, yes I could. I have absolutely no idea what to expect and go into this season with a strange nervous feeling in the pit of my stomach. It could be wind but I'm an expert on that, too. I have strangely alternating visions of Harry Kewell scoring and sulking. 1-0 tomorrow, just you wait and see.

```
-----Original Message-----
From: Firhad, Mohd, Eltelasia.ma
Sent: 15 August 2003 18:35
To: Shack, Dave, Ononon.co.uk
Subject: FW: LUFC Season 2002-3

All geared up for the new premier league. Last season's line up and a new
manager of great credentials. A Top 3 is what we should be looking
at...........A great perspective of new tactics incorporating continental
and Leeds gritty staright ahead attacking mode.

Come City ....you are on .
```

-----Original Message-----
From: Chris@captaindom.co.uk
Sent: 16 August 2002 18:51
To: Dave.Shack@Ononon.co.uk
Subject: Re: LUFC Season 2002-3

Managed to get 2 tickets for tomorrow. East Stand. Gonna wear my new white top with SMYITH 17 on the back. The girl at the shop was dyslexic.

Robbo's gonna be a star, cos he's got a point to prove.

City are gonna fight hard cos they've got a point to prove.(and 3 to win!)

Used to sitting in the west stand so am looking forward to lots of singing and cheering the lads on. Who knows, might even treat myself and have a pasty.

Marching on together, we're gonna see you . . . . .

* FOR THE RESULTS OF THIS LITTLE PREDICTORAMA : SEE APPENDIX

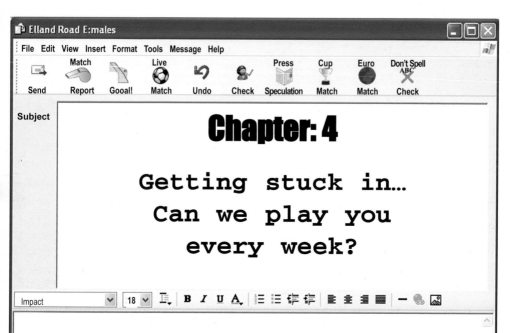

Chapter: 4

Getting stuck in... Can we play you every week?

PREFACE:

For the first time in many a season, I've had to miss the opening match. This time I'm away in L.A. - or actually on the way there as the game gets underway. But don't worry...steps have been taken to ensure I know exactly what's happening. There's nothing like the first weekend of the season and this was no exception...

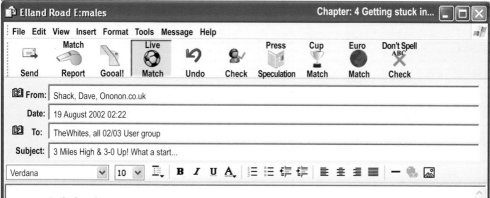

Elland Road E:males   Chapter: 4 Getting stuck in...

File   Edit   View   Insert   Format   Tools   Message   Help

Match   Live   Press   Cup   Euro   Don't Spell

Send   Report   Gooal!   Match   Undo   Check   Speculation   Match   Match   Check

From: Shack, Dave, Ononon.co.uk

Date: 19 August 2002 02:22

To: TheWhites, all 02/03 User group

Subject: 3 Miles High & 3-0 Up! What a start...

Verdana   10   B   I   U   A

-----Original Message-----
From: Shack, Dave, Ononon.co.uk
Sent: 19 August 2002 02:22
To: TheWhites, all 02/03 User group
Subject: 3 Miles High & 3-0 Up! What a start...

Lads - 3-0! Unbelieveable. Barmby too! Wow...2nd in the fledgling table I guess! Awesome. Lucas 'Man Of The Match" - wow!
The highlights were on ESPN 2 last night & I bloody missed 'em. Concierge bloke said - "Yeah, man -Leeds United - they're like baad ass, right! They have all the tough players from prison & stuff. Man they're cool. I love Leeds. I gave him my new Leeds T-Shirt & told him to keep up the good work! Don't think Ridsdale will thank me for that though...

Cheers to Moylesy for his mid-match e:mail which I got when we landed in L.A. Fortunately the wife was ordered to be by teletext & the phone at 5pm and so for £24 I called from 36,000 feet above Thunder Bay nr Lake Winnipeg. We were 3662 miles from Heathrow having gone North anyway so make that 3462 from Elland Road at minus70 degrees F (Kewell & Viduka would have worn their gloves!!) and crusing at 516 mph (according to the map thing on channel 59).

A 3-0 win! Mate,that was better than any Mile High Club entry...and the feeling has lasted a whole lot longer.

Gimme some vibes back guys - how was Robbo? Crowd? How lucky were man U to scab a 1-0, etc, etc.

Cheers ,

Shack
-         Flying on together, we're gonna see you win!

Comic Sans MS | 10 | B *I* U A

-----Original Message-----
From: Russ@VivaLeedspana.spa
Sent: 19 August 2002 10:45
To: Dave.Shack@Ononon.co.uk
Subject: Re: Oh Joyous L.A. vibes...

Dave Hola!

Due to my position on the map which i do not know the longitude south, i am unable to give you my feedback on crowd reaction! but i will do my best on the game:
Having lost our last two home games to City i think it was time that certain players on the park today made amendes.
And how! superb goal, taken with all the panache of a 30 goal plus season striker and that was our second! keep the diet going Cobber!
What a start for our man "Nicky Barmby, Nicky Barmby hello hello"
....................and he'll do that all season and my prediction that he'll play (i had a change of mind on friday afternoon sent you e-mail and had it returned i sent it again this morning so check the date) was a good call.
Dom & Lucas looked solid at the back so when Woodies back we should get stronger and stronger-this is where i ask for prayer for an injury free season.
Theres only one Keano theres only one Keano.................. who on earth gave the media a load of bull about we would swap him for sicknote!! hes fucking class pal and he was taking the piss with that class finish.
Graham poll needs to open he's fucking eyes, tosser-great to see Smithy not reacting, let hope he's grown up now.
after thoughts, el tel was happy but seems to like giving away alot of our game plan for others to pick up on, so it would be nice if he kept his trap shut.
Keegan honest as always, knew he had been outwitted, out classed by a far superior tactition.
LeedsLeedsLeeds marching on together...
ps, interesting comments by DO afterwards for the reasons behind he's sacking, he's Leeds through and through and not one of us would disagree with wanting ferdinand to go anywhere else but scum, we shouldn`t forget that is what he wanted for the fans and the injurys he was plagued with and of course the the court case saga
i think ....HE'll BE BACK
RTB

-----Original Message-----
From: chris@CaptDom.co.uk
Sent: 19 August 2002 12:59
To: 'Dave.Shack@Ononon.co.uk
Subject: 3 goals... 3 points

How cool was that?

So I drove up the M1 on Saturday morning. Checked into the hotel. Met my mate
and off we went. Sat down in our seats at 2.59. Left just after 5 very happy.
3 goals, could've been more. Then again was amazed City didn't score. They were
unlucky with that score line, we were lucky.
Few missed chances, few fuck ups. One dreadful kick back to Robbo from Bo, which
almost caused us a goal. It was a sitter for City
Smithy looked a bit pissed off. Don't know if it was cos he didn't score. (He has done
in the opening game for the past couple of years)
Lucus and Dom worked well together. Dukes looked good, played well but could've
been better (I love criticising when I can't play myself!)
Think this is gonna be a top season!!
Got you a programme too!!
Now don't go away to LA and miss a game again
Chris (got to wear my new smithy shirt) Moyles

-----Original Message-----
From: nelly@whitellie-phant.co.uk
Sent: 19 August 2002 09:27
To: Dave.Shack@Ononon.co.uk
Subject: 3 Miles High & 3-0 Up! What a start...

Wish I'd been there, too. First time in ages I've ever missed a first game of the
season too. My excuse? Missus' birthday so I was doing my best John Wayne
riding round Wimbledon Common. Actually, make that: my worst John
Wayne walking round Wimbledon Common. But at Leeds Ell Tel's lads won by
three clear lengths!!!

-----Original Message-----
From: Andy@Whitetoreply.co.uk
Sent: 19 August 2002 17:43
To: Dave.Shack@Ononon.co.uk
Subject: Re: 3 Miles High & 3-0 Up! What a start...

Feel a touch of Humble Pie may be in the air for me if this keeps o, but as long as
the boys are winning, who cares. Crowd was pretty lively singing for Bowyer to sign
for us. It was bloody hot and the lads ran their socks off. I was hot sitting in the

Tahoma   10   **B** *I* U A

shade of the Cop so what it was like on the pitch can only be guessed at. Watching Kewell and Keane towards the end makes you wonder whether there is a possible partnership there that can be tested. Excellent to see Lucas back. He was awesome.

Andy

-----**Original Message**-----
From: Wathen, Dorian, The Peacocks
Sent: 19 August 2002 13:03
To: Shack, Dave, On,on,on
Subject: RE: 3 Miles High & 3-0 Up! What a start...

Excellent - he should form a supporters club - L.A.nd Road - shocking I know ...

Looked a little shakey at the back and in midfield at times - overplaying it and generally a tad casual - gave the ball away too much in midfield again - Eirik the main culprit - we need a younger McAllister/Batty in there - Carrick would be ideal - Man City had a few shocking misses and hit post/bar, so a bit lucky not to concede.

Saying that - Keane looked great and Kewell looked back to something like former self - Barmby scoring one and making one was prob the MOTM. Robinson looked solid and made some great saves.

-----**Original Message**-----
From: Jeremy@Donsgloryyears.co.uk
Sent: 20 August 2002 10:48
To: Dave.Shack@Ononon.co.uk
Subject: Re: 3 Miles High & 3-0 Up! What a start...

Well, it was a pretty enjoyable day in the end. Bit weird though - there we were 2-0 up at halftime and I thought we'd played pretty crap. Maybe Ell Tel has brought with him a few sacks full of good luck as well as his renowned tactical nouse. Very comfortable victory in the end though.
Plenty of good points from the day:
 - Robbo in goal (feel sorry for Nige though - probably over the past 6 years the best keeper we've ever had. Anyone disagree with that? David Harvey, maybe....)
 - Interesting and effective substitutions. Keano looking like he had a point to prove scored one absolute beauty, and then missed a sitter. And Viduka substituted - have we ever seen that before?
 - Liked the fluid system that we seem to have between the forwards and the midfield; plenty of movement and changing of positions. Barmby - dream debut, looks a bargain; Harry - did not look comfortable playing so narrow and so far forward in the first half, but much better second half when he went wider (on both flanks).

Times New Roman   10   B *I* U A | ≣ ≣ ⧾ ⧾ | ≣ ≣ ≣ ≣ | — 🦴 🖼

- Lucas - simply majestic; as good as he was a couple of years ago when the Man of the
Match Award became known as the Man of the Match Apart from Lucas Award.

-----Original Message-----
Firhad@Eltelasia.ma
Sent: 21 August 2002 14:31
To: dave.shack@Ononon.co.uk
Cc: The Whites, all 02/03 user group
Subject: Leeds vs M. City

What an opener. As predicted by yours truly "Man. City will bite the dust
fast". An assessment of the match.

Leeds new strategy of 4-3-3 alternating with 4-4-2 is an eye opener.
Kewell just behind the front 2 and at times the left flank is an eye
opener. The manner the goals were scored was of a master markmanship.
Barmby's goal is indeed what a poacher would sniff for. Speed is the
essence of Leeds frontline reminiscent of 99/00, 00/01.

El Tel's influnce over the team has clearly shown with a tight defensive
game and seem to push all players to a different level. Whats heartwarming
is that they are playing like a continental side would where on the
defense, they will pull as many people behind the ball. Matteo is a rock
and the silky skills and speed of Radebe makes one thinks "Who was it that
was in the center of defense last season ?". Man of the match indeed.

Robbo ??? Oh my. 3 great saves marks a new goalkeeping force. Nigel may
find it hard to get back.

Am a big fan of El Tel. 2002/2003 will be ours !!!!!!!!!!!!!Will try to tape
for you my good Leed buddy. For the westlife match , the LUFC vs MUFC
jersey is on. MUFC for Westlife and BMG staffs whilst LUFC for RTM (radio
deejays) and local artists. I will than play for RTM as will never ever
wear MU.
Understand MU is loved by all of Westlife and Clive also other BMG staffs.
Hope my good Shacko will come and play alongside me.

Regards, Firhad

-----Original Message-----
From: chris@noredscum.co.uk
Sent: 22 August 2002 14:28
To: Dave.Shack@Ononon.co.uk
Subject: Re: 3 Miles High & 3-0 Up! What a start…

Courier New   10   **B** *I* U A

Sorry mate been busy as hell this week so I've only just found time now to reply.

The guys looked great the defence was good - Rioscum is totally un-needed - the biggest cheers of the day were for the mighty chief's return. Robbo looked great in the nets and I recon Sven will soon have him in the England squad.

Certainly one of the better opening day performances from the lads.

Man U were decidly average (the goal was offside but linesmen aren't allowed to flag at that ground) - Liverpool were the same - Arsenal were f**king awesome against B'ham on the Sunday live game and Newcastle looked pretty tasty on Monday - but it was against West Ham!

My strikers card finally arrived on Monday - that's only 8 weeks after I sent off the application - hopefully all my tickets will still come through as I booked them using the number on last years card. If not I'll be hassling everyone for a spare.

Thoughts for the Baggies on Saturday - think it will be difficult to start with - they did a great job against Munich - but I reckon we'll win 2-0 with Smithy getting both. Put it this way we better win - our CD manufacturer is based in the West Midlands and I have bets with about 30 people that we'll win.

I will be at the Reading Festival this weekend so I'll have to find somewhere to get the results from.

Enjoy LA. Chris

-----Original Message-----
From: Shack, Dave, Ononon.co.uk
Sent: 23 August 2002 19:19
To: TheWhites, all 02/03 User group
Subject: Boing, Boing! The Baggies are going down...

Lads! 3rd in the table - no goals conceeded - and the baggies up next. I'm not far from going to Mexico now, but I'm hopeful of finding a bar tomorrow for the match here in L.A. Looks like everyone at the club wants to stay & win something this season - which is great to read on the website & Football365 this week - especially Robbie Keane & Olly. Is Woody crocked? Link went down as I tried to open 'New Blow for Woody' - I'm praying it's a new hair-style, but I somehow doubt it. Let's hope for a draw tonight between the Red & Blue shite - pls send me a note on how 'loyalty' played - & is there any truth in Jimmy who? going to Barcelona? Oh please...

Being this far away at this crucial time is killing me, but optimism is burning hot & you'll be pleased to know that I've got a couple of great new superstitions that helped us on Saturday (sure, they did) & I'll be doing the same just as soon as I work out the time difference for Saturday's game!

On,On On...Shacky

-----Original Message-----
From: chris@noredscum.co.uk
Sent: 27 August 2002 10:46
To: Dave.Shack@Ononon.co.uk
Subject: Re: Boing, Boing! The Baggies are going down...

We are top of the league!!!

Bowyer scored one of the goals of the season - we again looked so good on Saturday - lets hope we can keep it up for the rest of the season. El Tel seems to have brought out a new sense of belief in the lads - we look like we may win something this season if this continues.

On a more personal note I have won several bets with our CD manufacturing company and look forward to collecting the money soon!

Newcastle, Arsenal and Manure have all dropped points so far this season - Liverpool are shaping up to be a force to be reckoned with this season - that Diouf looked very good. Arsenal went to sleep against the Hammers and only after West Ham missed a penalty did Arsenal wake up and claw their way back to a draw.

Well its the stadium of shite on Wednesday - lets hope Peter Reed will need cheering up on Thursday.

Courier New   10   **B** *I* U A

Chris

-----Original Message-----
From: russ@Vivaleespana.esp
Sent: 27 August 2002 11:33
To: Dave.Shack@ Ononon.co.uk
Subject: Re: Boing, Boing! The Baggies are going down...

My My Shagger you are missing out a bit out there, Top Top Top Top..........Top
of the league!
Sad isn't it getting so exited after just two games and against medioca
opposition!+
But has el tel says it will give the lads encouragement to keep things going and
build confidence.
It's amazing because they looked in the first half as if they were not confident
in themselves, harry hardly touched the ball, viduka seemed to go back into he's
world of dreams and the defence was, well i can't be to hard on them, lets just
say it was not good.
Although the first and third goals were great in there build up and for vidukas
clever finish, you have got to marvel at the second, that come the end of the
season we will still be purring over, superb build up play, fantastic lay off and
class finish and the celebraition i am sure every white fan wanted to
see.......................Bowyer back.......lets hope its to stay.
Next.........Sunderland..........my dads team.........lets just hope the phillips stays in
the form that he has showed of late and can't see any thing other than 3 more
points.
hope you had a great holiday, when you back?
Laters
R.T.B.

-----Original Message-----
From: Wathen, Dorian, The Peacocks
Sent: 27 August 2002 16:06
To: Shack, Dave, On,on,on
Subject: RE: Boing, Boing! The Baggies are going down...

JF now not going to Barca - Chelsea refused their offer of a hilarious £5 mill.
They obviously realise that he'll only be with them for a season before joining
Real Madrid.

Great result on Saturday. We seriously need to address the Bakke situation -

how many times is he giving the ball away in dangerous positions - lucky we were against West Brom. Get Olly in there.

H is looking the business.

----Original Message-----
From: Nelly@whitellie-phant.co.uk
Sent: 27 August 2002 11:21
To: Dave.Shack@Ononon.co.uk
Subject: Re: Boing, Boing! The Baggies are going down...

Headless chickens for 35 minutes then Kewell turned it on. A couple of things he did were pure David Copperfield - and no, I don't mean Dickens.
In the end, we walloped them. It was Harvey Nicks versus Asda. Shame about the late consolation - but they did (kinda) deserve it...

-----Original Message-----
From: Shack, Dave, On on on
Sent: 30 August 2002 16:09
To: TheWhites, all 02/03 User group
Subject: I wish I'd stayed abroad...

It's all gone tits up the minute I step off the plane! There I was in Mexico City, largeing it up, top of the league lah de dar...the next minute we've lost against the Black Kittens (pussies?) for the first time since we wore blue & yellow halves, full facial mustaches & really did play with a well 'dubbined' pigs bladder! Not only that but we drew some Ukrainian muppets in the Uefa & most damning of all we have sold Robbie Keano for less than we paid for him! He's just had an amazing World Cup & has scored a wonder goal for us. They need a striker almost as bad as Sunderland do (McAteer excepted!) and are only paying £7million! Shocker - are there still some El Tel debts there that the rest of the fee is going against - are there some GG ones? We deserve to be told!

And, when I woke up at 4.10 this morning & couldn't get back to sleep I started watching all the tapes the missus had kindly made for me of the Premiership. Two things: 1) Where are we in the opening sequence? A bit of Nige, a corridor shot of Kewell - it's bobbins - I think Southampton have got more time on there than us & that's not right...& 2) The Venables interviews are bloody annoying - he says 'done' far too much & he smiles too much. The smiling really got to me after the defeat against Sunderland interview. You don't smile or joke - you get angry & terse. Well, I do anyway. Blues tomorrow...? Should be OK for the players - I worry for the fans mostly after our little 'event' back in '96. Never again.

Verdana | 10 | B *I* U A

Cheers lads, sorry I'm miserable today. For the last two weeks I could have been largeing it up all round the office & the day I come back we're nowhere & all the Yiddos here have got grins like cheshire cats.I hate Tottenham.

On,on,on. Shack

-----Original Message-----
From: Wathen, Dorian, The Peacocks
Sent: 30 August 2002 16:21
To: Shack, Dave, On.on,on
Subject: RE: I wish I'd stayed abroad...

Perhaps you should stay in Mexico - surely not a bad thing for a season.

Keano - 7 Mill and the last piece I saw on the website stated not on your nelly for less than 9.

I agree. I think we've been conned.

On TV Ell Tel appears as tactical genius, waxing lyrical about formations, strategies et al. A true footballing creative genius demi god.

Put him in a managers tracksuit and suddenly he's had a footballing lobotomy, stuttering "done good" all the time and "stone bonker" and looking decidedly uncomfortable in front of the camera and hoping Des has kept his seat warm in the Premiership panel.

-----Original Message-----
From: Jeremy@Donsgloryears.co.uk
Sent: 30 August 2002 17:31
To: Dave.Shack@ononon.co.uk
Subject: Re: I wish I'd stayed abroad...

Not a great week to say the least. I know we shouldn't have got carried away with good wins against two of the promoted teams, but Wednesday night was pretty miserable. What the fuck has happened to Eirik Bakke?
Is he on drugs? He gives the ball away about half a dozen times per half! And he's normally a top player. Surely he can't keep Ollie out of the team any longer.

And as for selling Keano - why now ? (apart from the obvious transfer window). We've got 6 strikers on the books (inc.Harry), of whom one (Fowler) is out till Oct/Nov, one (Bridges) is still to prove that he has/will recover from a career-threatening injury, one (Viduka) saying in the papers today that his achilles are fucked and that he probably needs an operation sooner or later. If Keano goes that leaves us potentially with just Smithy and Harry for the next few weeks. Not ideal!

Anyway off to loathsome Birmingham tomorrow - the nastiest fans in the country. Last time I was there (in 1996) me and my son (then aged 13) were spat at and had bottles thrown at us as we were penned in the car park after the game. It wouldn't be quite so bad if they didn't have those stupid accents...

-----Original Message-----
From: russ@Vivaleedspana.esp
Sent: 30 August 2002 17:58
To: Dave.Shack@Ononon.co.uk
Subject: Re: I wish I'd stayed abroad...

yeh hola amigo!
i wish you had stayed abroad as well you miserable git!!!
but i agree with everything you have said.
listen am i sending you what you need for this book of yours?
good luck tomorrow where ever you may be im playing golf in the morning and will be around by kick off time if you want to converse

see ya pal
rtb

-----Original Message-----
From: Nelly J [mailto:nelly@whitellie-phant.co.uk]
Sent: 02 September 2002 10:36
To: Dave.Shack@ononon.co.uk
Subject: Re: RE: I wish I'd stayed abroad...

It was bloody awful - Bakke shit again but Dacourt fantastic: WHY won't Tel start with him? When I talked to him last week he kept talking about "hard work", maybe Olly is a lazy trainer? Who knows, but he's fantastic when it matters so give Bakke (and all of us) a break.
Collectively they were dismal although most individuals weren't too bad.

Smithy was a giant - in attitude, ability AND application. Just nine more like him and we'd have won. They really weren't that good and Savage tired badly towards the end despite what the reports seem to say... That's when we should have made our class count.

-----Original Message-----
From: Firhad, Mohd, Eltelasia.ma
Sent: 03 September 2002 05:40
To: Shack, Dave, Ononon.co.uk
Subject: Bouncin' Back We shall

Oh my!!!!!!!!!! El Tel let Keano go......Unless Bridges is back we may lose
a natural poacher. Again Bowyer in the middle tends to to flactuate
between fast attacking and no control at all. But great scoring
positionings by them.My fave Dacourt is alright but with new El tel fast
attacking mode tend to slow it down.....Need a playmaker in the middle to
dictate terms. dacourt form the start with Bowyer back at the side with
Bakke and/or Barmby would be fine.

Sunderland 10 men behind the ball but Leeds can do better. Birmingham ????
Oh My. What a shocker. We should have won hands downs but the 2 goals is
indeed unstoppable. 2 balls hit the bar and there is this on going
superstition that if a team end up on the woodworks mo than 2x will fall.
here we are....

There were boos in the turnstiles in the Sunderland match. Hope my man El
tel sees the Leeds way of vintage soccer 1999/2000. But on the upside,
remember 2000/2001. We lose at the star and bounce back after heavy
injuries. As not to repeat 99/00 and 01/02 where midway after in the lead
we falter its good that El Tel rectify the mistakes now than later. Good
omen. Think it is...Never a quitter and forever an optimist we shall
prevail and a Treble (UEFA/League/FA Cup) is on.

Regards,
Fir

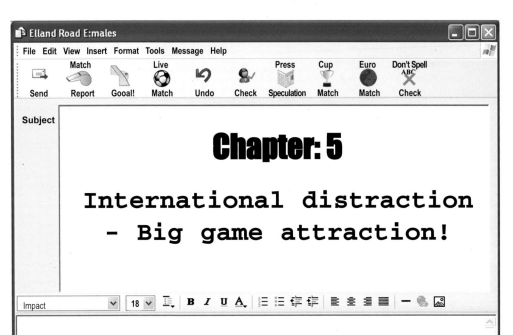

Elland Road E:males

File Edit View Insert Format Tools Message Help

Match | Live | Press | Cup | Euro | Don't Spell
Send | Report | Gooal! | Match | Undo | Check | Speculation | Match | Match | Check

Subject

Chapter: 5

International distraction - Big game attraction!

Impact | 18 | B *I* U A

PREFACE:

So the season just gets started & bloody England come & get in the way! As ever, International matches are a real quandary for club soccer fans. Of course you want your players to be recognised, but then you certainly don't want them to a) have a 'mare or b) much worse: get injured! For his England game vs Portugal, Sven finally gave not only, Robbo, Mills & Smith their chance but he also called up Woody & Bowyer too. Smithy played a blinder & scored a great first senior goal. It was great - but the up & coming battles versus the Geordies &, more importantly, Man. Utd were far more consuming...

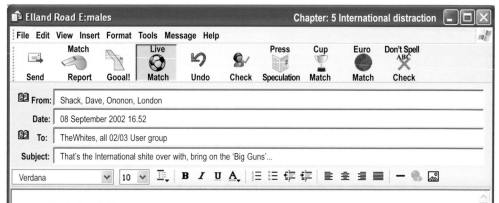

File Edit View Insert Format Tools Message Help

Match   Live   Press   Cup   Euro   Don't Spell ABC

Send   Report   Gooal!   Match   Undo   Check   Speculation   Match   Match   Check

From: Shack, Dave, Ononon, London

Date: 08 September 2002 16.52

To: TheWhites, all 02/03 User group

Subject: That's the International shite over with, bring on the 'Big Guns'...

Verdana   10   B   I   U   A

-----**Original Message**-----
From: Shack, Dave, Ononon, London
Sent: 08 September 2002 16:52
To: TheWhites, all 02/03 user group
Subject: That's the International shite over with, bring on the 'Big Guns'...

Well done Smithy - and admirable mentions in despatches to Millsy, Woody
& Bow. Unlucky to Hartey, & Keano (shit - scrub the last one!) Not sure if
Bakke played for Norway, but maybe a niggle would be good for him at
the moment so that Olly or Batts could show him how to hold onto a ball
for a while. It was probably good for Capt. Dom not to have made the
embarassing trip to the Faroe Islands - maybe some of their players will be
changing jobs when the transfer window opens again in January!
So, a bloody big week - the Geordies & the Scum. I look back to two
games last season as being the catalysts for all that followed and they
were the throw-away goal debacles against Leicester (2-2) & Newcastle
(3-4) both at home in December.
What really winds me up about Scum is their cynical tactics against us -
twice they have taken Kewell out of the game in the opening exchanges
and if they do that again now that he's flying then I am gonna compile a
tape of at least three incidents over the years & take it myself to Soho
Square to demand a viewing. There'll be no Keane to bait, no Barthez to
laugh at - but oh will our focus be framed on one man alone - Yep Rio-
scum as Tamsy so eloquently calls him. I wish him a shocker of the
magnitude of his v Leicester debut a couple of seasons ago.
Keep the faith, let's hope we really do see some tactical nouce this week
or the defeats against Sunderland & The Blues are going to appear very
insignificant.

-----Original Message-----
From: Davidharveysmonkey@aol.com
Sent: 09 September 2002 10:06
To: Thewhites, all 02/03 User group

Garamond   10   𝐄,   **B** *I* U A,   ≣ ≣ 💷 💷   ≣ ≣ ≣ ≣   — 🌑 🖼

Subject: Re: That's the International shite over with ...

Sunday and Sat night I had london mates and liverpool fans telling me how good alan smith is, like it was news DH'sM

-----Original Message-----
From: Andy@Whitetoreply.co.uk
Sent: 09 September 2002 17:41
To: Dave.Shack@Ononon.co.uk
Subject: Re: That's the International shite over with,...

Was Smithy the bees knees or what. The all in one complete striker. Michael Owen eat your heart out mate .. if indeed he has one. I think Smithies bagged them all. Great intro for Bowyer. Why was he taken off. This wholesale change of Personnel is ridiculous. Let's get a team playing. They'll be doing fish and chips next to decide who's on who's side.
Not looking forward to the next 3 weeks. Four big games (yes even Blackburn). Looking at the team, as long as Bakke's dropped and replaced by Dacourt, and as you say, protect Harte as well, them we should have a good chance on all the games. But persist in the keep ball but get nowhere philosophy and we're doomed. See ya, Andy

-----Original Message-----
From: Jeremy@Donsgloryears.co.uk
Sent: 09 September 2002 10:27
To: Dave.Shack@Ononon.co.uk
Subject: Re: That's the International shite over with...

It's amazing how my interest level in an England team rises when there is a good Leeds representation (not just England, but I used to really support Scotland in the 70's, Eire in the last World Cup, but funnily enough never N.Ireland not even when Nigel "Fossil" Worthington captained them as a Leeds player). Anyway, Smithy rightly got all the plaudits for Saturday; let's hope Ell Tel was watching and starts playing him in his best position - upfront, playing with his back to goal, holding the ball up, and getting into scoring positions. As for the two upcoming games, two draws would seem like good results right now. Let's see if Venables' great tactical acumen recognises the shortcomings of the last two games, from a selection, tactical, and motivational point of view

-----Original Message-----
From: Wathen, Dorian, ThePeacocks
Sent: 09 September 2002 11:41
To: Shack, Dave, Ononon
Subject: RE: That's the International shite over with...

I have a feeling that this useless friendly could now be a catalyst. Surely all the great performances are going to lead to a much needed injection of confidence for the next few crucial games.

-----Original Message-----
From: Firhad, Mohd, Eltelasia.ma
Sent: 09 September 2002 08:29
To: Shack, Dave, Ononon.co.uk
Subject: That's the International shite over with...

Smithy the new Allan Clarke ??!!! Hope he'd have a better break for the nation than the legendary man.Owen / Smithy. Thats an interesting one. Smithy may be the man to unlock the defense with a defence splitting pass or two. Owen will indeed shine. Just ask Viduka. Millsy the man...........Eat yer heart out Neville and other wanna bes. El Hell is whats in stote for Rio. Who cares he pleads for his loyalty in the past. A Scum is a scum. El tel will have learned the team better and come up with a scheme to stamp the sums into oblivion.

-----Original Message-----
From: nelly@whitellie-phant.co.uk
Sent: 09 September 2002 10:32
To: Dave.Shack@Ononon.co.uk
Subject: Re: That's the International shite over with ...

Fantastic - how proud did that make you feel? Bow and Smudger waltz into the team as we all knew they could and were the best on display. And did you see Smithy's Leeds salute as he walked back after scoring the goal?!? Just a shame Eriksson took Mills off - did he needed to play Hargreaves for 45 minutes at right-back to know he wasn't as good as Bulldog?

-----Original Message-----
From: chris@CaptDom.co.uk
Sent: 11 September 2002 12:42
To: Dave.Shack@Ononon.co.uk
Subject: tonight's the night ...... gonna get 3 points

Rod Stewart 1979

-----Original Message-----
From: Shack, Dave, Ononon.co.uk
Sent: 12 September 2002 10:14
To: TheWhites, all 02/03 User group
Subject: 6 points in one night!

In one night Leeds overcame their Newcastle curse, Man United perpetuated their Bolton one & even Liverpool & Spurs decided to do a Dr Barnados & make donations to Birmingham & Fulham respectively. Oh glorious 4-4-2! Oh glorious Olly Dacourt, Oh striking duo heaven, oh young, safest hands in soccer! Yes, with Kewell & Woody also on top of their game I only hope this peak isn't 3 days too early. There's no question that with Barthez back on Saturday & without the backbone of their midfield for once we will not be the underdogs. I know we will win on Saturday, because after being at evey home & away game against them since 1992 I cannot get to this one. Chances are we'll kill 'em too and all I'll have is a programme & a club video that'll be rush released within two weeks of this Saturday.

Tamsy text'd me last night & made a great point about the Ref last night being lucky for us - we should make every attempt to book him for all our big games. Dorian also said to me today that just having Bridges on the bench on Saturday would be a massive boost for the crowd (like they need it at home versus them...), but he's right.

Oh it all feels great after last night - and the funniest thing of all - was Robbie Keane's position for Tottenham last night. Striker? Left wing? Slotted in just behind Sheringham? Well, kind of...right behind Sheringham - on the fuckin bench! What a night....if only they were all like this. To the next one!

-----Original Message-----
From: Jeremy@Donsgloryears.co.uk
Sent: 12 September 2002 10:35
To: Dave.Shack@Ononon.co.uk
Subject: Re: 6 points in one night!

Let's not get too carried away - it's only three points and we've got a long way to go this season..... No, fuck it, let's get carried away! It was a truly joyous night. We came, we scored, we defended, and we conquered.

Everything about the game was perfect - Smithy scoring, Harry running them ragged, Ollie in the team (!), world-class defending especially from Woody, and of course Robbo showing that we have the best two English keepers at the same club. And then, thinking that the grin on my face couldn't get any wider, came the news from across the Pennines. If only every football day was like this...

-----Original Message-----
From:chris@Noredscum.co.uk
Sent: 12 September 2002 14:04
To: TheWhites, all 02/03 User group
Subject: Re: 6 points in one night!

Courier New   10   **B** *I* U A

Three points on Saturday would say more to tRaItOr than a million boos, sneers or hisses. The tabloids are having a field day - The Sun today has a back page of "I'll shake your hand" tRaItOr to Ridsdale - Don't do it Peter he's probably after nicking your watch and wedding ring. Never mind having 6 ex-SAS men protecting tRaItOr - how about placing them in the Ladies' loos so that the women in them wont be pestered by Manure directors trying to have a quick peek.

-----Original Message-----
From: russ@vivaleedspana.esp
Sent: 12 September 2002 18:33
To: Dave.Shack@Ononon.co.uk
Subject: ectasy

Ecstasy so thats what it is, shutting those f***ing geordies up and of course playing as well as that.
I think i told all you loveley laddies we needed to have more cohonies (spanish for bollocks) in the opening part of our game!!
Brilliant performance by all and now bring the scum and talking about that, nice bit of chest control that DB ha ha ha ah ah ah ah ah oh f*** i have just spilt a drink all over my poxy desk its 19.35 and i really should be out of here
Marching on...........................adios

-----Original Message-----
From: nelly@whitellie-phant.co.uk
Sent: 13 September 2002 11:11
To: Dave.Shack@Ononon.co.uk
Subject: Re: 6 points in one night!

We mullered them. If it was there to be done, we did it better. We out-defended and out-attacked them. Woodgate and Robbo were heroes. Oh, and Ameobi - it's the white stringy thing with wood around it that you're supposed to be aiming for.

-----Original Message-----
From: Firhad, Mohd, Eltelasia.ma
Sent: 13 September 2002 12:01
To: Shack, Dave, Ononon
Cc: Wathen, Dorian, The Peacocks
Subject: 6 points in one night!

Batang | 10 | B *I* U A

The time has come. Great to see my man Olly rockin. El Tel...I told ya so. The shift of Kewell / Viduka upfront and Smithy on the right is shrewd. El tel The man is understanding da flow. Robbo for England

Newcastle curse gone...MU will bite da bullet.

-----Original Message-----
From: Andy@Whitetoreply.co.uk
Sent: 13 September 2002 01:40
To: Dave Shack , On on on
Subject: Re: 6 points in one night!

Sorry not to get back to you before now. Had a few things to sort and think about. Got to watch the Newcastle match at a mates who was feeling pretty depressed at the time. It's amazing what the wonders of football can do to change a mood. If ever there was a great advert for football, I think that was it. It was pure attack and defence, edge of seat stuff. Although we didn't make many chances, I think we were deserved winners. Viduka, Smith and Robinson had marvellous games. Even Bakke looked OK. Where was Barmby? He seems to be the one that doesn't seem part of the game. But anyway, a superb 3 points for the boys.

```
-----Original Message-----
From: chris@noredscum.co.uk
Sent: 13 September 2002 09:30
To: Dave.Shack@Ononon.co.uk
Subject: Marching on with Dermot


Don't know if you're aware of this but we have know gone 16
games unbeaten with Dermott Gallagher as a referee - thought
we carved out a solid defensive result t'other night - Robbo
certainly kept us in it. Roll on the Scum on tomorrow! You
going up or watching it down here?
```

-----Original Message-----
From: Shack, Dave, Ononon
Sent: 13 September 2002 09:31
To: chris@ noredscum.co.uk
Subject: RE: Marching on with Dermot

f*ckin' trainspotter! Welsh Mountains (hopefully.) Don't ask...
On on on. Shacky

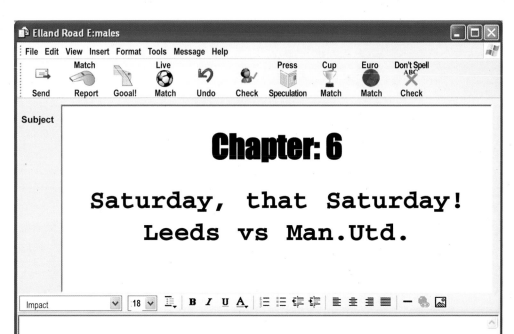

Chapter: 6

Saturday, that Saturday!
Leeds vs Man.Utd.

PREFACE:

It's the chapter of chapters - it's the one that all Leeds fans will read first - it's the one game that everyone makes sure they can get to/watch/listen to etc. Everyone that is except me. My 11 year old golf society, Monkey Island G.C., plays a Ryder cup format home & away against the Poker Sharks each year & this year it's fallen on this damn weekend. As playing Vice-Captain of a 12 man team there's nothing I can do. It's the first home Leeds vs Man Utd match I have missed since about 1991. Firhad's boss, a big Man Utd fan, surprises me with a congratulatory e:mail before I have time to send out the victory note:

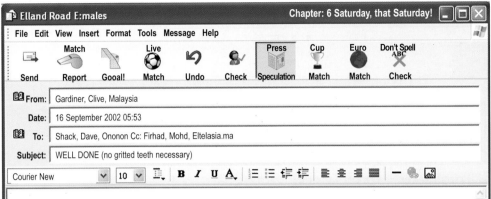

Elland Road E:males

File   Edit   View   Insert   Format   Tools   Message   Help

Match   Live   Press   Cup   Euro   Don't Spell
                                              ABC

Send   Report   Gooal!   Match   Undo   Check   Speculation   Match   Match   Check

From: Gardiner, Clive, Malaysia

Date: 16 September 2002 05:53

To: Shack, Dave, Ononon Cc: Firhad, Mohd, Eltelasia.ma

Subject: WELL DONE (no gritted teeth necessary)

Courier New   10   B I U A

-----Original Message-----
From: Gardiner, Clive, Malaysia
Sent: 16 September 2002 05:53
To: Shack, Dave, Ononon
Cc: Firhad, Mohd, Eltelasia.ma
Subject: WELL DONE (no gritted teeth necessary)

Hard fought victory against a petulant undeserving Scum.

Came to the conclusion pre-season that I support my team, but don't like them very much right now. It was much more fun before they started winning so much, and would go out with "death or glory" attitude. So much sour grapes these days. Can't stand all this preening and posing and different colour boots....(I haven't scored for a few games ....but maybe this new line of natty grey ones available at your local JB Sports will do the trick !)

These days, much prefer to see a decent game of footy such as Leeds vs Newcastle from earlier in the week....or Man City or Fulham against anybody.

Your boyz are definitely on the upswing again, difference being
1) Olly..the vital missing link
2) Robbo.....for England....please
3) Tel - a man with plan (even brave enough to take off Viduka now and then)

If Smiffy can go upfront, it can only look good for all at Tel-land Road.

cheers Clive

-----Original Message-----
From: Shack, Dave, Ononon.co.uk
Sent: 19 September 2002 09:44
To: Gardiner, Clive Malaysia
Subject: re:WELL DONE (no gritted teeth necessary)

51

Mate - are you sure you're a Man U fan? None I know talk like this (or can write!) - maybe it's that Southall influence from your days before you went out there to further the empire... see you in KL soon for our football extravaganza.

-----Original Message-----
From: Shack, Dave, Ononon.co.uk
Sent: 19 September 2002 09:44
To: Whites, all 02/03 User group
Subject: High Noon - Low handicap. How I spent my Saturday

So picture the scene - it's 12.25 and in a relatively sedate pub in the middle of the Welsh Mountains a car screeches into a gravel car park. Running from the car is a sweaty, flustered golfer - resplendent in golf shoes, posh trousers, shirt, slipover & cap. In his hand is the crumpled white standard of Leeds United. Pushing into the room, the cap, sunglasses & top half of the golfing gear are removed in one fluid motion to be replaced by the Leeds shirt. The golf spikes slide slightly on the wooden floor, but I find a chair order a strongbow & focus on the big screen promising me 0-0 with 28 minutes gone at Elland Road. We're taking a battering...

Within the next 25 minutes 20 more golf-gear clad guys enter the pub & the feeling of intimidation is gone. Chicken pie at half-time refreshes us and then in mirror image on the screen a revitalised Leeds team take the game to Man U and, when Kewell, Salmon-like (or should that be sheep in this place?) evades both Silvestre & Ferdinand to score a peach all the golfers go mad! The rest of the pub - who as you can imagine are far more in tune with a Hughes or a Giggs than a Flynn or a Yorath, begin to mumble & gradually filter out to the beer garden. Such is the feeling of desperation now about the Man United team. Rio's pass to Kewell finished off the stragglers who swear at me as they leave. I'm all smiles and know that I'm gonna play the golf round of my life that afternoon with an almighty smile on my face.

That was my lunch-time in the Welsh mountains. My Dad was there to hug me at the end & all the golfers - my Monkey team mates & the Shark opposition all said well done as though I had contributed to it. In all honesty, it can't have been much better than this at the ground...

So lads - was it? Olly - awesome. Woody -awesome. Becks - jammy git (although they would have got a penalty if he hadn't done that!), Smithy

- how he wanted it! Hartey's cross (with the right foot), Robbo! Lucas! What a second half eh? Indulge me with where you were when we won & let's make this the biggest chapter yet. Get typing...

Shack

-----Original Message-----
chris@Captdom.co.uk
Sent: 15 September 2002 17:37
To: Whites, all 02/03 User group
Subject: so then . .

I had to get up at 6.45 in the pissing morning on Saturday.
I had to drive up the M1 avoiding all the Red fans coming up from the south.
I passed about 15 cars full of Leeds shirts or scarfs
I saw 4 busses with LEEDS in the window
I got to the ground with my old man at 11.10
I had a pint and couple of ciggies before doing the 'excuse me' 'sorry' 'thanks pal' dance to get to my seats in the middle of the row.
I watched 45 mins of football predicting how monday's gonna be shite at work with 500 e-mails from man u fans taking the piss
Half time, at least we're not losing

AND THEN . . .

The Boys in white start playing their socks off, The Chief saves our ass a few times, as does Robbo and Dacourt. Woody is bloody marvelous, Smith wants it, viduka wants it .. KEWELL GETS IT!

Leeds 1 Man Utd 0.

Now that's what I call getting up early to have a fucking good day.

-----Original Message-----
From: Davidharveysmonkey@aol.com
Sent: 16 September 2002 09:25
To: chris@ Captaindom.co.uk
Cc: whites, all 02/03 user group
Subject: Re: so then . .

You think you had it hard!!!!!

I ended up on a bus with man U hooligans! shepherded back to the station and had to virtually fight with the police to srtop them shipping me back to manchester!!! DH'sM

Century Gothic   ⌄   10   ⌄   ≣⌄   **B** *I* U A⌄   ≣ ≣ ≣ ≣   ≣ ≣ ≣ ≣   — ◉ 🖼

-----Original Message-----
From: nelly@whitellie-phant.co.uk
Sent: 16 September 2002 13:59
To: Dave.Shack@Ononon.co.uk
Subject: Re: RE: so then . .

I was so delirious (and unaccustomed to travelling home by train) that I decided to walk to the station. I went out of the West Stand hit a massive jam of people so went into the Kop, behind the goal, then out again and joined the happy throng going out and through the Lowfields Road underpass. Everyone was smiling and winking and talking to total strangers, those driving were hooting their horns and waving flags and scarves. Walking six inches taller on this wave of euphoria I turned right on Gelderd Road - and spent nearly an hour finding my way back to the city square.
But did I care? Not a bit!

-----Original Message-----
From: russ@vivaespana.sp
Sent: 16 September 2002 14:29
To: Dave.Shack@Ononon.co.uk
Subject: RE: so then . .

shagger how long oh how long have we waited for that!
doing the scum and the geordies in one week, awesome, shame we weren`t there where we should have been.
Thought the first half was back to the same performance as the 1st half against wba, slow

-----Original Message-----
From: russ@vivaleedspana
Sent: 16 September 2002 14:33
To: Dave.Shack@Ononon.co.uk
Subject: RE: so then . .

dave i keep hitting a send button on my computer before i have finnished the bloody e-mail, so i will continue.
.....................wba, slow indecisive and not being able to put anything together especially Vid and Harry

-----Original Message-----
From: russ@vivaleedspana

Comic Sans MS   10   B *I* U A

Sent: 16 September 2002 14:38
To: Dave.Shack@ Ononon.co.uk
Subject: RE: so then . .

fuck i done it again!
i thought vid and harry looked lazy again, but maybe am being a bit hard on them
as el tel did say after he thought their work rate in the magpie game was
outstanding, but then in saying that their second half performances on sat were
brill!!
10 out of 10 to tel for taking vid off just when he was tiring, and using a great
squad player like bakke, that somthing DO would never have done, and taking
barmby off.

-----Original Message-----
From: Firhad, Mohd, Eltelasia.ma
Sent: 19 September 2002 10:07
To: Shack, Dave, Ononon.co.uk
Subject: Ole Ole Leeds !!!!!!!!!!!!!!!

Here's how my Super Saturday went

Travel the country from KL to Johor Bahru (bordering to Singapore on a
mind blowing Elvis 30 # 1 Hits Nationwide Tour with a convoy of 30 multi
colored kelisa starting off at 8.30 am and travelling over 500 km. A
Malaysian car called Kelisa made up to resemble a Mini. Malaysian Job
comes to mind and Michael Caine step aside.Mind is gettin there before 7
pm Malaysian time kick off. made it indeed and here I am rushing into a
bar to watch. MD Clive had to go take an artists out for dinner and am not
gonna miss this for anything in this world. The one with me is an Arsenal
fan, my radio man. The bar if filled with 12 MU die hards. here I am all
alone.

Game starts and the "Scummians" raoar their approval.We are on the ropes.
Becky elbow Bowyer and they dare to see its a dive. Shut up guys. Jez
Becky's sour grapes warning to Bowyer that the right midfield for England
is his. Gotta do something and pray El Tel send in a ball winner.

Second half, Bakke's in. Though not a great player but hardworking enuff.
With him in Olly can dictate terms to the hilt.Radebe adds steel and speed
in the middle.El Tel weaves his magic and now we can see why he is one of
the "brains" of today's soccer.

55

Batang   10   **B** *I* <u>U</u> <u>A</u>

Kewell teasing the defense is a delight. Smithy's persistence and dogged
determination is making MU nervous. Sense somethings coming. Out goes Harte
and suddenly the cross came in. Kewell's head in and Goal. I raise my
hands. Oh!!! Oh !!!!! I am the only one in a barof 12 MU fans and 1 Arse
man. Hey who cares !!!!!!!!!!

The crowd surely got to Rio when he fluff a pass to Kewell who very nearly
scored. The pressure has got to him. As for line up 2nd half is more
solid. Bakke in the squad adds balance as with Olly running things in the
middle of the park, a ball winner is indeed needed. A Batty for the El Tel
era. The ERl tel LU is versatile where a player can be rotated in any
position seem fir and all in one match. Smithy right, left middle
etc.Kewell here, there everywhere.

A Wins A Win !!!!!!!!!!!!! Till we thrash Scums again in The Theatre Of
Dreams its sweet victory for now !!!!!!!!!!!!!!! Talked to my MD Clive and
after he sees the game had to admit that Leeds rules OK !!!!!!!!!!!

-----Original Message-----
From: Andy@whitetoreply.com
Sent: 21 September 2002 02:25
To: Dave.Shack@Ononon.co.uk

Subject: Re: High Noon - Low handicap. How I spent my Saturday
Without doubt the game of the season (unless of course we do the double at their
place). Smithy looks like the only footballer still in the game who truly wants to win.
And what an engine. He is the hottest player in England at the moment.
I was of course on the terrace with my three mates, and the crowd went absolutely
wild. We had that crowd roll where everyone is jumping with no direction, and
bodies just go in every direction and you find it hard to stand up. Outside afterwards
cries of " Let's go fucking mental" were of course the order of the day, but apart
from the Scumbus, I think it was all good humoured.

-----Original Message-----
From: chris@noredscum.co.uk
Sent: 19 September 2002 13:15
To: Dave.Shack@ Ononon.co.uk
Subject: Re: High Noon - Low handicap. How I spent my Saturday

Imagine the scene - the Townhouse pub in Ealing (the one that
the IRA let off a car bomb outside last summer!) - yours truly
having only just failed in last minute bid to get a spare
ticket resigned to watching the game on telly.

Courier New   ⌄   10   ⌄   🇪⌄   **B** *I* U A⌄   ⬚ ⬚ ⬚ ⬚   ⬚ ⬚ ⬚ ⬚   — 🔗 🖾

```
Out of a crowd of about 100 people I recognised two people who
were Leeds fans - the rest were a motley collection of
"Cockney Reds" - I knew for a fact that I've been to more Man
U games than the lot of them and seeing as I've only ever been
to Leeds Man U games we're hardly calling them dedicated fans.

What can I say about the goal - Hartey finally uses his right
foot and delivers a peach of a cross right on Harry's head -
tRaItOr and the rest of Manure's shambollic defence look on in
amazement as the ball thuds past the clown Barthez. The Team
go crazy, Elland road goes crazy - I go crazy!!!! 97 Cockney
Reds utter something under their breaths but I'm too happy to
even be bothered.

Then for the rest of the match Manure look like they've all
been drugged - they look a shadow of their former selves and
boy do I enjoy every single minute of it!!!

Final score hits I go mental the pub clears in two minutes and
me and the other two Leeds fans just hug each other and cant
stop smiling. We all howl with derision at Fergie's post match
synopsis - funny how he saw clearly the two "penalty incidents"
which were about 60 meters away from him but he failed to see
Beckhams elbow which was about 10 yards away from him.

Who cares? Certainly not me - we've beaten them and are,
albeit briefly, on top of the league where we belong.

Marching on together.
```

-----Original Message-----
From: Jeremy@Donsgloryears.com
Sent: 19 September 2002 15:31
To: Dave.Shack@ Ononon.co.uk
Subject: Re: High Noon - Low handicap. How I spent my Saturday

The first thing I want to know is - what the fuck were you doing playing golf on a day like that? Don't you check the fixture list before making such absurd arrangements?

The truth is Shacky, you really did have to be there, and I am lucky enough to be able to say I was (the first time I'd seen us beat the old enemy since the 79's!!). The game was no classic, but who gives a fuck!?

For sheer drama guts and determination it was as good as it gets (and that was just us lot in

Times New Roman   10   **B** *I* U A

the stands!). Strangers were hugging andhigh-fiving after the game - it really did feel like we'd won the European Cup or something.

The crowd were absolutely brilliant - Rio got booed every time he went near the ball, but there wasn't the same intensity of hatred that I've seen and heard directed at Cantona or Hasselbaink in the past. Better still, it was more focused on supporting our team than hating another one, which after all is the point of the whole thing.

The game itself has been well enough documented, but all I can say is thank God we've got Olly back in the team, thank God Smithy was born the right side of the Pennines, thank God for having the best two goalkeepers in the country (a pity we can't play them both at the same time), thank God for Harry's head, and just thank God in general for Lucas - a hero really worthy of that much abused epithet.

-----Original Message-----
From: Shack, Dave, Ononon.co.uk
Sent: 20 September 2002 09:14
To: TheWhites, all 02/03 user group
Subject: Triple Word score - Metalurh
ZaporizhzhyZZZZZZzzzzzzzzzzzzzzzzzzz!

Well 1-0 at home to some miners (reminds me of the bad old days versus Doncaster or Barnsley). Maybe we should be kicking off an hour later in all our matches then we might start brightly...
Well done Robbo, Welcome back Bridges & nice lay off. Well done Smithy for getting behind the 11 men too & scoring! I thought Tv might have given Nige a run tonight - did anyone else? or would that be a bit patronising? At the moment Robbo is not letting anything go & God bless him for it!
30k crowd - sounded like a hell of a lot of school kids, but that was still 100% more than Chelsea got which was embarrassing.

-----Original Message-----
From: Firhad, Mohd, Eltelasia.ma
Sent: 20 September 2002 10:31
To: Shack, Dave, Ononon.co.uk
Subject: Re: Triple Word score - Metalurh Zaporizhzhya
ZZZZZZzzzzzzzzzzzzzzzzzzzzzzzzzz!

What are the guys doing ????? From a master blaster performance they are now slumbering thrugh the game. Bridges is back and is lookin' sharp and deadly. Smithy is ever sharp.

-----Original Message-----

Century Gothic   10   B *I* U A

From: nelly@whitellie-phant.co.uk
Sent: 21 September 2002 11:42
To: Dave.Shack@ Ononon.co.uk
Subject: Triple Word score - Metalurh ZaporizhzhyaZZZZZZzzzzzzzzzzzzzz

30,000 exactly?!? Did they round it down for tax reasons - or round it up to avoid the embarrassment. Roll on that shiny new 60,000 seater stadium so we can play European no-hopers somewhere that looks REALLY empty

-----Original Message-----
From: russ@vivaleedspana
Sent: 21 September 2002 16:18
To: Dave.Shack@ Ononon.co.uk
Subject: Re: Triple Word score - Metalurh ZaporizhzhyZZZZzzzzz!

Dave its the same as before we seem to be asleep in the first half, dont want to get out of bed! when was the last time we had a decent start?
If we start against the arsoles like we normally do we could be 4 down by h/t and my brother would not let me live that down, because he is a gooner. adios & come on you whites

-----Original Message-----
From: Shack, Dave, Ononon.co.uk
Sent: 22 September 2002 15:03
To: TheWhites, all 02/03 User group
Subject: Anyone on line? I'm listening to the match on www.Lufc.com

Come on you whites! No Kewell...

-----Original Message-----
From: Shack, Dave, Ononon.co.uk
Sent: 22 September 2002 15:17
To: TheWhites, all 02/03 User group
Subject: RE: Anyone on line? I'm listening to the match on www.Lufc.com

We're getting done here! We don't seem to be attacking at all...

-----Original Message-----
From: Shack, Dave, Ononon.co.uk
Sent: 22 September 2002 15:26
To: TheWhites, all 02/03 User group

Verdana   10   B *I* U A

Subject: RE: Anyone on line? I'm listening to the match on www.Lufc.com

Balls! 0-1 Deflection off Woody. Bakke keeps giving the ball away in midfield. Great biased commentators on here from Radio Aire's Bradders & Brendan Ormsby too!

-----Original Message-----
From: Shack, Dave, Ononon.co.uk
Sent: 22 September 2002 16:24
To: TheWhites, all 02/03 User group
Subject: RE: Anyone on line? I'm listening to the match on www.Lufc.com

McMaster, Kelly & Mcphail for Viduka (again!) Harte & Dacourt -- YEESSSSSSSSSSSSSSS!!!!!!!!!!!!!!Penalty. Where's Hartey?

-----Original Message-----
From: Shack, Dave, Ononon.co.uk
Sent: 22 September 2002 16:25
To: TheWhites, all 02/03 User group
Subject: RE: Anyone on line? I'm listening to the match on www.Lufc.com

Smithy's missed it! Oh no...

-----Original Message-----
From: Shack, Dave, Ononon.co.uk
Sent: 22 September 2002 16:55
To: TheWhites, all 02/03 User group
Subject: RE: Anyone on line? I'm listening to the match on www.Lufc.com

Oh shit, another frustrating match. Robinson has been the best player on the pitch by the sound of it. The substitution was a couple of minutes too early for Harte to take the penalty. Viduka seems to be out of sorts, we missed Kewell & the pace of Gillespie & Dunn caught us out again.
Again we've had a strong second half - but why are our first halves so bad?
Oh, well - 2 hours on line - probably the same price as a pie & some bovril, but without the indigestion & the long drive home. Radio Aire was fun, but it's never lucky for me when I'm listening at home on the radio/net.
The highs & the lows...you're not kinding.

-----Original Message-----
From: Davidharveysmonkey@aol.com
Sent: 23 September 2002 09:09
To: TheWhites, all 02/03 User group
Subject: Re: RE: Anyone on line? I'm listening to the match on
www.Lufc.com

You are fucking mental shacky, i am blotting this out and awaitinhg the arrival of the scum fan who sits opposite me who i've been giving hell to for the last month.good to see mcmaster getting promoted after some blinding games in the reserves. where's batts?

DH'sM

-----Original Message-----
From: Firhad, Mohd, Eltelasia.ma
Sent: 23 September 2002 10:36
To: Shack, Dave, Ononon.co.uk
Subject: Anyone on line? I'm listening to the match on www.Lufc.com

What has happened ?????? The fear is confounded where consistency is concerned. McPhail for Viduka is not healthy as we need a striker. El Tel, whats up ??!! Bring on Bridges "Lorimer" anyttime to parner Smithy "Clarke".

Penalty miss ??!! Well it happens . Guess its just bad luck. We need to be more consistent and balanced esp. in the first half. El tel, bring on your matador skilss right now. We need em.

-----Original Message-----
From: chris@Captdom.co.uk
Sent: 22 September 2002 20:26
To: Dave.Shack@Ononon.co.uk
Subject: Re: Anyone on line?

Well that was fun -today I ran the Nike 10K race in Richmond Park.

My trainer had run the course last week and assured me the hills weren't that bad

...SHE'D RAN THE WRONG WAY!!

Anyway, did a top time of 52.36 .. which I'm very happy with. Straight into the waiting car, home, shower, pub!

Arial   10   **B** *I* U A ≣ ⋮≣ 仨 ⫶ ≣ ≣ ≣ ≣ — 🔗 🖼

Dave (off of the radio) wanted to watch Everton. Whilst this is going on, and my legs are aching like hell, I double check the LEEDS game is on.

"No, it's not mate!"
"yeah it is 3 o;clock"
"Not in here pal"
"Yeah it is"
"No it's not ...etc"

Eventually, the man at said pub (no names for obvious reasons) finds out the game is on, ONE HOUR DELAYED, on RTL5!
Which, thank god, he has.

So, the question is, can I survive not finding out the score till, 4 o;clock. Simple answer .... NO. Text comes in; "Leeds are 1 - 0 down mate" "Oh cheers you ****!"

Anyway, 4 oclock arrives, I sit down to watch the game. Now, I know the score is 1-0 anyway, but I don't know the result.
Till, a LEEDS fan walks in, looking pissed off and saying;

"What a shit result. And we missed a penalty!"

aaaaaaaaarrrrrrrrrrrrrgggggggggggggghhhhhhhhhhhhhhhhhh

Shit afternoon, shit game, shit legs. Bollocks

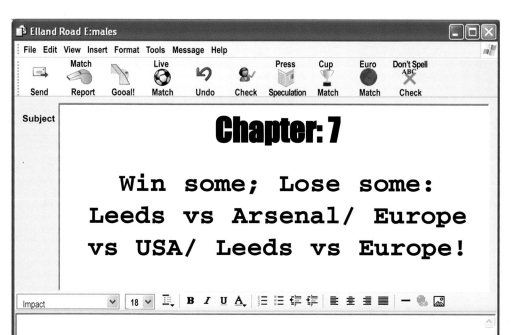

Chapter: 7

Win some; Lose some: Leeds vs Arsenal/ Europe vs USA/ Leeds vs Europe!

PREFACE:

Normally the lure of the Gooners @ Elland Road would have me up the M1 like a shot - but hey! Golf's my second passion (sorry Mrs S!) so with the Ryder Cup only in the UK every four years & with 2 complimentary tickets & a sympathetic Villa fan, Phil Jordan, in tow, there was never any doubt as to where I would be on that fateful day/weekend. And a funny thing happened there too...

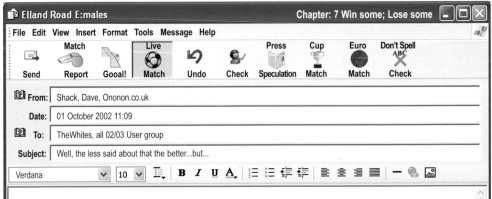

File Edit View Insert Format Tools Message Help

Match · Live · Press · Cup · Euro · Don't Spell

Send · Report · Gooal! · Match · Undo · Check · Speculation · Match · Match · Check

From: Shack, Dave, Ononon.co.uk

Date: 01 October 2002 11:09

To: TheWhites, all 02/03 User group

Subject: Well, the less said about that the better...but...

Verdana   10   B I U A

-----**Original Message**-----
From: Shack, Dave, Ononon.co.uk
Sent: 01 October 2002 11:09
To: The Whites, all 02/03 User group
Subject: Well, the less said about that the better...but...

...there I was at the Belfry watching some of the most amazing golf ever, but in true fan mode I managed to ascertain that the Victor Chandler tent had at least one screen showing the Leeds game. Beer in hand I stood amidst hundreds of not even remotely interested golf attired punters to watch the kick-off. Wow I thought - that'll throw Arsenal - that back four in those positions. It didn't take long to realise that it would throw us too! Well done Tel! Good on paper - crap on grass!! Again & again we are leaking goals after midfield lose the ball...& the defenders forget their man or which part of the pitch they should be protecting.

At 2-0 down I opted for more golf & for the first time ever dragged myself away from a live Leeds game. Not proud of it, but it seemed the right thing to do. I had a great moment though on the way out of the 'tent'. I mentioned, but never explained properly, that I had a great new talisman for Leeds victories which started back in America - and that is a pair of Leeds United specially logo'd adidas golf shoes. They are awesome & were a gift from my Dad from a Yorkshire golf pro called Simon Hurd, who's a massive Leeds fan & obviously has a bit of sway with adidas!

So, I'm leaving this tent and this bloke in a Yorkshire accent, with a great looking girlfriend asks where I got my shoes. I told him about this Yorkshire Pro giving them to my Dad for me & it turned out to be him! Simon Hurd. Freaky or what? In a crowd of 35,000 people at the Ryder Cup I met the guy who got the shoes done! I don't think he even stayed for the rest of the game...

Finally, you may know that European hero Colin 'Monty' Montgomerie is a

Leeds fan and so before he tee'd off in the afternoon I was close enough
to remind him to "Forget the Leeds score Monty, Let's take it out on the
Yanks!" to which he smiled and proceeded to kick arse! What a man!

Bring on the Euro distraction - blood some more rookies & pls come back
Fowler & Bridges 'cos Viduka's out of sorts again. Nice that we didn't lie
down though on Saturday - which was a small consolation.

Shack - EUROPE & LEEDS

-----Original Message-----
From: Davidharveysmonkey@aol.com
Sent: 01 October 2002 12:54
To: Dave.Shack@Ononon
Cc: thewhites, all 02/03 user group
Subject:Re: Well,the less said about that the better...but...

Shacky, do you ever go to the games anymore or is it just co-incidence that most of these e:mails
start with "So there I was in Hollywood/the Virgin Lounge/the Hospitality Tent/etc etc" .
You're worse than me.
Also I'm thinking of adding some more guys to this list, how do I go about it?
and good to see you last thurs

- DH'sM

P.S Re the football. One word: Batty!
He's been treated like Pierre Van Hoydonk at Forest when he said the team were shit and went
on strike.

-----Original Message-----
From: Andy@Whitetoreply.co.uk
Sent: 04 October 2002 17:36
To: Davidharveysmonkey; Dave Shack
Subject: Re: Well, the less said about that the better...but...

I thought it was just me that thought this. I'm starting to think that Dave's going for
a record on how many different places he can watch Leeds from. Are we going to
see you at Elland Road this year to catch some of the real atmosphere?
Mind you, after the debacle against Arsenal, perhaps Dave's doing the best thing.
We showed that we are desparately lacking in any real pace throughout the whole
team. Although the work ethic got better in the second half, we are also lacking
creativity and tactics. The only good thing that can be got out of a match like that is
that it's easier to get back to my car when the final whistle goes as half the crowd
had left!!

65

Arial   10   **B** *I* U A

-----Original Message-----
From: Chris@Captdom.co.uk
Sent: 01 October 2002 20:34
To: Davidharveysmonkey@aol.com
Cc: Dave.Shack@Ononon.co.uk
Subject: Re: Well, the less said about that the better...but...

I seem to start mine with .. ".. well i went to the game .." AND I'M NOT EVEN A
PROPER FAN (as I keep getting told!)
Sat next to my new pal in my season seats. This time he'd brought his son along.
Ahhw bless. (Not by the end of it, he could be done for child abuse! a poor kid in a
leeds shirt seeing us get stuffed by the arse).
Well i have lots of thoughts but am too depressed to write them. The Arsenalfans did
make me laugh though. They started singing;

"Stand up if you hate Man u .. Stand up ......"

A good few Leeds fans rose to their feet and stuck their arms in the air ...only to hear
the song ... slightly change to ...

"Stand up .. for the champions .. stand up ...."

You have never seen Leeds fans sit down so quick!!

Anyway, looking forward to Thursday. I'm on the radio during the Leeds game, then
on telly before the chelsea match. Can't somebody swap them round please??

-----Original Message-----
From: chris@noredscum.co.uk
Sent: 01 October 2002 11:24
To: Dave.Shack@Ononon.co.uk
Subject: Re: Well, the less said about that the better...

I watched in amazement as Arsenal absolutely demolished our
team - I've not seen such a complete and utter total football
performance since England vs.Germany in Munich or England vs.
Holland at Wembley - quite simply they were magnificent and we
didn't actually play that bad we were simply outclassed.

Marching on...

----- Original Message -----
From: Dave.Shack@Ononon.co.uk

Verdana   10   **B** *I* U A

**To: chris@noredscum.co.uk
Sent: Tuesday, October 01, 2002 11:29 AM
Subject: RE: Well, the less said about that the better...but...**

Fuck me! Humble Tams! What's up mate?

Chris Tams writes:

Well I have the feeling that Manure's reign at the top has
come to an end its a shame we're not taking their place but we
can all laugh at their downfall.

Arsenal are going to take the piss this season so I think we
should
concentrate on finishing second to them in the League.

Every now and again in football we have to take a reality
check - this is one of them!

-----Original Message-----
From: Jeremy@Donsgloryears.co.uk
Sent: 01 October 2002 10:45
To: Dave.Shack@Ononon.co.uk
Subject: Re: Well, the less said about that the better...but...

I watched the game in an Irish bar in Atlanta, Georgia. It didn't make it any less painful....

>>> <Dave.Shack@Ononon.co.uk> 10/01/02 11:09 >>>

Thank fuck! someone who understands me... away for Leeds games!

-----**Original Message**-----
**From: Shack, Dave, Ononon.co.uk
Sent: 08 October 2002 10:05
To: whites, all 02/03 User group
Subject: ZZZZZZZZZZzzzzzzzz & Villa: Searching for Inspiration -
on & off the pitch!**

Where's the passion gone? The motivation levels seem pretty bloody low
at the moment - I really, really hope we're not turning into another
Chelsea (ie Big Game Charlies), but the evidence in front of us really does
seem to point that way. In fairness I'd go along with the 'line' that we got
ourselves a 'result' in the Ukraine, we defended well away at Villa & we
now have a break (the players all have this week off) before a massive

game against Liverpool.
Negative points recently: Viduka not scoring, no Dacourt, no Batty.
Hartey not making decent dead-balls, Woody & Dom being injured,
Bowyer 'out of sorts', Bakke giving the ball away. Kewell dis-interested for
most of the 90 minutes.Smithy getting wound up again.

Plus points recently: Robbo, McPhail back (but not playing his best),
Barmby scoring & getting well stuck in, Lucic & McMaster on the bench,
Viduka on the bench, Fowler beginning training. Smithy trying his bollocks
off.

Hmmm, not the most impressive 'Plus' list is it?

-----Original Message-----
From: Jeremy@Donsgloryears.co.uk
Sent: 08 October 2002 09:58
To: Dave.Shack@Ononon.co.uk
Subject: Re: ZZZZZZZZZZZzzzzzzzz & Villa: Searching for Inspiration - on & off the
pitch!

I couldn't agree more - you must have read my mind (or maybe it was our conversation
during the long car journey back from Villa!).

No passion, and no real tempo in our game. No Batty was bad enough, but why has he
decided (seemingly) to dump Dacourt as well? And as for Hartey's deadballs - as a highly
paid professional who (presumably)practices such things every day in training (and we know
that he has the ability to deliver killer deadballs) for him to fluff - either too long or not
missing the front defender - maybe 40-50% of them is unforgiveable.

And can someone please tell me the last time we scored from a corner?
And why are all our freekicks within shooting range only ever taken by Hartey? Where are
Venables' much-trumpeted innovative freekick ideas?(I think I'd better stop now before I turn
into the kind of whingeing supporter that I most despise....)

-----Original Message-----
From: Firhad, Mohd, Eltelasia.ma
Sent: 08 October 2002 10:17
To: Shack, Dave, On on on
Subject: FW: ZZZZZZZZZZZzzzzzzzz & Villa: Searching for Inspiration - on &
off the pitch!

Oh !!!! Oh !!!!! Its happening. When are we gonna be on a bull run ??!!
Now its like when are we gonna hit a winning trail. After MU all leads to
a strong run but instead its down to another draw.

Batang   ⌄ 10 ⌄ ⅀↓ **B** *I* U A⌄ ⌄Ξ ːΞ 拝 拝 ≣ ≣ ≣ ≣ — 🦋 🖼

Euro run was due to Hartey's free kick. Since last season its all gone.
Bridges must come forward. Liverpool is a surefire battle but they are a
defensive counterattacking lot. Thats where Bats can come in and hold the
fort. Let lose Dacourt. The only way is to get Bats beside him.

-----Original Message-----
From: nelly@whitellie-phant.co.uk
Sent: 08 October 2002 10:34
To: Dave.Shack@Ononon.co.uk
Subject: Re: ZZZZZZZZZZzzzzzzzz & Villa: Searching for Inspiration - on & off the
pitch!

If only we knew. My theory is that they've been told how good they were so
many times by O'Leary without any proper coaching that when they ran out
of luck their confidence went too. Footballers can only get so far on youthful
enthusiasm and self-belief.

-----Original Message-----
From: Chris@Captdom.co.uk
Sent: 12 October 2002 12:16
To: Dave.Shack@Ononon.co.uk
Cc: The Whites, all 02/03 User group
Subject: ZZZZZZZZZZZZZZzzzzzzzzzzzzzzzz, Villa & Up & down Hilla!

Hello all,

Sorry I didn't make the Villa game, but I was running The Great North Run!!
13.1 miles of bastard hills and roundabouts. I must be insane!
I woke up in Newcastle Sunday morning at 7.00AM, and then had to make my way
to a nearby hotel where the 'celebrity coach' was turning up ... I shit you not! Imagine
this, me and my trainer Jane, with a coach that included Frank Bruno, Ray Stubbs
and Motty!! I even got interviewed by Sue Bloody Barker. How showbiz am I?

Highlight of the day had to be when I was getting back on the 'celebrity
coach'(!!) Stubbs and Motty were sitting on the front 2 seats. The radio wason 5 Live,
so I asked; "You don't know the Leeds result do you Ray?"

"Sorry Chris I don't"   Replied Mr. Stubbs.

"Actually don't they kick off later Chris?"

"Oh yeah, think it's 4 o'clock actually Ray"

Then Motty looked at me as if I'd just shit on his shoes and said; "Well how would we know the score if it hasn't kicked off then yet!!!"

Moody bastard. Still a legend though!

Anyway, Leeds didn't score, but I finished the race in 1hr 57 m.

Limping on together . . .

-----Original Message-----
From: Shack, Dave, Ononon
Sent: 08 October 2002 11:50
To: TheWhites, all 02/03 User group
Subject: Bulgaria it is!

Well, knock me down with a feather! Let's send Leeds to the least glamorous places in the world shall we? Long gone are the glamour ties... It's taken me 35 minutes to find a selection of flights to Sofia (Where Tel Aviv are playing this year - why? What's up? Are they re-building a Wembley? Only kidding...)I got about 6 reasonable priced onces £ 288 via Istanbul (surely some sick Uefa conspiracy) ot £600 via Greece! Then I ticked the direct flight only button & saw one on BA at £998 plus tax in Economy! Hey fantastic! I think I'll go see Blackburn vs Celtic instead. Bugger, bugger, bugger? Anyone fancy 4 hours in Istanbul or Thessalonika? No, me neither.

Shack (miserable of Europe...)

-----Original Message-----
From: Davidharveysmonkey@aol.com
Sent: 08 October 2002 12:20
To: Dave.Shack@Ononon.co.uk
Subject: Re: Bulgaria it is!

Can I be the first to say EL TEL AVIV!

-----Original Message-----
From: Jeremy@Donsgloryears.co.uk
Sent: 08 October 2002 12:24
To: Dave.Shack@Ononon.co.uk
Subject: Re: Bulgaria it is!

I think I'll give that one a miss (plus it's the MTV Awards in Barcelona that night -are you going?)

70

Comic Sans MS ⌄ | 10 ⌄ | ▤, | **B** *I* U A̲ | ☱ ☲ ⸬ ⸬ | ▤ ▤ ▤ ▤ | — 🖈 🖻

-----Original Message-----
From: russ@vivaleedspana.esp
Sent: 08 October 2002 12:29
To: Dave.Shack@Ononon.co.uk
Subject: Re: Bulgaria it is!

No comment on villa but i will use radio 5 live as my inserts.
caller one: wheres the passion gone? the players do not look as if they care? if
we carry on the way were playing we will be fighting relegation this season!
caller two: where the passion gone? all the fight? its a disgrace, bowyer should
go he does not want to play for us any more.
caller three: wheres the passion gone? the players don't seem to care anymore,
they just stroll about like oh someone else can run for that, whats kewell doing,
he is so lazy caller four: no you get the message...
I'm now dreading what liverpool are going to do to us.
We'll just all have to go out & get lagging!!
adios from sunny spain

-----Original Message-----
From: Chris@Captdom.co.uk
Sent: 12 October 2002 12:22
To: Dave.Shack@Ononon.co.uk
Subject: Re: Bulgaria it is!

So, let me get this straight ...

You checked the details of getting to Sofia, via Istanbul and Greece!!

Here's how you can see the boys any other week;

From your house, Mister Big Shot Shackey, round North Circ, get on the M1. Travel
197 miles in a STRAIGHT LINE, then get off at the ELLAND ROAD exit. It's that
fucking easy!!!

Anyway, love you! xx

-----Original Message-----
From: chris@Noredscum.co.uk
Sent: 08 October 2002 11:48
To: Dave.Shack@Ononon.co.uk
Subject: Re: ZZZZZZZZZzzzzzzzz & Villa

71

Courier New   10   **B** *I* U A   ≣ ≣ ⁅ ⁆   ▤ ▥ ▦ ▤   — 🖉 🖼

Well it could have been worse - we could have done a Chelsea
in Europe (They are becoming as big a laughing stock as the
Scottish National team).

Talking of which we have drawn Hapoel Tel-Aviv in the next
round of the UEFA cup - sunny away trip to Cyprus anyone?

-----Original Message-----
From: Shack, Dave, On on on
Sent: 13 October 2002 19:48
To: whites, all 02/03 User group
Subject: Leeds Utd 'Fantasy XI' to face Liverpool next weekend.

Well, bit of a week in football eh? Wilko for the Black cats (wonder if any
ex-Leeds players will join him? Whelan? Whitlow? Wallace? Speed? Nige?
Batts?), Eriksson bowing to pressure (not from Ulrika or Nancy - know
which one I'd go for & she's got more in common with Teddy Lucic than
err...John Charles! Have we ever had an Italian player at Elland Road? -
oh well you get my drift....) to re-instate one of the Ugly twins in
preference to Millsy.

Olly to go? Batts still frozen out (these two combine to tell me that
Anderton is on his way to us - no seriously - you watch...) Mmm, things
need brightening up with a win against Liverpool on Saturday and so for a
bit of light relief I think we should all name our team that would start (no
injuries, no suspensions matter, just current form) if all the squad were at
Thorp Arch raring to go (told you it was a fantasy!). Here's mine:

Robbo
Mills Woody Matteo Lucic
Bowyer Olly Batts Kewell
Smith Fowler
Subs Bridges McPhail Johnson Radebe (with Goal-keeping gloves)

PS Russ is over from Spain for the game on Saturday - beers in Leeds
Friday night - Laws? All meet on Saturday after the game for a chat/
beer/fish & chips?

-----Original Message-----
From: Andy@whitetoreply.co.uk
Sent: 14 October 2002 06:14
To: Dave Shack; The Whites, all
Subject: Re: Leeds Utd 'Fantasy XI' to face Liverpool next weekend.

Tahoma   10   B   *I*   U   A

Please don't even joke about Anderton. It was bad enough when El Tel was recruited and worse when Barmby followed. If Sick Note joins, that's gunna be it. Klinsman would follow out of retirement, or possibly a new Ferdinand!!

Fantasy Eleven much like yours except Viduka instead of Fowler (the big guy always scores - who can forget that famous game at Elland Road 2 years ago), and Harte still at right back as I haven't seen Lucic. Subs all sound good except maybe Fowler instead of Johnson.
Andy

-----**Original Message**-----
From: Nelly@whitellie-phant.co.uk
Sent: 14 October 2002 10:04
To: Dave.Shack@Ononon.co.uk
Subject: Re: Leeds Utd 'Fantasy XI' to face Liverpool next weekend.

jones clarke
gray bremner giles lorimer
cooper hunter charlton reaney
Harvey sub madeley

<dave.shack@Ononon wrote:
time-warp, hippie - your flares are fashionable again -tosser!

-----**Original Message**-----
From: Wathen, Dorian, The Peacocks
Sent: 14 October 2002 10:21
To: Shack, Dave, On on on
Subject: RE: Leeds Utd 'Fantasy XI' to face Liverpool next weekend.

Would be tempted to go the 3 at the back route ... seems to look better shape to me and more alternatives going forward.

Robinson

Woodgate   Chief   Matteo

Mills   Harte   Bowyer   Olly   Kewell

Smith   Viduka

Verdana   10   **B** *I* U A

-----Original Message-----
From: Shack, Dave, On on on
Sent: 14 October 2002 02:42
To: Wathen, Dorian, The Peacocks
Subject: RE: Leeds Utd 'Fantasy XI' to face Liverpool next
weekend.

how long did it take you to space this reply?

-----Original Message-----
From: Jeremy@Donsgloryears.co.uk
Sent: 14 October 2002 10:27
To: Dave.Shack@Ononon.co.uk
Subject: Re: Leeds Utd 'Fantasy XI' to face Liverpool next weekend.

Best team?

Robbo
Mills, Woody, Lucas, Matteo
Bowyer. Batts, Olly, Harry
Smithy, Viduka

Will we ever see this line-up? Not under Ell Tel (see central midfield pairing).

-----Original Message-----
From: russ@Vivaleedspana.esp
Sent: 15 October 2002 16:26
To: Dave.Shack@Ononon.co.uk
Subject: Re: Leeds Utd 'Fantasy XI' to face Liverpool next weekend.

martyn, kelly, dubery, the chief, harte, burns, wilcox, johnson, singh, barmby,
okon
subs, oh fuck it i've lost interest.
blinding move from el tel, buys barmy (back injury) buys okon(injured when
bought, now injured again) and wants to buy sicknote!!!!!! come on what the fuck
is going on?
adios

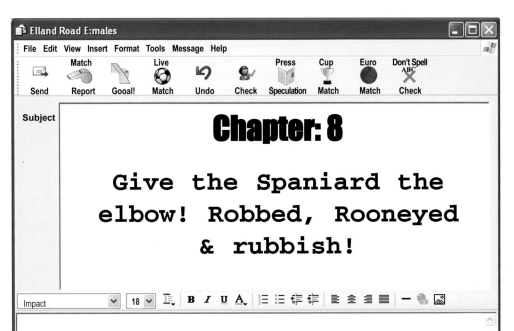

Chapter: 8

Give the Spaniard the elbow! Robbed, Rooneyed & rubbish!

Impact | 18 | B *I* U A | lists/formatting toolbar

PREFACE:

Spectacularly uninspiring recent form should have been forgotten for our usually feisty & exciting home Liverpool encounter. The Lads (as many as were able) got together for some golf & then beers prior to the game (Russ & our kid lost to me & Dad - but Russ definitely won the subsequent drinking!). Match day saw a meet at Billy & then a very sociable de-brief at Lorimer's pub after the event. But the weekend rose & fell on the presence & actions of one man: he calls himself RTB - Russ the Boss - and I call him the Spanish Jinx! Oh, and lowly Yorkie rivals Sheff United made an impact on us not for the last time this season...

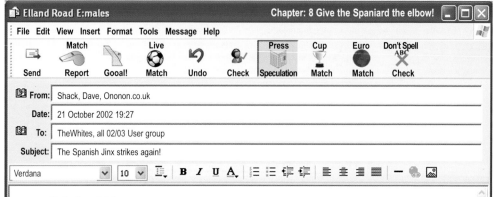

File   Edit   View   Insert   Format   Tools   Message   Help

Match   Live   Press   Cup   Euro   Don't Spell

Send   Report   Gooal!   Match   Undo   Check   Speculation   Match   Match   Check

From: Shack, Dave, Ononon.co.uk

Date: 21 October 2002 19:27

To: TheWhites, all 02/03 User group

Subject: The Spanish Jinx strikes again!

Verdana   10

-----**Original Message**-----
From: Shack, Dave, Ononon.co.uk
Sent: 21 October 2002 19:27
To: TheWhites, all 02/03 User group
Subject: The Spanish Jinx strikes again!

We came, we saw, we conkered. Actually, we might have won a good old playground conker fight - we could have used the shaven pates of Lucic, Mills & Matteo - one more slap-head at the back & we'll at least look the hardest back four in the country...
we didn't deserve to lose on Saturday - Kewell went from hero to zero after his 2 bullet headers turned into the kind of miss that we all thought only Derek Parlane could make. As soon as we lost the goal, our heads went down & we became resigned to the fact that we were going to be beaten by a very average Liverpool side.
At least I was there to witness our age old Kop disappoint us with a chant for O'Leary. What good does that possibly do? Fine the chants for Batty & Olly - but what is the point of O'Leary? He's gone, we sacked him. Shut up.
The best organisation & formation today was from the community office (Hi Emms!) people who sorted out the anti-racism demonstration for the whole of the East stand that looked great, it was nothing to do with the wanderings of Bowyer (he has to be dropped - he's never, ever been so out of sorts), the roving of all the make-shift back four - or indeed Kewell, Smith & later, Dukes.

I still believe we can make this all great - but we need someone to marshall the troops on the pitch and give them belief like Strach or Billy used to do.

It was good to get there at last this season - it was just a shame I coincided it with the Spanish jinx that is Russ! Everytime he comes we lose. Full stop. It was good to see you Moylesy, Andy & Russ at Lorimer's pub (he agreed they should not have lost) & next time we'll organise a proper get together, win, & all get ruined!.

I'm glad Boro lost yesterday, I'm gutted Keano got 2 goals - I'm fearful of high fliers Sheffield Utd, hate Barthez & am not sure about Arsenal losing.

There you have it. Loads to think about - let me AVE IT!

-----Original Message-----
From: nelly@whitellie-phant.co.uk
Sent: 22 October 2002 11:13
To: Dave.Shack@Ononon.co.uk
Subject: Re: The Spanish Jinx strikes again!

Why is it any one of us can not only pick a better starting XI but it takes a tactical genius to arrange a lesser one in a formation that not even the players can understand?

As for the Spaniard? Time to give him the elbow...

-----Original Message-----
From: Wathen, Dorian, The Peacocks
Sent: 22 October 2002 11:46
To: Shack, Dave, Ononon
Subject: RE: The Spanish Jinx strikes again!

Speculation is rife at present - out with Olly and Dukes and in with Argentinian Sorin (how we need a left back) and Brazilian Kleberson.
Who was the last South American to play for Leeds - Alex Sabella?

We're badly missing the drive of Olly and stabilising influence of Batts in the middle - McPhail is a luxury player - good for 2 or 3 quality passes a game but can't impose himself.

----Original Message-----
From: Jeremy@Donsgloryears.co
Sent: 22 October 2002 15:42
To: Dave.Shack@Ononon.co.uk
Subject: Re: The Spanish Jinx strikes again!

There's only 3 things wrong at the moment - wrong team selection, wrong formation, and a distinct lack of motivation. Apart from that, the new manger's doing a fine job.

Batang | 10 | B *I* U A

-----Original Message-----
From: Firhad, Mohd, Eltelasia.ma
Sent: 22 October 2002 16:51
To: Shack, Dave, Ononon
Subject: Leeds Renaissance In The Wings ???!!!!

Signs are there but we have to stick 'em into the net. Kewell's 2 headers plus the miss of the season (??!!). Brilliant pull back but liftin' high over the post.

Liverpool have been lucky and we should have won em'.

Barthez, da fool is at work again. A devil indeed. Fulham could have got em' but they got off da hook. His gamesmanship that makes you wanna puke.

We are gettin' there. The flow of play gives us hope. Still feel we can bounce back.

-----Original Message-----
From: Andy@Whitetoreply.co.uk
Sent: 23 October 2002 01:59
To: Dave Shack @Ononon
Subject: Re: The Spanish Jinx strikes again!

Was it just me or were Lucic's legs destined for a shorter body. It was like one of those puzzles where you match a head, body and legs and get something that doesn't quite fit.
The scouser game is still one of those where you believe it was a nightmare you're remembering, not the real result. I agree we need to get hold of the midfield and start controlling the game rather than panicking on the ball and being very sloppy with our passing. Why do we continue with Bakke. It's getting like England and the left midfield scouser donkey (do you need the name?).
How many times has Russ been incidentally?

-----Original Message-----
From: russ@Vivaleedspana.esp
Sent: 22 October 2002 18:01
To: Dave.Shack@Ononon.co.uk
Subject: Re: The Spanish Jinx strikes again!

Hola Dave!!!
If only i came back every game, then we could blame me for my spanish jinx for

Comic Sans MS   10   **B** *I* U A   ≣ ≣ ≣ ≣   ≣ ≣ ≣ ≣   — 🔗 🖼

losing all the time, fortunatley I don't, unfortunatley we do!!
We did manage to salvage some pride though this week, with kewell producing a great display of forward play with his head, although his work rate off the ball was still poor and his miss at the end unbearable for all us suffering whites.
Dudic producing save of the season and a carpenter making our bar with liverpool wood, just to stop the ball going in.
The disappointment for me though is the continuing poor performances of bow and vid.
Last of all it was fantastic to see the Shack family and you, the most relaxed i have seen you for some time, and you can still thank your dad for winning the golf!!! Take care russ

-----Original Message-----
From: Shack, Dave, Ononon.co.uk
Sent: 26 October 2002 15:00
To: TheWhites, all 02/03 User group
Subject: Onwards & upwards - and that's not just me on a plane again!

So last time I got on a plane for a long journey & Leeds were playing -it helped us to two wins. I promise to repeat this feat against Middlesboro if today's flights to Hong Kong & then KL do the same.
What a week for Venables articles eh? There's a lot of his mates coming out of the woodwork to say that he might have bitten off more than he can chew... I still feel the transfer window has really hurt us - and that everyone should make it very clear to TV what we'll think if he does buy Darren Anderton in January - because that's when I'll start griping from the Kop. Until then, let's get behind the team & pray for some luck.

Shack - With his lucky LUFC golf shoes & loads of Leeds gifts for Firhad in his luggage.

From: Nelly@whitellie-phant.co.uk
Sent: 29 October 2002 10:37
To: Dave.Shack@Ononon.co.uk
Subject: Re: Onwards & upwards

Saw Barmby yesterday, he looked like someone has studded him across the face - which, as he was just comiong off the training pitch, is what I assumed had happened. Boateng, though, had apparently tried to scratch his eyes out in the tunnel. Lucas, Dom and Fowler in physio, everyone else looking glum - until they found out someone from O2 was there to give them

Comic Sans MS · 10 · **B** *I* U A

all a free phone.

-----Original Message-----
From: russ@Vivaleedspana.esp
Sent: 31 October 2002 09:28
To: Dave.Shack@Ononon.co.uk
Cc: The Peacock; Davidharveysmonkey;Whitellie-phant
Subject: Re: Onwards & upwards

Well as usual shagger you were wrong about that result!!
Although we did deserve the 3 points as we did against the reds.
Smithy as usual letting everybody down with a ridiculous display of petulance again and this after the ref warned him of his language and wreckless challenges.
Its okay the crowd singing there praises for the way he fights and shows that yorkshire grit but please Smithy do it with a degree of cleverness!!
Last point on it, take the fight out of a player and he some what becomes a completely different player and a very ordinary one as well; Enter Bowyer!
As soon as the court case ended and he was told off by the F.A about not playing for England unless he curbed his manner of play, he has turned into a nothing player, let hope this dose not happen to Smithy, but going up to the refs face a calling him a "fucking wanker" will not help keep him on the pitch.
I hear hapoel are worried about Vid return of form! please have i missed somthing?
Adios come on you whites
Rtb

-----Original Message-----
From: Shack, Dave, Ononon.co.uk
Sent: 01 November 2002 09:57
To: Whites all, 02/03 User group
Subject: 1-0 to the Mighty Whites!

Hong Kong Airport - not kicked off! Mexico City Airport - logged on 1-0 Leeds! Cheers to the two of you who sent me texts that said things like - hope you're watching this' & 'Come on Leeds' - without any clue of the fuckin Tel Aviv score! You bastards!

Bring on Everton & Sheff Utd. See you all at West Ham - how about a beer meeting?

Times New Roman   10   ▼   **B** *I* U A   ☰ ☰ ⇥ ⇤   ▤ ▤ ▤ ▤   — 🌐 🖼

Cheers. Shack In the BA lounge on-line!

-----Original Message-----
From: Jeremy@Donsgloryears.co.uk
Sent: 01 November 2002 13:07
To: Dave.Shack@Ononon.co.uk
Subject: Re: 1-0 to the Mighty Whites!

1-0 yes, but far from convincing. Can someone please explain why it took our tactically enlightened manager until half time before changing the shape of the team and playing Harry wide left and Barmby right in a conventional 4-4-2 instead of the horrible narrow diamond shape midfield that has been the main cause of our ineptitude this season. The second half was halfway decent as a consequence, but what a waste of 45 minutes; and what a waste of the first dozen games of the season.

I'm also getting increasingly angry (sorry to bang on here) when I hear Venables talk about a "period of transition". I thought he was hired to take the club forward with the tlented squad of players we currently have, not sidewards. Just think, two seasons ago we were competing with - and in many cases beating - the likes of Lazio, Deportivo la Coruna, Barcelona. Anderlecht etc. We wouldn't stand a chance against them now. And we've basically got the same group of players, probably an improved squad if anything. Progress? I don't think so...

----Original Message-----
From: Andy@whitetoreply.co.uk
Sent: 04 November 2002 02:24
To: Dave Shack@ On on on.
Subject: Re: 1-0 to the Mighty Whites!

And what an awful showing first half. 4-3-3 was crap. Much better second half when we went to 4-4-2, a bit more commitment and nounce. Bit unlucky that it was only 1-0, but at least no away goals against us and a draw against another less than fantastic side will see us through.

--Original Message-----
From: chris@noredscum.co.uk
Sent: 07 November 2002 11:07
To: Dave.Shack@Ononon.co.uk
Subject: Re: 1-0 to the Mighty Whites!---

What the hell has happened to our team? One player leaves and we fall to pieces - the final insult losing to Sheff Utd!! I hate to say it but I think it's time we and Mr Venables parted company. Put it this way one manager will be out of a job on

Verdana   10   **B** *I* U A

Sunday.

-----Original Message-----
From: Shack, Dave, Ononon.co.uk
Sent: 07 November 2002 11:07
To: Whites all, 02/03 User group
Subject: Why don't we all just take a deep breath &....

...realise that this season is going to yield nothing for us. Allow this tosser until the end of January to get things right & then judge him properly. I totally accept that he can't do what he wants to do until January (because he obviously wants to change players), but I hate the fact that he will not use all the resources open to him (Batty) and that he does not seem that passionate about the predicament.

I still maintain that we need someone to look at our physio/training regime as too many players are not recovering/ getting crocked in training. Which also makes me think we reap what we sow on the pitch - ie if we are a bit snidey & dirty on the pitch teams will kick us extra hard - hence the worse injuries we receive. Cut out some of the more cynical play & teams don't react to you as badly. Right?

The fans? Fuck the idiots last night - we lost to a team who didn't give up, when we were happy to sit on an own goal & cruise into the next round. That's not a reason to dislike The Blades for beating us or their fans for running on the pitch after scoring 2 goals in 2 minutes to win the game.

Anyone fancy a moan, sorry a meet, on Sunday at say 12 noon out East for a beer & some pie n' mash? Let me know...

-----Original Message-----
From: Firhad, Mohd, Eltelasia.ma
Sent: 07 November 2002 11:15
To: Shack, Dave, Ononon
Subject: Why don't we all just take a deep breath &....

My optimism is running thin. here is a man who is El Tel's big fan and see him as Elland Road's messiah but 2 losses in a row makes me re think. McPhail being used regularly instead of Bats baffls me. get Dacourt with Bats. The new system seem to stifle my fave player Dacourt;s movement. Playing deep it stops his creatvity. Bats will do that and let Olly free. Lets hope the revival begings with knockin The Hammers. Still optimistic but rather cautious.

Thanks Dave "Bremner" Shack for the gifts last week in KL. It sure is great to have you in the same team in soccer. Cherish the moment you don my Leeds away jersey 29th. Oct and prancing as coach on the 30th on the sideline of the Kuala Lumpur National stadium with the new season white kit. Ole Shacky . Sincerely from Firhad "Clarke".

-----Original Message-----
From: nelly@whitellie-phant.co.uk
Sent: 07 November 2002 11:16
To: Dave.Shack@Ononon.co.uk
Subject: Re: Why don't we all just take a deep breath &....

Dave.Shack@Ononon.co.uk writes:
...realise that this season is going to yield nothing for us.

what took you so long?

-----Original Message-----
From: chris@noredscum.co.uk
Sent: 07 November 2002 11:09
To: Dave.Shack@Ononon.co.uk
Subject: Re: Why don't we all just take a deep breath &....

I'm up for a beer before the game - let me know the details
I've a few mates coming with me

-----Original Message-----
From: nelly@whitellie-phant.co.uk
Sent: 07 November 2002 11:23
To: Dave.Shack@Ononon.co.uk
Subject: Re: Why don't we all just take a deep breath &....

Dave.Shack@Ononon.co.uk writes:
>I hate the fact that he will not use all the resources open to him (Batty) and that he does not seem that passionate about the predicament.

Batty was good for one more season, then they'd have let hm go. we shouldn't fixated on him... Why not Kelly at right-back instead of Mills or Lee Chapman up front. Time passes... it's the future that worries me more than the present.

>regime as too many players are not recovering/ getting crocked in

Verdana   10   B *I* U A

training.

I doubt it's that - this guy HAncock is top drawer, apparently. But your next piont about the tough tackling is interesting…

>The fans? Fuck the idiots last night

That's not a reason to dislike The Blades for beating us or their fans for running on the pitch after scoring 2 goals in 2 minutes to win the game.

You're spot on. I was gutted.

As for the trouble…
They kept us in for 15 minutes. The two guys I took with me were too scared to hurry back to the car (it wasn't as bad as Cardiff, but similar) and I had to ask a copper in full riot gear if I could go back into the street where I'd parked the car. While a team of mounted policemen pushed away a mob of Blades fans. Overhead a chopper and spotlight. We just leapt in and fucked off. Got to M1. Funny noise. Some wanker had let down my right rear tyre (my fault, should've removed stickers). Result: £60 or so for a new one. 70 minute wait for AA. Bed at 2.30.

I'll be in Blind Beggar at that very time. Fuck ,me I'm fed up. DH'sM and I had the trip to Florence as light relief. But then they brought the kick-off forward so we've cancelled flights. Fuck em. they don't deserve out support anyway. Hope the board spend the TV revenue wisely.

-----Original Message-----
From: Jeremy@Donsgloryears.co.uk
Sent: 07 November 2002 11:18
To: Dave.Shack@Ononon.co.uk
Subject: Re: Why don't we all just take a deep breath &....

I'm too depressed to think about things right now. I've got nothing more to say that I haven't already in earlier e-mails.

I'm meeting Nelly on Sunday at a pub called the Blind Beggars (which is I think where the Krays perpetrated many of their foul deeds). I'll forward his e-mail with directions. Fancy meeting up there? Batty for player/manager!!

-----Original Message-----
From: Wathen, Dorian, The Peacocks
Sent: 07 November 2002 11:26
To: Shack, Dave, On, on,on
Subject: RE: Why don't we all just take a deep breath &....

Century Gothic   10   **B** *I* U A   ☰ ☷ ☰ ☰   ☰ ☰ ☰ ☰   — 🔗 🖼

I get the feeling Sunday could be lively...from both sets of supporters!

-----Original Message-----
From: russ@vivaleedspana.esp
Sent: 08 November 2002 10:18
To: Dave.Shack@Ononon.co.uk
Subject: Re: Why don't we all just take a deep breath &....

sorry guys i have had major problems with my phone line and now i am off to valderrama, so my comments will have to wait until monday, so i can moan about losing to the hammers at the same time as moaning about the rest of the shit!!!!

-----Original Message-----
From: chris@noredscum.co.uk
Sent: 07 November 2002 17:09
To: Whites all, 02/03 user group
Subject: Re: Re(2): Why don't we all just take a deep breath &....

Put it this way I've a feeling one team will be without a manager after Sunday...

-----Original Message-----
From: Andy@whitetoreply.co.uk
Sent: 08 November 2002 02:39
To: Whites all, 02/03 user group
Subject: Re: Re(2): Why don't we all just take a deep breath &....

Please god, an early Xmas presie, Venables out. I've had nothing else from Leeds this year, so is it too much to ask?

----Original Message-----
From: Nelly@whitellie-phant.co.uk
Sent: 07 November 2002 17:30
To: Dave.Shack@Ononon.co.uk
Subject: Re: Re:Why don't we all just take a deep breath &....

Dave.Shack@Ononon.co.uk writes:
>realise that this season is going to yield nothing for us...

It's just dawned on me. I came straight back to you and said I knew this ages

ago and I DID - but it hasn't helped because I haven't wholly and truly accepted it. I know we will win nothing but I still expect us to.
This is the path to disappointment. We need to be more Zen about it. We need to accept it, remember it, and get on with it (as a wise football captain I played with once said).

Dave.Shack@Ononon.co.uk writes:
>Ah, Nelly - that was me when we played for Kerrang! FC right???

There lies the way to true enlightenment.

With that kind of inner peace even watching George Graham's eight defenders grinding out a succsession of 0-0 draws became fun. I know now where we need to go...

But let's stop at the Blind Beggar first!

-----Original Message-----
From: Shack, Dave, Ononon.co.uk
Sent: 09 November 2002 19:44
To: Whites all, 02/03 user group
Subject: The real cream of Manchester...

Lads! So The real cream of Manchester (City!) rose to the top today! Lovely. Even Liverpool slipped up & so it was really only Chelsea winning that marred a great day of football scores. Sheff United didn't win (proving they are actually shite) and our own website denies a punch-up rumour from after the Sheff match - yet indicates that Mills isn't avaialable for selection tomorrow.

Jeez - I'll see Tams, Dorian, Jeremy & Nelly in the Blind Beggar for a pint tomorrow.

Cheers & pray for the lads! (it's come to that!)

Shacky

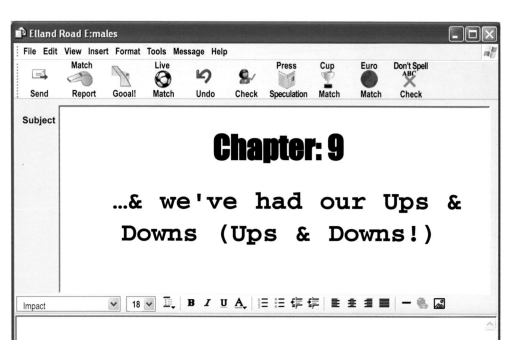

Chapter: 9

...& we've had our Ups & Downs (Ups & Downs!)

PREFACE:

Well, a roller-coaster ride doesn't normally have this many Ups & Downs (Ups & Downs) does it? Leeds manage the most ridiculous victory over the self proclaimed worst team in the league (at that time), West Ham, before heading off to smash Hapoel Tel Aviv. On the back of being dumped out of the Worthless Cup to a lesser (not as it would later transpire!) team we had to endure debacles with Bolton and a resurgent Everton. Up & Down indeed...

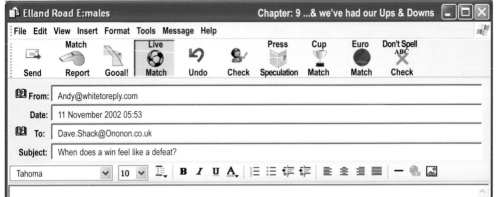

-----Original Message-----
From: Andy@whitetoreply.com
Sent: 11 November 2002 05:53
To: Dave.Shack@ Ononon.co.uk
Subject: When does a win feel like a defeat?

What a game. 4-1 at half time and we're running them ragged, more out of mistakes by West Ham than excellence by us, but what the hell. I think El Tel needs to work on his half time talks. More of a Master Bater than a Master Tactician. Leeds press the self destruct button again and only just come away with the 3 points. For those of us with nervous dispositions, this was not good.
On the positive side, I thought Lukic was excellent which made one out of eleven. Nice to see the young blood as well. Could we have a Wayne Rooney. Did he get a touch at all?
Let's hope that we do the business in Florence and then bring on the mighty Bolton.
Andy

-----Original Message-----
From: russ@Leedsvivaspana.esp
Sent: 11 November 2002 08:49
To: Dave.Shack@Ononon.co.uk
Subject: When does a win feel like a defeat?

yeah, pray no more! 3 points at last!!
i think only the hammers could provide us with 3 points like that, but well take them anyway we can at the moment.
kewell was more of himself and i thought we looked a bit more lively than of late, but you have to say our back line looks incredibly weak.
was that kelly getting skinned or his other half, those too are becoming the only regular things happening to leeds and there bad.
i don't know why el tel keeps going on about the transfer window, we have what we have and if he dose'nt think batty is better than what we have

Comic Sans MS   10   B I U A

mmmmmmmmm?
bring on tel a heave!

----Original Message-----
From: chris@noredscum.co.uk
Sent: 11 November 2002 16:16
To: Shack, Dave, Ononon
Subject: Yesterday's game

Well despite the best intentions of London Underground I
managed to make it in time to meet you at the pub.
  What can I say about the game? Definitely a Phirric victory
(schoolboy Latin anyone?) - but 3 points is 3 points. I
actually felt quite sorry for West Ham in the end but there's
no room for sentimentality in this game! I'm dying to see the
highlights tonight because I want to see how dreadful De
Canio's dive for that penalty.
  Good to see young Milner making his debut - thought he played
well (apart from that one awful pass) which leads me on to why
aren't we giving more of our youngsters a chance - Singh,
Candsell-Sheriff etc etc
Roll on Thursday - what sort of a kick off time is 4pm?
  Chris

-----Original Message-----
From: Firhad, Mohd, Eltelasia.ma
Sent: 11 November 2002 02:43
To: Shack, Dave, Ononon
Subject: Leeds Knocks The Hammers - Barely

Phew !!!!!!!!!! What a game. But rather leave it to another rather than
Leeds. The 45 minutes syndrome strikes back.Where was our lads in the
second half ??!!

Complacency breeds lackadaisical concentration and there you go 3 goals.
Although we were 4 up , the question mark remains as the West Ham's
defence serve it up on a silver platter with one of the worst defensive
displays yet this season.

Will reserve optimism till the next 2 games. Bowyer in the middle is a
waste. Shift him back on the right flank. Lucic is cool and is an asset.
Await Robbie and Matteo's return.

Verdana   10   B *I* U A

-----Original Message-----
From: Shack, Dave, Ononon.co.uk
Sent: 14 November 2002 17:44
To: TheWhites, all 02/03 User group
Subject: Smiffy rules Tel Aviv Ok!

Four goals - what a star!

Let's have 10!

...Wow live action: Robbo great 1 on 1 save. What a hero too!

-----Original Message-----
From: chris@Captdom.co.uk
Sent: 20 November 2002 11:58
To: Dave.Shack@Ononon.co.uk
Subject: Re: Smiffy rules Tel Aviv Ok!

So I'm on the air at Radio One. It's my dream job, and LEEDS are playing on 5 (nice channel that!), divided loyalties for me today.

I must apologize to my listeners about talking rubbish very quickly for 10 seconds between each song so I could watch the match in the studio!!

Alan Bloody Brillaint Smith. How ace was that. See, we're not that bad, and we have great players. Things could turn around soon ... we hope

-----Original Message-----
From: chris@Noredscum.co.uk
Sent: 14 November 2002 17:45
To: TheWhites, all 02/03 User group
Subject: Re: Smiffy rules Tel Aviv Ok!

and to think they put Chelsea out last year...

-----Original Message-----
From: Davidharveysmonkey@aol.com
Sent: 15 November 2002 11:10
To: Dave.Shack@Ononon.co.uk
Subject: Re: Smiffy rules Tel Aviv Ok!

8 goals in a week!!!

DH'sM

Tahoma | 10 | 🛂 | **B** *I* U A | ☰ ☰ ☰ ☰ | ▤ ▤ ▤ ▤ | ▬ 🔗 🖼

-----Original Message-----
From: Andy@Whitetoreply.co.uk
Sent: 16 November 2002 02:11
To: Dave.Shack@Ononon.co.uk
Subject: Re: Smiffy rules Tel Aviv Ok!

I can't think of anyone I would rather have seen score 1 goal let alone 4. It's a great reward for the commitment that he shows the team. If he isn't up front for England from now on, Sven is mad.

Ye you're right about Robbo as well. Marvellous performance and nice to see 2 more new faces given a run. Mind you, central defence is looking a bit sparse.

-----Original Message-----
From: Shack, Dave, Ononon.co.uk
Sent: 15 November 2002 10:36
To: TheWhites, all 02/03 User group
Subject: Pre Uefa draws jitters....

Something tells me that we will draw a Turkish side in this 3rd round draw...anyone else feel the same? Denizlispor (where?)here we come. Nice to know we're the 3rd seeds behind Lazio & Liverpool & above Celta Vigo!

Fingers crossed for Malaga & a stay at Russ' house!

-----Original Message-----
From: Davidharveysmonkey@aol.com
Sent: 15 November 2002 11:16
To: TheWhites, all 02/03 User group
Subject: Re: Pre Uefa draws jitters....

No spanish teams (football) or turkish teams (history), is there anywhere in france

-----Original Message-----
From: Russ@VivaLeedspana.esp
Sent: 15 November 2002 11:30
To:Dave.Shack@Ononon.co.uk;Davidharveysmonkey@aol.com
Subject: Re: Pre Uefa draws jitters....

yeh Malaga party party!!

Courier New | 10

```
-----Original Message-----
From: Chris@Noredscum.co.uk
Sent: 15 November 2002 11:45
To: TheWhites, all 02/03 User group
Subject: Re: Pre Uefa draws jitters....

Its Malaga
```

-----Original Message-----
From: Chris@Captdom.co.uk
Sent: 20 November 2002 11:59
To: Dave.Shack@Ononon.co.uk
Subject: Re: Pre Uefa draws jitters....

I know they've got an airport & some nightclubs. Do they have a team as well ...!!?

-----Original Message-----
From: Nelly@theWhitellie-phant.co.uk
Sent: 15 November 2002 11:51
To: Dave.Shack@Ononon.co.uk
Subject: Re: Pre Uefa draws jitters....

Russ here we come - can I have the big room?

```
-----Original Message-----
From: Russ@Vivaleedspana.spa
Sent: 15 November 2002 11:43
To: Dave Shack; Whites, all 02/03 User group
Subject: Re: Pre Uefa draws jitters....
```

yeeeeeeeeeeeeeeeeeeeeeeeeeeeeeeeeeeeessssssssssssssssssssssssssssssssssssss!!!!!!!!!!!!

-----Original Message-----
From: Nelly@theWhitellie-phant.co.uk
Sent: 15 November 2002 12:07
To: Dave.Shack@Ononon.co.uk
Subject: Re: RE: Pre Uefa draws jitters....

we are the champions, champions of europe!!!
we are the champions, champions of europe!!!
we are the champions, champions of europe!!!
we are the champions, champions of europe!!!

-----Original Message-----
From: Shack, Dave, Ononon.co.uk
Sent: 18 November 2002 14:36
To: TheWhites, all 02/03 User group
Subject: Match day foreign travel Leeds Utd blues...

I can't remember being so disappointed in Leeds. I'm here in bloody Brolin-land (he's getting a lifetime achievement award at the Swedish football awards here tonight, Fat Git!)and met another long-time Leeds fan yesterday - Mark Plunkett who looks after Ronan Keating. We both were sat in the dressing room getting more & more miserable as text alerts came in.

2 goals in the last 2 minutes - how can a fully professional team switch off like that? It's a disgrace. It's like any of us with a job to do packing in an hour before it's finished & pissing off home.

I'd like to see Smithy's face & hear his comments when the rest of the team let's his team down. What did Terry say? Ha, Ha, keep my seat warm Des/ Gabby I may need it sooner than you think... Oi, Mr agent get me a Christmas Panto quick I'll be out of work by Xmas...?

Fortress Elland Road! Ha - it's a shit show.

-----Original Message-----
From: Nelly@theWhitellie-phant.co.uk
Sent: 18 November 2002 14:51
To: Dave.Shack@Ononon.co.uk
Subject: Re: Match day foreign travel Leeds Utd blues...

Is that "Crouching" Mark Plunkett formerly keyboard wizard of Little Angles? Very nice man...

Exactly... This from a 16-year-old match reporter I read:

So the Elland Road faithful are treated to a third four-goal display? Yes, but they didn't, in there wildest dreams, expect the four goals to be scored by the team anchored to the bottom of the league!

-----Original Message-----
From: Wathen, Dorian, The Peacocks
Sent: 18 November 2002 14:55
To: TheWhites, all 02/03 User group
Subject: RE: Match day foreign travel Leeds Utd blues...

Century Gothic   10   B *I* U A

True - but you look at the 2 team sheets and Bolton had the better players - Djorkaeff, Campo, Jay Jay Okocha, N'Gotty etc are all world class players - we had Burns and McPhail in midfield - says it all - I can't recall a worse midfield that at present - we've got too many injuries and not enough back up - roll on January transfers - hopefully we won't be far enough down the table to turn the better players off ...

-----Original Message-----
From: Jeremy@Donsgloryears.co.uk
Sent: 18 November 2002 15:13
To: Dave.Shack@Ononon.co.uk
Subject: Re: Match day foreign travel Leeds Utd blues...

It's not that complicated - we are losing games because our midfield is totally inadequate in terms of shape, tactics and personnel. What othermanager on the planet would pick Jake Burns over David Batty? And how can a defence defend properly when there is no protection being given it by the midfiled?

-----Original Message-----
From: Chris@Captdom.co.uk
Sent: 20 November 2002 12:07
To: Shack, Dave, Ononon
Subject: Re: Match day foreign travel Leeds Utd blues...

I sat having a bit of lunch with 'our lass' and my mate was texting me the score from a pub down the road.

With my limited knowledge of football, how does it work?

We equalize in the 87th minute to make it 2-2. Then we lose 4-2. WHAT THE FUCK!!??

-----Original Message-----
From: DavidHarveysmonkey@aol.com
Sent: 18 November 2002 18:36
To: TheWhites, all 02/03 User group.
Subject: Re: Match day foreign travel Leeds Utd blues...

You can't win if you don't have posession, Batts used to get us posession and then give it to the attacking midfielders. It's dead simple.

who's going to spain? & does eden still support leeds? has he fixed his trousers yet?

Courier New   ⌄   10   ⌄   ☰   **B** *I* U A   ☰ ☰ ☲ ☲   ☰ ☰ ☰ ☰   — 🌐 🖼

```
-----Original Message-----
From: Chris@Noredscum.co.uk
Sent: 18 November 2002 18:31
To: TheWhites, all 02/03 User group
Subject: Re: RE: Match day foreign travel Leeds Utd blues...


Hmm not sure yet - don't know if I should blow a lot of money
if we are going to play like we did on Sunday...More currently
- who's going to Spurs?


-----Original Message-----
From: Firhad, Mohd, Eltelasia
Sent: 19 November 2002 03:39
To: Shack, Dave, Ononon
Subject: Match day foreign travel Leeds Utd blues...


On Hapoel:
Smithy the spark........Go You Leeds. What worries me is the defense.
Hapoel could have 3- 4 themselves. Robbo's one on one save is great. 3 in
against West Ham is a dangerous situation.


Bolton:
Oh my God !!!!!!!!!!!!! Amateur defensive lead to another defeat. Writings
on the wall from our last 2 matches. Bar injuries but at least we can
shore up our defense. Still behind the bots and El Tel but for how long
???!!!! It will lead to feelings of disssatisfaction on the performers ie.
Kewell, Smithy etc. It may rub off on them. Mills come back. Be in the
center whilst awaiting the injured warriors return.
```

-----Original Message-----
From: Shack, Dave, Ononon.co.uk
Sent: 19 November 2002 20:57
To: TheWhites, all 02/03 User group
Subject: Gallows Humour - the Leeds website has it all!

Just how bad can it get? Looking for some light relief (ok I wanted to see
what positive spin they were gonna put on everything on the web-site) I
have taken some of the latest headlines (ha!) and re-written the stories
for you.

1. Batty Out for Six.
Leeds Legend David Batty (45) has been forced to retire from the Leeds
United First Team squad. He has now got a severe case of tendinitis in
both knees that he contracted by continually bending down on El Tel's

Verdana   10   **B** *I* U A

office floor begging to be given a chance. As the axminster gradually wore away, the Yorkshire granite has played havoc with his knees and it looks likely that Jacob Burns will now step into his position at the club. The perfect replacement, Burns (21), will add some much needed steel & experience to the Leeds midfield. He joined Leeds because the Pennines & Yorkshire moors provided him with so many sheep that he can keep his sheep shearing world record (25 in an hour) intact.

2. Pleasure Flights in the Leeds United Helicopter
A brand new service for fans not interested in watching the shite at Elland Road on matchday was announced today. The new Leeds United Helicopter (Please do not peel the plastic logo of the natty little red helicopter - & please let the office know if the Vodaphone logo shines through the paintwork again!) will fly a route over Old Trafford's training ground (with guaranteed views of Rio-Scum & Beckham laid up), then it will take in The Stadium of Shite with a view of Wilco & his mis-firing team before returning over the now forgotten about site for the new, state of the art, 50,000+ seater stadium on the edge of the A1. All in all a great day out for all the family.

3.McMaster set for Coventry Loan.
Right in the middle of a midfield crisis we are allowing one of our talented youngsters to piss off & help someone else. Brilliant. Why not send Jacob Burns?

4. Meet Nick Barmby. Nick Barmby Signing...
For any other club who will be in Europe next season and doesn't tell him a pack of lies on signing or pay him in knock off Rolexes & Armani whistles.

Also - in Ridsdales note about seeking re-election he mention's our team from the end of '96 Season. By doing this he then notes that he is making no judgement about them all compared to this current team. And guess what? Wetherall's in there again. So that's twice that PR has publicly humiliated him.

Laugh? I nearly booked a flight to Malaga!

-----Original Message-----
From: Shack, Dave, Ononon
Sent: 21 November 2002 09:25
To: TheWhites, all 02/03 User group
Subject: Password Change

Verdana | 10 | B *I* U A, | ≡ ≡ ≡ ≡ | ≡ ≡ ≡ ≡ | — 🔗 🖼

My computer made me change passwords today & it won't let me have any of the last 8 choices. Obviously I had no problem getting rid of 'Venables' - the now retired entry and I chose :   Battyback
Any better 8 letter minimum combinations?

---Original Message-----
From: Nelly@whitellie-phant.co.uk
Sent: 21 November 2002 11:16
To: Dave.Shack@Ononon.co.uk
Subject: Re: Password Change --

clarke1-0 leeds4eva DonRevie

-----Original Message-----
From: Chris@Noredscum.co.uk
Sent: 21 November 2002 10:04
To: Shack, Dave, On on on
Subject: Re: Password Change

Rio=scum Leedssos

-----Original Message-----
From: Nelly@whitellie-phant.co.uk
Sent: 21 November 2002 11:43
To: Dave.Shack@Ononon.co.uk
Subject: Re: RE: Password Change

>leeds4eva?

----- Original Message -----
From: Dave.Shack@Ononon.co.uk
To: Nelly@whitellie-phant.co.uk
Sent: November 21, 2002 11.44
Subject: RE: Password Change

How old are you 8?

-----Original Message-----
From: Nelly@ whitellie-phant.co.uk
Sent: 21 November 2002 11:45
To: Dave.Shack@Ononon.co.uk
Subject: Re: RE: Password Change

don't tell me you hadn't thought of it!!!

Arial   10   **B** *I* U A ...

-----Original Message-----
From: Chris@Captdom.co.uk
Sent: 22 November 2002 10:11
To: Shack, Dave, Ononon
Subject: Re: Password Change

"ElBollox" ...?   "Smithystay"   "Waynewhoney"
or how about;
"We'vegotsomanyinjuredplayersthebloodygroundsmanisplayingforusthisweekend"

----- Original Message -----
From: Dave.Shack@Ononon.co.uk>
To: Chris@Captdom.co.uk>
Sent: Friday, November 22, 2002 10:27 AM
Subject: RE: Password Change

> the last one has too many letters

-----Original Message-----
From: Chris@Captdom.co.uk
Sent: 30 November 2002 15:10
To: Dave.Shack@Ononon.co.uk
Subject: Re: Password Change

you think ...?

-----Original Message-----
From: Andy@Whitetoreply.co.uk
Sent: 21 November 2002 23:45
To: Dave.Shack@Ononon.co.uk
Subject: Re: Password Change

How about Whiteshite or Neverwin or Givingup or Noeffort or PleasesignSmiffy

----- Original Message -----
From: Dave.Shack@Ononon.co.uk
To: TheWhites, all 02/03 User group
Sent: Friday, November 22, 2002 10:27 AM
Subject: RE: Password Change

Enough!

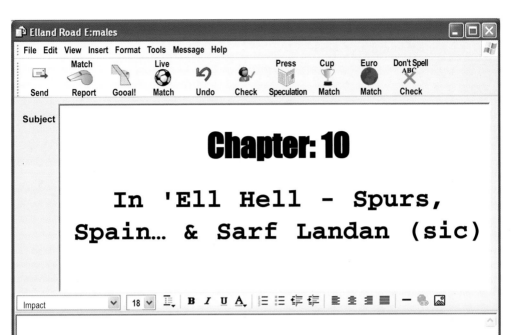

Chapter: 10

In 'Ell Hell - Spurs, Spain... & Sarf Landan (sic)

PREFACE:

Venables' reign is certainly not all it's cracked up to be. Consistency is not a word bandied about at Elland Road and the natives are getting increasingly restless. After the shocker against Spurs came even worse performances against Fulham & Charlton. European elimination was on the cards against Malaga - even the Spanish jinx couldn't be over-turned in it's own backyard and yes, Christmas was looking more like a tangerine & a couple of nuts than a Buzz Lightyear, a PS2 & a 'super-market sweep' in the club shop!

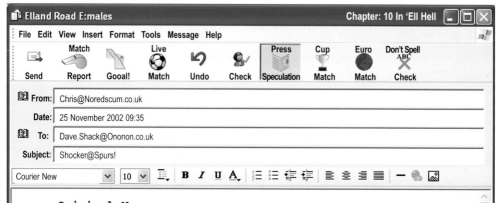

From: Chris@Noredscum.co.uk

Date: 25 November 2002 09:35

To: Dave.Shack@Ononon.co.uk

Subject: Shocker@Spurs!

-----Original Message-----
From: Chris@Noredscum.co.uk
Sent: 25 November 2002 09:35
To: Dave.Shack@Ononon.co.uk
Subject: Shocker@Spurs!

Well - I now know what its like to be a fan of the worst team in the league. We were absolutely abysmal yesterday - Spurs were bad and we were worse. To make it even worse Robbie Keane didn't even score first - so bang goes my £10 with William Hills!!

I was sat in the upper tier and I must say the Leeds fans were the loudest I've ever heard - for most of the game we sang out loud trying to encourage the team - I personally didn't hear any discouraging chants (apart from at the referee who was quite frankly the worse ref I've ever seen). Ridsdale was complaining last week about the boo boys - we had more reason than ever to boo yesterday but no-one did - the team let us all down, badly. Something has got to change at our club and its got to change right now or we will get relegated.

Most of the players seem to have no fighting spirit, no determination, no heart or spirit. When ever the fans show their distaste we get slated by the Chairman - he has got to realise that we are sick to death of all the spin that is emanating from Max Clifford - its time for a serious sort out at Elland road.
Just to end on a lighter note I woke up this morning to find a 12 foot long "Super Leeds" England flag in my flat - I have no idea where I got that or how or why - alcohol's great isn't it? Chris

Verdana ▾ | 10 ▾ | 🇪, B *I* U A, | ☰ ☷ ⏭ ⏮ | ☰ ☰ ☰ ☰ | — 🐌 🖼

-----Original Message-----
From: Shack, Dave, Ononon.co.uk
Sent: 25 November 2002 09:56
To: TheWhites, all 02/03 User group
Subject: Ell Hell but no way back!

On Saturday I started to kid myself with a fuzzy warm perception that - hey, maybe Bolton are not that bad - they nearly beat Chelsea after all (although they clearly tired in that game unlike ours). Everton too - they are solid right now & in fact it's certainly no disgrace to have been mugged 1-0 by their wonder bollocks. The Gooners could lose to Southampton & even Liverpool were having a wobble. Shitty Villa have won a few games since our bore draw and even Sunderland. Nah, forget them.

But then Sunday arrives & the 2 hour journey to the end of the London footballing earth ends (fortunately I wasn't driving for once and could bloody drink my mate's box bar tab) with a truly appalling result against a relatively pedestrian team & a striker with a point to prove. It was always gonna be a nightmare for us, but why, oh why can 11 guys (actually 8 because Smithy, Robbo & shop window (for obvious reasons) tried their best) turn up to play football with absolutely no desire to win? That first half was atrocious. Sure it was a shame about Barmby, but Jacob Burns? Come on he's played in Div 2 of the Aussie league & he's playing for Leeds. Yeah, he's really the bloody future isn't he? Blood another young 'un. The tactics were about right - man for man with wing backs played out fine, but for a lack-lustre clearance & an assist from the unluckiest manager in the premiership! Jesus.
The fans were great despite the shite & I just found my self laughing with the Spurs fans (& my host, Rich$ who is as funny as anyone) at how bad we were. The cheer from the Leeds end when Kewell finally had our first (albeit weak) attempt on goal was brilliant - the irony saying more than a thousand chants of _____ out (insert any of the following names: Venables, Ridsdale, Bowyer) ever could.

Believe me, that one moment of lucidity made me feel a whole lot better. It's shit, we know it, we can't do anything about it - so let's laugh with it and at least stop appearing like a bunch of sad, ungrateful bunch of Yorkshire tossers to everyone else in football. Que Sera Sera. We'll always be Leeds & if Malaga batter us on Thursday & the now seemingly inevitable does happen in both the boardroom & the managers office then let's not be responsible for it. The fans didn't get rid of O'Leary. The fans did not bring in Venables - but the fans might keep a future success story away.

Comic Sans MS   10   **B** *I* U A

Original Message-----
From: russ@vivaleedspana.esp
Sent: 25 November 2002 10:58
To: Dave.Shack@Ononon.co.uk
Subject: Re: Ell Hell but no way back!

eh eh nice speech dave, nelly better watch out i reckon you could take a top job in writing!!
what no talk about football? no fuck off im in a good humor today, so lets not spoil it.no pace thats our problem
adios

-----Original Message-----
From: chris@noredscum.co.uk
Sent: 26 November 2002 10:41
To: TheWhites, all 02/03 User group
Subject: Re: Ell Hell but no way back!

Two shots - we only had two shots

-----Original Message-----
From: Wathen, Dorian, The Peacocks
Sent: 26 November 2002 10:52
To: Shack, Dave, Ononon.co.uk
Subject: RE: Ell Hell but no way back!

True - but again player for player on paper and on the pitch we were the weaker side. We didn't create an opening all match.
Check out the defence - only one player would be there on merit - and woody was carrying an injury it seemed to me.
Same for the midfield - we have the worst midfield in the premiership it appears to me.
why did we start 3-5-2 seems strange to me too - it must have been last minute as a result of the Barmby injury but we looked better 4-4-2 after he changed it round when Burns (thank god) came off - he would struggle to get into a first division side, let alone premiership.

At present we just have a terrible side - and it's not really Venables' fault that all he has is strikers and no qualtity back up in defence and midfield.

Best Regards, Dorian

Century Gothic   10   **B** *I* U A ≔ ≡ ⧉ ⧉ ≣ ≣ ≣ ≣ — 🖉 🖼

-----Original Message-----
From: nelly@whitellie-phant.co.uk
Sent: 26 November 2002 11:22
To: Dave.Shack@Ononon.co.uk
Subject: Re: RE: Ell Hell but no way back!

half of me didn't want to go because I didnt think they deserved it. But your email said it all - this isnt about them, it's about US. I'm six inches taller since reading it.

-----Original Message-----
From: Jeremy@Donsgloryears.co.uk
Sent: 26 November 2002 12:32
To: Dave.Shack@Ononon.co.uk
Subject: Re: Ell Hell but no way back!

You're right, the gallows humour of the fans was the only bright spot on what has to be one of the gloomiest experiences I have had in recent years watching Leeds. I can't bring myself to talk about the football any more, as we are just going from bad to worse for all the reasons that have already been mentioned (although our injury situation is just compounding an already dire situation). Let's us as fans stay as positive and as humourous as possible. Things could be worse - imagine being a Sheffield Wednesday supporter!

-----Original Message-----
From: Andy@Whitetoreply.co.uk
Sent: 27 November 2002 02:08
To: Dave.Shack@Ononon
Subject: Re: Ell Hell but no way back!

No good Shack. Can't believe that anyone can stand up for him anymore. Venebles must go. OK the team are shite as well, but he picks them, he organises them and he should motivate them. There is no desire and that needs action at the managerial level. My pre season thoughts have been totally vindicated almost half way into the season. We have a number of "easy" games coming up and if we are to survive the most unexpected drop of the season, we must start winning - whatever the cost.
 Yours dejectedly Andy

-----Original Message-----
From: Shack, Dave, Ononon.co.uk
Sent: 29 November 2002 10:41
To: TheWhites, all 02/03 User group
Subject: A gutsy performance - so we did, to be sure!*

Malaga 0-0 Leeds

* Gary Kelly, Channel 5 post-match Interview

Well, we'll take what we can at the moment. What we got was some passion & some real desire to not let the ship sink any deeper. It was very interesting to hear Kells afterwards (didn't realize he was so 'comedy' irish still - Oh to be sure & Oh so we did! He's 100 times broader than nephew Ian that's for sure, anyway...) saying that all the lads were right behind 'the gaffer' and keen to display it. They have a great spirit there (to be sure) he said & he'd take anything in Europe & swap it all for a run of premiership wins (so he would!). The whole team takes the defeats & criticism personally & that the defence starts from the strikers backwards (I liked that bit). It was a good interview from an honest Leeds player who, whilst maybe a bit of a one-trick pony now (jump in, spin & hoof the ball like a sand iron down the line) can never be faulted for his career - long commitment to Leeds United.

We could have won it - so could they at the end with their fresh subs, but we always looked the more likely thanks to Harry & Smithy.

It's all about Charlton now. Win that & we'll make it to Xmas I think. The same commitment, a supportive home crowd & we should do it.

Shacky

P.S. Russ was there & we didn't lose! Maybe the Jinx is waning...

-----Original Message-----
From: Davidharveysmonkey@aol.com
Sent: 29 November 2002 10:57
To: TheWhites, all 02/03 User group
Subject: Re: A gutsy performance - so we did, to be sure!

I think Duberry get's a rough ride. At first he was just like a club
buffoon but remember when he filled in with Mills a couple of seasons
back? He was fucking ace. he just gives the impression of being a
simpleton, I'm sure if they hadn't all been given such big wages then he'd already be playing for
Bolton, West Ham or Cov or someone like that. DH'sM

-----Original Message-----
From: Wathen, Dorian, The Peacocks
Sent: 29 November 2002 11:27
To: Shack, Dave, Ononon
Subject: RE: A gutsy performance - so we did, to be sure!

Taped and seen this a.m....

I think Dubes' head is octagonal - there was one scary moment where a hopeful cross was looped in, he tried to head it out for a throw and it flew past Robbos right hand post.

Reports this morning from the tabs - Bow and Fowler to Man City and Olly given his marching orders to leave in Jan and an Argentine central defended called Milito being pursued....

-----Original Message-----
From: chris@Captdom.co.uk
Sent: 30 November 2002 15:27
To: TheWhites, all 02/03 User group
Subject: Re: A gutsy performance - so we did, to be sure!

I had to go see Jools Hooland at the RAH (big fan you see!) so I missed the game live.

Managed to get through the night without finding out the score, waiting to watch the replay on 5 at 12.50AM!!!

Got to bed at 2.30AM after watching a game with no goals ... makes a change actually!!!

-----Original Message-----
From: Shack, Dave, Ononon.co.uk
Sent: 01 December 2002 15:13
To: TheWhites, all 02/03 User group
Subject: About last night...

2.50 Sunday, December 1st

Man U have just beaten Liverpool (Dudek again) and I hate to say that the little turd Neville has had a stormer. But enough of that bad news...here's some more. At a dinner party last night I was talking to a really top bloke who buys sports rights for a living. We got talking about golf, the BBC loosing all theirs etc, etc & then we moved to football. He was a Liverpool fan & was pretty confident in giving me some shit about our pedicament relative to theirs. Anyway, then came the bombshell: He said that the real problem at Leeds was not a division in the dressing room versus the Manager, but between SIX WANT AWAY PLAYERS & the rest of the team. He was not 100% per cent on all six - but he did have the following names ending in the bombshell to follow:

The names - starting with the obvious....
Bowyer....Dacourt....Duberry...Mills (?) Viduka (?) and WOODGATE!!

Hey it's kick off now - I'm listening to RadioAire on the internet & they have announced the same team as Thursday (no Lucic for Dubes!) but with FOWLER on the bench -so come on Leeds!

Anyway, what about that? Woody wants to get away... Can you believe it? My question marks are about names he could not confirm - but wow! is all I could say.

6 minutes in & Harry nearly scored!

The only good thing that did happen yesterday was that when I got doubled up with 2 golfers at a place called Stockley Park - one of the lads turned out to be a mad Leeds fan called Mark who originally came from Barnsley. How did he become a Leeds fan I asked? Well, in the early 70's when Leeds were doing well & Barnsley were not, all his relatives bought him Leeds stuff & he became interested. Then come the Euro final his Uncle had been a Leeds Fan forever & never missed a game home or away for 10 years. The club failed to help him get a ticket so he gave all his stuff to Mark and never went to see Leeds again. Come on Leeds!

-----Original Message-----
From: Shack, Dave, Ononon.co.uk
Sent: 01 December 2002 16:54
To: TheWhites, all 02/03 User group
Subject: Last minute heartbreak...again

4.54pm Parker - solo run, length of field. 2-1. Shit.
Can it get any worse? I don't think so. Shit.

-----Original Message-----
From: Firhad, Mohd, Eltelasia.ma
Sent: 02 December 2002 03:08
To: Shack, Dave, Ononon.
Subject: Last minute heartbreak...again

Been busy.............Heere are all thoughts coming at once:

Spurs Reaction:
No clear chances. Players out of sorts. Tactical vision nowhere. Defensive discipline in shambles. El Tel, where are you ??!!! The 2 goals can be

avoided if we wree a litlle more focused to integrate meidfield and
defense.

Malaga:
A lil booster for a revival...........But knowing the season;s pattern
expect the worse. When are we gonna string a run that befits a club that
is poised for greater things - how come the last flourish by opponents
will open our floodgates?

Charlton:
Tempted to scream El Tel must go. Blame it on complacency or sheer
"bollocks".........As evidenced the last 10 minutes seems to be our down
fall and not forgetting the second half Mr., Hyde kinda performance.

-----Original Message-----
From: Wathen, Dorian, the Peacocks
Sent: 02 December 2002 10:54
To: Shack, Dave, Ononon
Subject: RE: Last minute heartbreak...again

The only positive is that I got rid of Robbo in my fantasy team a month ago ...
why are we so susceptible to players running at our defence ? Mind you we
didn't have the midfield tackling dynamo that is McFoul on at that point ...

-----Original Message-----
From: Nelly@thewhitellie-phant.co.uk
Sent: 02 December 2002 11:28
To: Dave.Shack@Ononon.com
Subject: Re: Last minute heartbreak...again

I don't think so. Shit.

To be honest, from where I was they have been a LOT worse. I thought the
whole scenario was vastly improved (even on Malaga - which I thought was
a really dull game, "gutsy" "determined" but ultimately, just really dull and
frustrating).

The crowd support for the team was superb. "Stand up and sing for Leeds!"led
The Kop, right from the off - and three sides of the ground picked it up!

You've got to admire TV for being that positive. Strangely, I think
that match might be a watershed. Best they've played for ages. I feel much
more encouraged, now...Malaga (except for the match) was a fanastic trip.

Century Gothic   10   B *I* U A

Russ says "Hi!" to you all!

-----Original Message-----
From: Jeremy@Donsgloryears.co.uk
Sent: 02 December 2002 11:07
To: Dave.Shack@Ononon
Subject: Re: Last minute heartbreak...again

I was listening to the second half on radio, and all through the commentary was going "and Leeds' midfield cannot retain possession" or "and Leeds keep giving the ball away" etc. etc. To be honest the two late goals came as no surprise. We seem to have currently the most ineffective midfield in the Premiership - teams must love playing against us because we make it so easy for them.

But the odd thing is this - remember 3 seasons ago; great run in the UEFA Cup, semi-final etc, finishing 4th in the Premiership and qualifying for the Champions League, despite all the post-Istanbul (not to mention the pre-trial) traumas? Who were our midfield for most of that season? Bowyer, Bakke, McPhail, Wilcox. Who are our current midfild? You got it... I don't remember our being such a powder-puff team then, and I don't remember a midfield that was anything other than competetive, combative and often extremely creative and effective.

So what the fuck's happening now?

-----Original Message-----
From: Andy@Whitetoreply.co.uk
Sent: 03 December 2002 02:06
To: Dave Shack @ On on on
Subject: Re: Last minute heartbreak...again

What the chuff? Do we not understand that we need to play the injury time as well as the opposition. This last minute goal leak has got to stop.
Regards the guys wanting out, no surprises there at all. How can you blame people who want to get on and don't believe that Leeds is the place to do it. It's desparately disappointing, particularly as with their salaries, they should give complete commitment. Perhaps this explains the absences and the lack of grit in their performances. Mind you, what would it leave us with? Come on you under 17's!!

-----Original Message-----
From: Russ@Vivaleedspana.spa
Sent: 03 December 2002 15:36
To: TheWhites, all 02/03 User group
Subject: Re: Last minute heartbreak...again

Comic Sans MS   ⏷   10 ⏷   ⲉ▾   **B** *I* <u>U</u> <u>A</u>▾   ☰ ☷ ⮒ ⮓   ▤ ▤ ▤ ▤   — 🌐 🖼

relegation?

-----Original Message-----
From: chris@Captdom.co.uk
Sent: 03 December 2002 22:09
To: Dave.Shack@Ononon.co.uk
Subject: Re: Last minute heartbreak...again

So I'm at work today and Viduka is on the news pretty much saying that he doesn't know why he wasnt played at the weekend. He went on and said that if they didn't want him there he would go!!

WHAT THE FUCK IS GOING ON THERE?

There's seems more to all of this then meets the eye, and let's be honest,are we really surprised??

Players talking to the press about how fucked off they are!! Marching on together? Maybe not

  -----Original Message-----
From: Firhad, Mohd, Eltelasia.ma
Sent: 04 December 2002 04:45
To: Shack, Dave, Ononon.co.uk
Subject: FW: Last minute heartbreak...again

Shocker !!!! Shocker !!!!!!!!! Charlton beat us. Now Batty's suing us......What happening. Still await the redemption but when, God knows. Fulham is another bite at it but still optimistic. Relegation. Nope it will not happen. Fowler / Smith and Bridges somewhwre upfront may work.

-----Original Message-----
From: Shack, Dave, Ononon.co.uk
Sent: 05 December 2002 13:56
To: TheWhites, all 02/03 User group
Subject: Like Father (First Team) like Son (Reserves) - The Elland Road Epidemic!

How spooky is this? Here's a report from the Reserves last night 1-1 vs WBA. My bold italics!

Substitute Simon Johnson could have secured the win for Leeds, but missed two good chances before Martyn was given a warning when West

Verdana   10   B *I* U A

Brom hit the bar again, this time with a header.
The Baggies equaliser with three minutes of normal time left saw Matthew
Collins direct his diving header past the outstretched arms of Nigel
Martyn.
Mark Viduka should have restored United's lead immediately by
converting Seth Johnson's cross, but allowed the keeper to make the
save.
Despite the disappointment of conceding late on, the major plus points
were seeing Radebe, Fowler and Seth Johnson get some more valuable
match practice, all on their way to bolster Terry Venables squad.
It's fucking epidemic in this club! Our training regime has got to be
altered for the guys to last until the final whistle.

Anyway, I'm (sorry James) off to Brazil for a week now - no e:mails, no
phones - just a private Island. Rest assured I'll be taking a speedboat to
the mainland on Saturday & Thursday to check the scores though!

In the meantime Tamsy please circulate the e:mails without me - oh have
a Happy Birthday too mate!

Shacky

P.S. The missus has washed my Leeds shirt with something left in the
machine - it's a bit pink now - it happened to me once before in about
1975 and we then went on a European run all the way to the final - do
you think it's an omen?

-----Original Message-----
From: Nelly@whitellie-phant.co.uk
Sent: 05 December 2002 14:16
To: Dave.Shack@Ononon.co.uk
Subject: Re: Like Father (First Team) like Son (Reserves) - The Elland Road
Epidemic!

Dave.Shack@Ononon.co.uk writes:
>do you think it's an omen?

Not sure about that, but it's definitely a pinken!

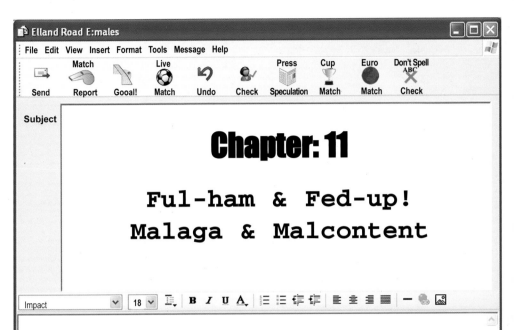

Chapter: 11

Ful-ham & Fed-up!
Malaga & Malcontent

PREFACE:

Whilst Shack sits on a secluded island in Brazil with George, a marginally more miserable Sunderland fan, Tamsy takes the reigns but not even this line-up change can breathe new life into a dire Leeds team that are in a league free-fall and for the first time in 12 years the dreaded 'R' word is being mentioned. No - it can't be... it is.

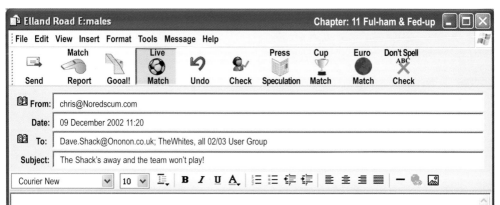

File   Edit   View   Insert   Format   Tools   Message   Help

Match   Live   Press   Cup   Euro   Don't Spell

Send   Report   Gooal! | Match   Undo   Check   Speculation   Match   Match   Check

From: chris@Noredscum.com

Date: 09 December 2002 11:20

To: Dave.Shack@Ononon.co.uk; TheWhites, all 02/03 User Group

Subject: The Shack's away and the team won't play!

Courier New   10   B *I* U A

```
---Original Message-----
From: chris@Noredscum.com
Sent: 09 December 2002 11:20
To: Dave.Shack@Ononon.co.uk; TheWhites all 02/03 User group
Subject: The Shack's away and the team won't play!
```

Another embarrassing afternoon stood watching a team of players who should be dominating only to see them roll over and lose to a second rate bunch of first division rate players.
The only shining light from the game was Robinson who pulled off a string of saves which we couldn't quite believe.
Yet again we sang and sang trying to rally the team - and yet again they let us all down. No one individual at the club is responsible for this poor run - not Ridsdale, not Venables, not individual players, not Brian Kidd -they should all collectively take responsibility and try and sort this problem out before the club dies.
Call me depressed if you want but I really don't see much hope of us surviving this season - all it takes is one of the teams below us to start a string of results and we will go down.
So if you have any spare places on your Christmas present lists this year please ask Santa for some points.

---Original Message-----
From: nelly@whitellie-phant.co.uk
Sent: 09 December 2002 11:39
To: chris@noredscum.com; dave shack@Ononon.co.uk
Subject: Re: The Shack's away and the team wont play

Billy Bremner died five years ago to the day on Saturday. All semblance of the team we were supporting just two years ago has just faded away. Pitiful. The Wee Man would be ashamed...Nelly

Tahoma | 10 | B *I* U A |

-----Original Message-----
From: Andy@whitetoreply.co.uk
Sent: 10 December 2002 01:45
To: TheWhites, all 02/03 User Group
Subject: Re: The Shack's away and the team wont play

There's no point asking Santa for any points - he wears red and doesn't live in Manchester so we know what that means!!

Mind you....I believe the original Santa was dressed in White and Coca Cola turned him red for Marketing, the fiendish devils. So I'll give it a go.

-----Original Message-----
From: Wathen, Dorian, The Peacocks
Sent: 10 December 2002 10:45
To: TheWhites, all 02/03 User group
Subject: RE: The Shack's away and the team wont play

I may eat my words later but having previously been a supporter of Venables, I have to say the way he's treated Batts and Dacourt is pretty unprofessional and lacking in any tact or foresight whatsoever - his latest public over-reaction over Olly in a mis-translation says it all - you'd never find Wenger or Ferguson publicly (Keane/Vieira) doing that over one of their leading players, as Olly as been over the past few seasons.

-----Original Message-----
From: Russ@vivaleedspana.spa
Sent: 10 December 2002 11:56
To: TheWhites, all 02/03 User group
Subject: Re: The Shack's away and the team wont play

they don't need shagger to go away to not play, they have been doing that for the last 7 matches?

-----Original Message-----
From: chris@Noredscum.co.uk
Sent: 10 December 2002 12:18
To: Russ Wood, Vivaleedspana
Subject: Re: The Shack's away and the team wont play

I thought it was more like the last year?

Comic Sans MS   10   B *I* U A

-----Original Message-----
From: Russ@vivaleedspana.spa
Sent: 10 December 2002 12:09
To: TheWhites, all 02/03 User group
Subject: RE: The Shack's away and the team wont play

yeh, its mind blowing, but nothing we say as a fan seems to be lifting the spirits
of the players and what ever tels telling them has the same effect, the main
problem is the chance pete took to elevate the club to the dizzy heights of the
champions leauge semi final and it was great while it lasted, problem was we
didn't win anything and haven't in the 4 seasons.
We don't need prayers or xmas presents we need a bit of good old fashion
fight, determination and few shots from any of our players who can remember
to have a go from anywhere near the fucking goal!!! come on you whites

-----Original Message-----
From: Davidharveysmonkey@aol.com
Sent: 10 December 2002 14:42
To: Dorian.Wathen@thepeacocks.co.uk
Cc: TheWhites, all 02/03 User group
Subject: Re: RE: The Shack's away and the team wont play

I agree, my biggest hope had been that he'd sort it out but I just can't see this team winning any
points. I sat in front of Lucas on saturday and he was fully fit and ready to play b ut didn'y even
make the bench. So that's no martyn, no batty, no dacourt, no rio due to financial mismanagement,
no van bommel or a right winger because we invested in 6 strikers and seth johnson. it's not all
venables fault but he's mis managed the squad spectacularly. who's next for the savaging in his
column - Kells and Lucas? We're seriously looking like relegation candidates. DH'sM

-----Original Message-----
From: Wathen, Dorian, The Peacocks
Sent: 10 December 2002 14:51
To: TheWhites, all 02/03 User group
Subject: RE: RE: The Shack's away and the team wont play

I've just had enough of his public criticism of players who have been
outstanding for Leeds in recent years and who we've worshipped as a result.
He's looking to save his reputation at the cost of Leeds players by making
feeble excuses instead of standing up and being counted. We aren't thick -
we know there are injuries, so tactically you change to accomodate that
and try to grind out results until you get your players back.

Courier New | 10 | B *I* U A | ≡ ≣ ≢ ≢ | ≣ ≣ ≣ ≣ | — 🖉 🖼

-----Original Message-----
From: chris@Noredscum.co.uk]
Sent: 12 December 2002 13:15
To: Shack, Dave, Ononon.co.uk
Cc: TheWhites, all 02/03 User group
Subject: European Tour...

Well what do our players have in store for us this evening?
Will it be one of those breathtaking European evenings that we
have come to love as Leeds fans? Will it be a re-run of the
European gladiators who so nearly got through to the Champions
League final? Will it be a re-run of those magnificent Leeds
warriors who made Europe quake in the late 60's? Or will it be
the weak willed poorly led team we've witnessed so often this
season? Without an away goal to count on we could be up
against but as our performances against Man Utd, Newcastle and
Harpoel Tel Aviv have shown we can turn on the magic when we
want to.

-----Original Message-----
From: Russ@vivaleedspana.spa
Sent: 12 December 2002 13:20
To: TheWhites, all 02/03 User group
Subject: Re: European Tour...

here here! breathtaking speech chris. cum on leeds give it some!!!

----Original Message-----
From: Davidharveysmonkey@aol.com
Sent: 12 December 2002 13:36
To: TheWhites, all 02/03 User group
Subject: Re(2): European Tour...

That Chris has gone mental. put batts, dacourt, radebe and martyn back in and we'd be sorted.

-----Original Message-----
From: russ@Vivaleedspana.esp
Sent: 12 December 2002 13:32
To: Davidharveysmonkey@aol.com
Cc: TheWhites, all 02/03 User group
Subject: Re: Re(2): European Tour...

ONE PROBLEM THERE : EL TEL DON'T LIKE THEM!!

-----Original Message-----
From: chris@Noredscum.co.uk
Sent: 13 December 2002 11:32
To: Dave.Shack@Ononon.co.uk
Cc: TheWhites, all 02/03 User group
Subject: (We're not going on a)... European Tour...

Well I suppose an optimist would say that we can now
concentrate on the league.
There were some moments last night when I thought we'd turned
the corner but they were far to few and far between and to
make matters worse Bridges looks like he's out with a
recurrence of his ankle injury - I'd be surprised if we ever
see him in a Leeds shirt again. Bowyer is going to get mauled
by Uefa for that "challenge" and I for one will not miss him
when he goes - I was appalled by that stamp last night and he
is going to attract even more bad press to our club.
It is very clear that there is no leadership on or off the
pitch and we need to sort this out now before we get relegated
- time for a new broom to be swept through Elland Road
methinks. Chris
PS Come back Shacky all is forgiven - writing these notes is
depressing the hell out me!!

-----Original Message-----
From: Jeremy@Donsgloryears.co.uk
Sent: 13 December 2002 16:31
Cc: TheWhites, all 02/03 User group
Subject: Re: European Tour...

We keep saying it can't get any worse, but it does.

Here are a few more reasons why Venables MUST GO NOW:

1) When he took over he spoke about how he finally had a team that he might be able to win the championship with. Within weeks, at the start of the disastrous run, he said that this was a team in a period of transition and he needed more time and patience.

2) After the Fulham game on Saturday he spoke of how pleased he was about how "positive" we were after going a goal down. Positive?!!? All you can say was that we went from embarrassing to just plain crap.

3) When we are crying out for leadership and inspiration, what does he do - leave Lucas out of the squad altogether on Saturday and only put him on the bench last night. And who does he play instead - fucking Duberry!!

4) If he is going to alienate the Leeds fans by first ditching Batts and then giving Ollie the cold shoulder, you might think he's got a plan to replace them with appropriate players in the crucial central midfield roles. But whoever he's tried there has been worse than useless. At Fulham, I counted one (yes, one) tackle that our midfield made in the entire first half.

I could go on...At least last night we had about half an hour when we actually played with a bit a fire and passion, and at a tempo that was close to how we played on those great European nights of the last few seasons. The fact of the matter is that right now we are the worst team in the Premiership - at least West Brom and Bolton try to make life difficult for the opposition. I bet every team must now really look forward to playing us, as they know how easy it is to win control of the midfield, and therefore the match. Please put us out of our misery. I know there is more wrong at the club than just Venables, but we have to make a change NOW. Hope and pray that we can get O'Neill for next season, and put Eddie Gray in charge for the rest of the season. Failing that, Paul Hart. He has done a great job with no money at Notts Forest and he was the guy in charge of the youth team that had Smithy, Harry, Woody, Robbo and the likes. But however bad we're feeling , spare a thought for Michael Bridges. I just hope that all the worst case scenarios about him never playing again turn out wrong. And remember - we just support the team, and (hopefully) have other things going on in our lives. This is his whole career and future on the line.

All the best, Bridgey.

-----Original Message-----
From: russ@Vivaleedspana.esp
Sent: 13 December 2002 11:55
To: chris@Noredscum.com; Dave.Shack@Ononon.co.uk
Cc: TheWhites, all 02/03 User group
Subject: Re: European Tour...

I think an industrial cleaner would be nearer to what we need!!!
Did woodgate really try on that tackle that led to there 2 goal?
Did danny mills try full stop?
Has smith forgotten how to shoot?
one piece of class all night was robbies pass to erik for the goal!!
Full marks to kelly bakke robinson wilcox for there effort they didn't stop
Bowyer for sicknote????????????? i don't think so, but i have to agree that i will not be sad to see him go now he fucking useless for us.
My brother saw arry in fulton and masons the other day and said he's just as

Comic Sans MS | 10 | **B** *I* U A

miserable off the pitch as he is on it!!
Imagine arry playing up at Carlisle no fucking way, the little twat will fine a stomach bug or somthing, come on Lazio put us out of our fucking misery and take him off of our hands!!!!!!
OOOOOOOOOOOWWWWWWWWWWW - I needed to get that off my chest!!!!!!!!!!!!!!!!!!!!!!!!!!!!!!!!!!!!

------Original Message-----
From: chris@Noredscum.co.uk
Sent: 13 December 2002 17:00
To: Jeremy@Donsgloryears.co.uk
Cc: TheWhites, all 02/03 User group
Subject: Re: European Tour...

Couldn't agree more. Terry Terry time to go...

-----Original Message-----
From: Firhad, Mohd, Eltelasia.ma
Sent: 16 December 2002 04:00
To: TheWhites, all 02/03 User Group
Subject: Leeds Overview

Agree to that................The problem is our midfirled. What has happened to El Tel's vision and strategic sense? Soccer are won via midfield control. The ideal one that may have worked for us will be Olly, Batty in the centre of the park. The cold shoulder treatment on Olly is unfair as look at how he performed against MU. All over the pitch and covering Harte when the right flank is under attack and like the French players are will be right in front of the back 4 as the extra man (vieira is one example). It is wrong from the start to let Bowyer in the center and Barmby?????

Await stillfor a miracle and a resurgence, but when. New manager? maybe as we have the goods and the team is basically the same as of previous years. Forget sophistication and continental intricacies. Just get the fast flowing straight ahead Leeds team of yesteryears.

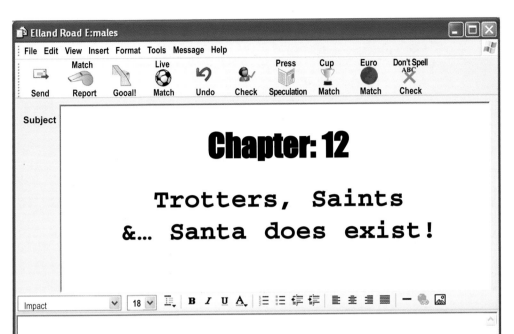

Elland Road E:males

File Edit View Insert Format Tools Message Help

Send | Report | Gooal! | Match | Undo | Check | Speculation | Match | Match | Check

Subject

Chapter: 12

Trotters, Saints &... Santa does exist!

Impact | 18 | B *I* U A

PREFACE:

It's the festive season but Leeds fans are in no mood for charity. They need points, they need consistency & they need goals to get them. Enter Bolton, enter a new pub for watching Leeds in London & then, except for a last minute give-away, see how there really is a Santa - and he certainly doesn't wear red!

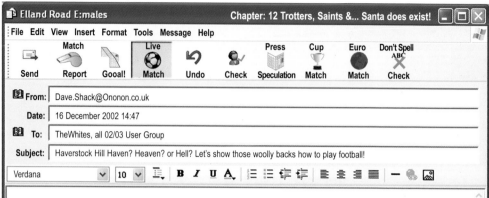

File   Edit   View   Insert   Format   Tools   Message   Help

Match	Live		Press	Cup	Euro	Don't Spell ABC
Send Report Gooal!	Match	Undo Check	Speculation	Match	Match	Check

From: Dave.Shack@Ononon.co.uk

Date: 16 December 2002 14:47

To: TheWhites, all 02/03 User Group

Subject: Haverstock Hill Haven? Heaven? or Hell? Let's show those woolly backs how to play football!

Verdana   10   B *I* U A   ...

-----Original Message-----
From: Shack, Dave, Ononon.co.uk
Sent: 16 December 2002 14:47
To: The Whites all, 02/03 User Group
Subject: Haverstock Hill Haven? Heaven? or Hell? Let's show those woolly backs how to play football!

Lads - How about the Haverstock Arms, Haverstock Hill tonight? - a drink per goal from me (not for theirs!)& a bag of your favoured Crisps/nuts/pork scratchings for each tackle our midfield makes...
I'm there with Tamsy (Free drinks all night for being such a good editor)& Moylesy plus possibly Dorian & DH'sM.
I'm brown, browned off & need something with brown sauce on it!
Like Big Brother - there could be an eviction at 10pm tonight...

El Shacko (the boy back from Bra - zil)

-----Original Message-----
From: Wathen, Dorian, The Peacocks
Sent: 16 December 2002 14:49
To: Shack, Dave, Ononon.co.uk
Subject: RE: Haverstock Hill Haven? Heaven? or Hell? Let's show those woolly backs how to play football!

I have a night pass, so am OK for it. Shall I ask Eden and Pete ?

-----Original Message-----
From: chris@noredscum.co.uk
Sent: 16 December 2002 15:57
To: Dave.Shack@Ononon.co.uk
Subject: Tonight

Hi mate

Courier New   10   B *I* U A

I'm gonna give tonight a swerve - I'm going out every other
night this week and so I recon I should save my liver for the
really serious trip to see Peter Kay tomorrow.Chris

-----Original Message-----
From: Shack, Dave, Ononon.co.uk
Sent: 16 December 2002 17:04
To: Chris@Noredscum.co.uk
Subject: Re: Tonight

Ga-arlic Bread...Garlic & Bread. I'll buy it for you....

-----Original Message-----
From: Shack, Dave, Ononon.co.uk
Sent: 17 December 2002 11:04
To: The Whites, all 02'03 User group
Subject: That's more like it! But it's only BOLTON...

Now, I know I should be screaming from the roof-tops about that
superlative football lesson we served up last night - but as my dear old
Grandad likes to say; one swallow does not a summer make (he does get
the order of his words mixed up a bit!)and so one win (against bloody
Bolton) does not a season ignite!Southampton will provide a more stiff
test at the weekend and then, and only then should we start to believe
that we have started to climb off rock-bottom.
Last night, for me, was about strong individual performances - Kewell,
Hartey, Woody, Robbo (Hey! It was Venables who promoted him - and
look at the genius of that decision!), Mills & even Kelly.
I spoke to Hartey last night & he told me just how fired up everyone was
- how the whole dressing room changed & just how well Kewell did last
night after the virus that has kept him out. It was good to hear him say
that all that matters is beating Southampton on Saturday now and getting
a real run together.
So, we've found a new lucky pub (Haverstock Arms) & they do a mean
chicken & mushroom pie! On the way there I showed Dorian the old pub
in Belsize Park where Russ & I celebrated after driving back from Sheff
Utd on 26th April 1992 - so the area certainly has good omens for me -
incidentally - Swiss cottage roundabout is another significant landmark for
me - because when Scum lost to West Ham that year I was driving home
from work & going round the roundabout when West Ham scored that
freak bounce goal. I continued going round the roundabout until the game
ended & West Ham had secured the win! Thank god it's a big
roundabout...

| Comic Sans MS ▾ | 10 ▾ | 🖳 | **B** *I* U A̲ | ⦂≡ ≡ 拝 拝 | ≣ ≣ ≣ ≣ | — 🌑 🖼 |

-----Original Message-----
From: russ@vivaleedspana.esp
Sent: 17 December 2002 09:08
To: Dave.shack@Ononon.co.uk
Subject: Re: That's more like it! But it's only BOLTON...

we love ya el tel we do................. fucking brill, i told ya shoot from anywhere and look what happens, smithy, vid take note!!!!!
were gunna win the league, were gunna win the league and now ya gunna believe us......................after all we have been through our supporters still have a great sense of humour!!!!!!

-----Original Message-----
From: Jeremy@donsgloryyears.co.uk
Sent: 17 December 2002 11:12
To: Dave.Shack@Ononon.co.uk
Subject: Re: That's more like it! But it's only BOLTON...

Crisis, what crisis? I always said that Terry Venables was the best manager on the whole planet....

-----Original Message-----
From: chris@noredscum.co.uk
Sent: 17 December 2002 11:14
To: Dave.Shack@Ononon.co.uk
Subject: Re: That's more like it! But it's only BOLTON...

Wasn't it great watching Mills' celebrations after his goal - after what he's been through recently I'm really happy for the guy. Looks like our wishes to Santa might start bearing some fruit.

-----Original Message-----
From: Jeremy@Donsgloryears.co.uk
Sent: 17 December 2002 11:23
To: The Whites, all 02/03 user group
Subject: Re: That's more like it! But it's only BOLTON...

If you're really looking for sad pieces of trivia... er, sorry lucky omens - at the end of Sky's coverage last night the outro music theyplayed over the closing credits was my new Feeder single "Just the way I'm feeling" which (I hope) is going to be a big hit in January. A satisfying end to a very satisfying evening, or (if I was Shacky) a surefire sign that the corner is turned and that Leeds United (and Feeder) are headed for the galaxy next year!

-----Original Message-----
From: Wathen, Dorian, the Peacocks
Sent: 17 December 2002 11:25
To: Jeremy@ Donsgloryears.co.uk
Cc: Dave.Shack@Ononon.co.uk
Subject: RE: That's more like it! But it's only BOLTON...

what a difference a day makes... now Feeder are going to have a hit.

-----Original Message-----
From: Davidharveysmonkey@aol.com
Sent: 17 December 2002 11:37
To: The Whites, all 02/03 User group
Subject: Re(2): That's more like it! But it's only BOLTON...

Let's hope this is a sign of things to come. Everyone knows I'd prefer to see Batts playing, but it was just great to see two absolute cracking goals!!! Both from players who should score more often. Did you see Ridsdale on Sky at 3-0 up, he didn't exactly look chuffed, ever get the feeling he's already offered someone else the post? DH'sM

-----Original Message-----
From: Shack, Dave, Ononon.co.uk
Sent: 17 December 2002 11:41
To: TheWhites, all 02/03 User group
Subject: RE: Re(2): That's more like it! But it's only BOLTON...

...and yesterday DH'sM told me off for starting rumours...
the conspiracy theory falls down when you consider the match wasn't in the last 10 minutes when you saw him & so we still could have lost or drawn...

There was a great moment when after Robinson got 'concussed' & the physio was checking him out - imagine the conversation:

Robbo: Err...where am I?
Physio: Robbo - you're at Bolton - you saved a penalty & we're 3-0 up!
Robbo: Piss off Physio I'm concussed! Lovely. Shack

-----Original Message-----
From: Davidharveysmonkey@aol.com
Sent: 17 December 2002 11:55
To: Dave.Shack@Ononon.co.uk
Subject: Re: RE: Re(2): That's more like it! But it's only BOLTON...

Garamond   10   **B** *I* U A

I think Venables was concussed, at one poinjt it must have looked likePompey versus Spurs, no wonder we won, he forgot who he was managing.

-----Original Message-----
From: Firhad, Mohd, Eltelasia.ma
Sent: 18 December 2002 03:05
To: Shack, Dave, Ononon.co.uk
Subject: That's more like it! But it's only BOLTON...

Great to see us smiling again !!!!!!!!!!!!!! Indeed we tried but maybe El tel is right luck has deserted us in games but I rather see it as new startegizing that needs understanding and system of El which is more of patient build ups. We wrere a fast moving team and against Bolton it shows. El must now balance that and Bolton is indeed a start.

-----Original Message-----
From: Shack, Dave, Ononon.co.uk
Sent: 23 December 2002 09:49
To: TheWhites, all 02/03 User group
Subject: Happy Xmas Saints! 'Ere 'ave a goal on us!

Well, drawing is one point better than losing! On a day when all around us lost we went & threw 2 points away that would have raised us a couple more spots up the table for Xmas. But in a way I think we were bloody lucky to draw - they should have had a hat-full!
There's not a lot to say really at this time (there would have been if Kewell's goal had won it)other than Viduka looked bright after he came on, Woody continues to be outstanding as does Robbo (was the goal his fault?)and ,of course, Kewell. Let's face it when he plays like this he virtually carries the whole midfield & attacking line. Imagine him playing in a great team (ie the one of 2 years ago) whilst he's in this sort of form - god! we'd be mashing people.
So, I'm up for the Chelsea game (shit they look great at the moment!) and I can only pray that we repay Sunderland in the same way we reminded Bolton that it's not really their place to beat us in the Premiership!

-----Original Message-----
From: russ@vivaleedspana.esp
Sent: 23 December 2002 10:29
To: Dave.Shack@Ononon.co.uk
Subject: Re: Happy Xmas Saints! 'Ere 'ave a goal on us!

Elland Road E:males   Chapter: 12 Trotters, Saints &... Santa does exist!

Comic Sans MS   10   B *I* U A

yeh but at least now we are only talking about dissapointment at getting a point, know one this morning is slagging off tb or the rest of the team and lets face it if we could have got a second there late lucky goal would not have mattered!! as EG says we need to start killing off games like bolton.

-----Original Message-----
From: Davidharveysmonkey@aol.com
Sent: 23 December 2002 11:55
To: Dave.Shack@Ononon.co.uk
Subject: Re: RE: Happy Xmas Saints! 'Ere 'ave a goal on us!

unbelievable, the fans were amazing, I'll writye you something about that later.

-----Original Message-----
From: Chris@Noredscum.co.uk
Sent: 23 December 2002 15:58
To: Dave.Shack@Ononon.co.uk
Subject: Re: RE: Happy Xmas Saints! 'Ere 'ave a goal on us!

Southampton - well I raced like a madman to Elland Road to watch yet another lacklustre performance. However it looked like we were going to scrape a one nil victory until the French midget Fernandez stepped up for the free kick in the dying seconds. Like you said though they could have had a hatful and considering some of the results we've had at home this season a point from this game is not a bad result.

-----Original Message-----
From: Andy@whitetoreply.co.uk
Sent: 23 December 2002 21:58
To: Dave.Shack@Ononon.co.uk
Subject: Re: Happy Xmas Saints! 'Ere 'ave a goal on us!

Sorry I'm a bit late on the replies recently, but it's Xmas and you must know how it gets. I thought Saturday was a big improvement. The Saints did look good, but as soon as Viduuka came on, we were a different team. Some clever hold up and lay offs were a pleaseure to watch. We put them under pressure as much as they had to us earlier.
In the end though, must agree that we gifted them a goal. Had Leeds thought that the whistle for the free kick was the final whistle. It was 88 minutes after all and that seems to be where we assume the game stops. As I walked to the end of our aisle, all I could hear from the guy in the row behind was "WE don't fucking play 90 minutes. It's shit. We never play fucking 90 minutes anymore".

Ah well, half way there and to use the old BJ phrase, "Livnin' on a prayer, 21 more points will see us there-re, oh lord, livin' on a prayer".
Ave an especially good one, polish your father's gun and let's hunt us some Chelsea scum. White to Reply signing out.

-----Original Message-----
From: Shack, Dave, Ononon.co.uk
Sent: 26 December 2002 20:59
To: The Whites, all 02'03 User group
Subject: Black Cats, White points!

It had to happen! Riding Oop North in a car loaded to the gills with the missus & a boot full of prezzies, feeling like shite after some dodgy bug or food poisoning on Xmas Day and the radio's going in & out on either 909 or 693 depending on where we are on the M1 - but one thing is clear - no make that 2 things 1 - we've won! & two we've got a new star that hasn't cost us a bloody penny! In fact if you take the fact that his Mum & Dad have season tickets & we're only paying him £80 a week then we're making money out of the Milner Family.
No more to say - it's Dad's phone line afterall - we won on Boxing Day & bring on the cardboard team from The Stamford Bridge Hotel!
Yeeeesssssssssss!!!!!!!!!!!!!!

-----Original Message-----
From: russ@vivaleedspana.esp
Sent: 27 December 2002 12:24
To: Dave.Shack@Ononon.co.uk
Subject: Re: Black Cats, White points!

shit hot comes to mind about that performance because at last it was nice to see a positive result at the end of all the hard work put in from the players. Robbie class act with the penalty and young james is a wonder, how long will that last? Hopefully until the xmas period!!!! And at last Arry is coming to life
Can you imagine putting all the good bits at the club and finding a way of making it all work together with no injuries, bust up's or bullshitters i think have a team to win the league?

-----Original Message-----
From: Shack, Dave, Ononon
Sent: 27 December 2002 12:28
To: Russ@Vivaleedspana
Subject: RE: Black Cats, White points!

Verdana   10   B *I* U A

Only you & me on line son!
There's no doubt we have the team if we had all the other conditions & no one else did. Where would Arsenal be without Henry & Cole & Campbell? Where would they be if Viera was slagging them off in France & was desperate to move? Where would they be if Wenger didn't rate all the players there but couldn't buy anymore?

-----Original Message-----
From: Andy@whitetoreply.co.uk
Sent: 27th December 19:58
To: Dave.Shack@Ononon.co.uk
Subject: Re: Black Cats, White points!

Ah-way the lads. A powim (sic) for Leeds

Why aye. We're better ah-way than at 'ome
We don't need to buy we've got 'ome grow-en
The boys 'ave done good
They're no slouch in the mud
They've made the three points owl their 'owen

Sorry for the shite Mackem accent. Go on my sonsssssssss!!!!

-----Original Message-----
From: Chris@Noredscum.co.uk
Sent: 27 December 2002 15:28
To: Dave.Shack@Ononon.co.uk
Subject: Re: Black Cats, White points!

Sunderland - At bloody last we've won a game!!!!!!! Santa listened to my prayers and has given the team some confidence. I missed my first Boxing Day game for six years and if we get this sort of result again I'm never going again on Boxing day!!!

-----Original Message-----
From: Firhad, Mohd, Eltelasia.ma
Sent: 27th December 2002 02:00
To: Shack, Dave, Ononon.co.uk
Subject: Black Cats, White points!

Yes we have done it.............A lil more consistency is needed. Nearly gave up on El tel but deep inside theres a voice that tells me that

a"legendary" man cannot turn "shitty" overnight.
Milner, 16 plus ???!!!! Maturity and a record breaker. Rooney who ??!!!
Come on Chelsea, you're next.

-----Original Message-----
From: Jeremy@donsgloryyears.com
Sent: 28 December 2002 05:44
To: Dave.shack@Ononon.co.uk
Subject: Leeds 2 Chelsea 0

Well it's a funny old (or should I say new) world! Here I am in India (on a cricket tour,
hoping to get more runs from my bat than my backside) having just watched the game live on
TV - something I couldn't have done if I was in England (other than - obviously - being at
Elland Road).

So I was on the phone from my hotel room in Delhi to my son, who is a season ticket holder
but stuck in London over Christmas, giving him constant updates on the staste of the game
(no, I haven't checked my phone bill yet).

As for the game, well it was no classic, and the football we played could hardly be described
as pretty, but who cares!! It was also great to see Kells regain some of his recently lost
confidence - I thought he was outstanding too.

As for the young 'un - well, I don't suppose Jamie Milner is going toland himself a Clearasil
ad modelling contract, but boy oh boy have we got ourselves a serious prospect!

Roll on Birmingham (I'll be in Agra, having hopefully just visited the Taj Mahal). Please try
not to feel too sorry for me...

----Original Message-----
From: Shack, Dave, Ononon.co.uk
Sent: 29 December 2002 11:41
To: 'Jeremy@Dongloryears'
Subject: RE: Leeds 2 Chelsea 0

Hero! It was awesome being there! Proper mail to all to follow! You sound
like me - "I'm away at the Taj Mahal with Westlife, etc, etc. Top man! Get
a picture in a Leeds shirt!

-----Original Message-----
From: Shack, Dave, Ononon,co.uk
Sent: 29 December 2002 13:19
To: The Whites, all 02/03 User group
Subject: Leeds re-United. Bye Bye Chelsea, Stand up Milner!

Verdana   10   **B** *I* U A

Oh my God! I have just witnessed Leeds Utd playing like Leeds United of old! The midfield tackled, the attackers ran at the defence, the defenders defended & passed out of trouble & , well, the keeper just played his usual game! The crowd - over 40k were awesome, the bench looked genuinely animated & excited & together and it really was the best end to an Xmas trip up home for a hell of a long time. I mean doesn't that journey fly by when you've won! That Woody scored (wonder what the boob juggling celebration was all about? In fact it's maybe better we don't know!) and that Milner out Rooneyed Roony again is just too awesome to believe. The fact that I can mention all this before saying it was CHELSEA that we beat makes this even more special. It kind of really wasn't about beating our fiercest of rivals(for me recently anyway); it was about Leeds United playing together like a team. Even with bloody Bakke taking Harry Kewell out (The premiership didn't show that did it?)we still looked the only team likely to win this game. We exposed Chelsea as not really title pretenders and we set up a run that if it includes Birmingham & Scunthorpe is gonna make this transfer window opening very exciting indeed!

Kelly deserves some real credit fo his performance today - what a captain he was - he kept reigning the players back (especially Smithy from Stanic), motivating them & leading by supreme example. You know that if anyone was really hurt by the shite run it was him every bit as much as Smithy. He showed it today and he will keep that armband until Matteo comes back I would expect!

So Milner! He does look good(actually he doesn't look great with that skin!)but with a ball at his feet he reminds me with some of his step-overs of Johnny Giles. I love the way he calls for the ball all the time too - and the fact that he can take a tackle without looking quite as bulldog as Rooney undoubtedly is. A great flair prospect for us.

Interestingly the speculation up north (particularly for the YP & the YEP) is that Kewell is off to Inter Milan at the end of the season (Sheree has wasted her Spanish lessons then!), Fowler is off to Man City, Bowyer to Spurs & O'Neill either to Leeds or Scum.

Just thought you should know!

Bring on the Blues - those bastards are due a right old kicking from us after starting the wobble back in August!

Bring on 2003 - it holds no fear now.

129

Comic Sans MS   10   **B** *I* <u>U</u> A

-----Original Message-----
From: russ@vivaleedspana.esp
Sent: 30 December 2002 12:48
To: Dave.Shack@Ononon.co.uk
Subject: chelsea

Hush your north & south me sun and go get ya fathers gun and shoot the chelsea scum, shoot the chelses scum, we hate chelsea!!!!!!!! Fucking brilliant, what a xmas wer'e having a may long it continue.

Funny innit Robbie scores a brilliant penaltey after being out for so long and now planning to get back to he's best and all of a sudden the scummy media come out with this man shitty story about being after him
Heres a very large happy new year to all my fellow whites and FUCK THE MEDIA Adios

-----Original Message-----
From: Andy@whitetoreply.co.uk
Sent: 30th December 2002. 18.32
To: Dave.Shack@Ononon.co.uk
Subject: Re: Leeds re-United. Bye Bye Chelsea, Stand up Milner!

Agree with most of what you say. Was a great game with plenty of committment and flair. Viduka's touches are wonderful to watch and I love the little skip he does before taking a step away from the opposition and laying the ball off. Wilcox is playing well also.

Let's hope Birmingham is another win.

-----Original Message-----
From: Firhad, Mohd, Eltelasia.ma
Sent: 31st December 2002 02:08
To: Shack, Dave, Ononon.co.uk
Subject: Leeds re-United. Bye Bye Chelsea, Stand up Milner!

Yes....it is the peformance that we have been waiting for. Forget the Continental slow build up. Leeds are built on fast attacking mode. Tel is finally understanding it and have forge a bridge of this two styles.

Can see El Tel's vision slowly unravelling. Hardworking midfield. To me the turning point of the revival is Jason Wilcox. His never say die, hard working attitude has rubbed on all the others and is his him to me that

Batang   10   ☰⌄   **B** *I* <u>U</u> A⌄   ☰ ☰ ☰ ☰   ☰ ☰ ☰ ☰   — 🔗 🖼

sparked this resurgence. Milner can see is the one to take over from
Kewell. Bakke is the new Batty. Smithy right midfield is fine as Bowyer
cannot defend. We have a "jewel' but still "raw" and thats Seth Johnson.
Certain touches reminds me of Trevor Brooking. Give him time.

Viva Leeds !!!!!!!!!!!!

-----Original Message-----
From: chris@noredscum.co.uk
Sent: 29 December 2002 11:14
To: Dave Shack@Ononon.co.uk
Subject: Re Re: Leeds re-United. Bye Bye Chelsea, Stand up
Milner!

Chelsea - Yesssssssssssssssssssssssssssss!!!!!!!!

Poor Judas Jimmy never ever ever gonna win a cup!!!!!! I had
a fantastic time shouting abuse to Piggybank all afternoon.
What a fantastic display - finally we are playing like the
side we all know we are!! The defence was outstanding -the
midfield was amazing and the forwards were superb - and what
about Milner? How good is that lad?

In years to come I'll be able to tell everyone about watching
him as he made his debut at West Ham and almost gave away a
goal with one of his first touches!!

Well all I can say after watching the highlights on TV is how
appalled I am about the lack of coverage our Jamie got - all
we've heard this season is Rooney this Rooney that and someone
comes along and beats one of his records and we get a 30
second mention. I hate to think what would have happened if
the lad in question played for Manure - we would have never
heard the end of it!!

A very enjoyable day out even if I had to share the train back
to Leicester with hundreds of Chelsea fans - I kept my coat
done up until I got off the train and the doors were locked
and then I ran down the platform showing my Leeds shirt
flicking the V's to all the Chelsea Scum glumly sat on the
train. Immature I know but thoroughly enjoyable!!!

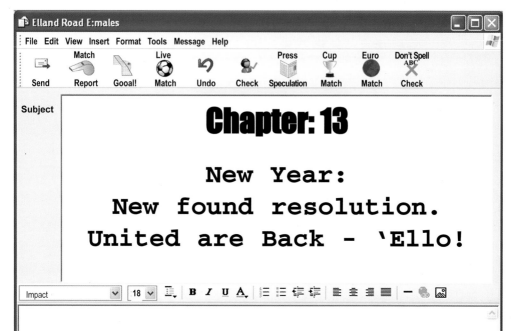

Elland Road E:males

File Edit View Insert Format Tools Message Help

Send Report Gooal! Match Undo Check Speculation Match Match Check

Subject

Chapter: 13

New Year:
New found resolution.
United are Back - 'Ello!

Impact | 18 | B *I* U A

PREFACE:

With hope in our hearts, the second half of the season
began as only we could have dreamed it on the pitch.
The other Blues got their come-uppance, a dodgy away
FA Cup game (with far too many reminders of last
year's debacle lurking in the press & on TV) was
negociated and then it was the 4th round draw, live!
Back to the league & - oh yes! The transfer window was
open...and that meant trouble. Big trouble...

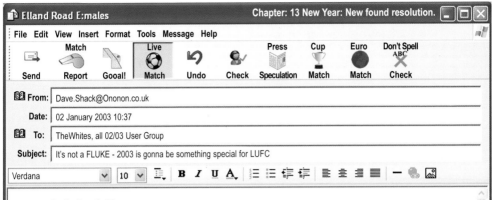

Elland Road E:males

File Edit View Insert Format Tools Message Help

Send Report Gooal! Match Undo Check Speculation Match Match Check

From: Dave.Shack@Ononon.co.uk

Date: 02 January 2003 10:37

To: TheWhites, all 02/03 User Group

Subject: It's not a FLUKE - 2003 is gonna be something special for LUFC

Verdana   10

-----Original Message-----
From: Shack, Dave, Ononon.co.uk
Sent: 02 January 2003 10:37
To: The Whites, all 02'03 User group
Subject: It's not a FLUKE - 2003 is gonna be something special for
LUFC

Harry New Year Lads!

13 points out of a possible 15 certainly isn't an unlucky number for us
and I don't think this run is over yet. Repaying Birmingham is just what
we needed for causing that early season blip - and having a second
40,000 crowd is really gratifying against a none 'glamour' team.
Don't you almost feel really bloody sorry for Liverpool & Sunderland now?
Boy do we know what they are going through - especially Sunderland
who are really emulating out last minute disasters to a tee!

So - it's transfer window time & if Ridsdale's programme address yesterday
is anything to go by there will be some to-ing & fro-ing shortly. What do
you guys think? How about a in/out/want/get rid of list? Here's mine:

Who do you think might come in?
-Anderton -Milito -A.n.other

Who do you think will go?
-Duberry -Martyn -Fowler

Who do you want? -Wayne Bridge -Kleberson -Gallas

Who do you want to go?
-Bowyer (a million or 2) -Dacourt (5 million)
-Burns (we'll give anyone his plane ticket)
-Duberry (ditto - don't need the heart attacks)

133

Verdana   10   B *I* U A

Remember this time last year - we beat West Ham to go top (the high) & then we lost to Cardiff (the low) - which pretty much sums up 2002 for our club. There's no doubt that things look pretty optimistic at the moment - and realistically we can once more set our sights on Europe - but I think that Venables is gonna go all out for the FA Cup (Europe & Cardiff glory)so stick some money on us before we play Scunny this weekend. They are playing well, but with our confidence (& Tel's plan & pure need to do something tangible)we will have a great run. Believe me - this is that year - no Worthington, no Europe, no relegation fear - put all your eggs in one basket & chase the FA Cup. I'm up for it.

Cheers Lads, we're back & doesn't work seem so much more 'do-able' now? Now, where are those Liverpool fans...

-----Original Message-----
From: Wathen, Dorian, The Peacocks
Sent: 02 January 2003 14:34
To: Shack, Dave, Ononon.co.uk
Subject: RE: It's not a FLUKE

So the Xmas wish was almost granted - top half of the table by the time we get back to work.

Can't say I saw much football over Xmas, due to a biting central midfield pairing of no satellite TV and girlfriend in tow, but Milners strike vs Chelsea was a cracker - I didn't know 16 year olds could kick the ball that far - or was that a version of the orange Wembley Trophy ball that swerved past Cudicini due to a freak gust of wind.

Anyway I agree - Dubes and Fowler look like being bought and Nige seems to be interesting Arsenal as back up.

In is a tricky one - but would be ideal if we bought Bridge or Konchesky as left back cover - midfield I'd like to see Carrick/Kevin Nolan or Sean Davis and Javier Zanetti of Inter Milan (dream on ...) as central and right midfield players to replace Okon and Bow. Would also strangely enough like to see Gary Speed back at Elland Road - call me nostalgic.

----Original Message-----
From: Shack, Dave, Ononon.co.uk
Sent: 02 January 2003 15:32
To: Wathen, Dorian, The Peacocks
Subject: RE: It's not a FLUKE

Speed! Yeah. That thought did cross my mind - he's overdue a return home! I also missed out ALPAY - he might well come to Leeds. Welcome back mate!

-----Original Message-----
From: russ@Vivaleedspana.esp
Sent: 02 January 2003 15:37
To: TheWhites, all 02/03 User group
Subject: Re: It's not a FLUKE

Great start just a shame we could not get a quick 2nd and maybe start a bit of a knees up and go on and get another 5 or 6, im happy with two though and three points, what a game next in the league, Man city.
As far as players are concerned
My choice is as follows
In: Ronaldo, Figo & anyonethat is not FUCKING INJURED
Out: Duberry, Burns, Dacourt (only because of the farcical situation he finds himself in), Bowyer if he does not want to play
And please please please Peter DO NOT LET tel buy sick note!!!!!!!!!!!!!!
Happy new year to ya all
r t b

-----Original Message-----
From: Andy@whitetoreply.co.uk
Sent: 02 January 2003 20:13
To: Dave.Shack@Ononon.co.uk
Subject: Re: It's not a FLUKE

Another great match with plenty of end to end action. Some superb performances and some dire performances. You asked about people leaving and forgot Harte. Uncle Gary wasn't best pleased with his nephew's passing yesterday. At times it was like a game of attack and defense. They'd try to attack and we'd get the ball off them, pass it around to look calm and in control, then Harte passed it back sportinglt for another go. Harte's taken my scorn away from Bakke who seems to have picked up the last few outings.

Incoming, I guess any left back with a bit of skill, and any controlling midfielder who Veneballs will let play. As long as there's no major leavers, I don't think we need anyone else. I guess though that Bowyer will go somewhere and his recent form was not that good, certainly not the Bowyer of last season. Perhaps he needs another trial to perk him up.

Tahoma   10   B *I* U A

Happy New Year mate. Andy

P.S. Mine was shite. my mum came out on Monday from LGI and Julie went in to BRI with Pneumonia the same day. Fab!!!!

```
-----Original Message-----
From: Firhad, Mohd, Eltelasia.ma
Sent: 03 January 2003 05:13
To: Shack, Dave, Ononon
Subject: FW: It's not a FLUKE

Who do you think might come in?
A South American centerback.(Forgot his name)

Who do you think will go?
Fowler- Duberry- Burns

Who do you want? - Kleberson

Who do you want to go?
Same actually.............

This season is a rollercoaster ride for all whereby a team can be caught
on a downward spiral of form and run thru' a losing streak. Scum seem to
have it and now they have survived Sunderland - barely. Liverpool and
Sunderland indeed feel what we feel. El Tel can focus our boys solely on
the FA Cup and also the league.
```

-----Original Message-----
From: nelly@whitellie-phant.co.uk
Sent: 06 January 2003 13:52
To: Dave.Shack@Ononon.co.uk
Subject: Re: It's not a FLUKE

I'll be happy with any changes because we need to move on. O'Leary and Ridsdale got us the best squad we've ever had and it won sod-all. So let's just mix and match. It would be great to see the tail end of Bowyer (once never stopped running, now hardly moves at all - perhaps because he's carrying so much baggage and - who knows? - the weight of a guilty consicence) and Dacourt (international class but a money-grabber who would jump on the first ship that paid him more) but I don't mind who comes in. As long as it's not Anderton. Anyone remember a player called Stephen McPhail?

-----Original Message-----
From: Shack, Dave, Ononon
Sent: 06 January 2003 12:04
To: TheWhites, all 02/03 User group
Subject: Take a bow, Bowyer!

Looks like he's off to west Ham (Him & Rieper - nice!)Good luck & good riddance really I'd say. Happy Birthday El Tel - let's hope the Chairman buys him a player (or 2) for it!

-----Original Message-----
From: nelly@whitellie-phant.co.uk
Sent: 06 January 2003 12:20
To: Dave.Shack@Ononon.co.uk
Subject: Re: Take a bow, Bowyer!

I've stuck by Bowyer all bloody season. To those who said we should sell him I said (a) he was found innocent and (b) if it's right for us to sell him, it's wrong for anyone else to buy him - for good or ill, he was our problem. But after that "challenge" against Tel-Aviv I lost it with him.
If he could do that in front of his manager (the dug-out was ten yards away), his team-mates, the home crowd and the millions watching on TV... what might he do if ever he was on his own, out of sight, and drunk down a dark alley? I really wanted to believe he had grown up and hoped he had reformed. I'm delighted to see that - as neither of these ideals were true - Venables has not picked him since. I can't wait for him to leave. He's a disgrace to our club. Not sure what West Ham have done to deserve him,though...

-----Original Message-----
From: russ@Vivaleedspana.esp
Sent: 06 January 2003 12:06
To: TheWhites, all 02/03 User group
Subject: Now they know how last January was!

That's better now the toffees and the magpies know how much it hurts to go out at stage one to the underdog .Its just a shame the welsh c**** hung on in the last few moments.

Can anyone tell me whats happening with robbie?
rtb

Verdana   10   **B** *I* U A

-----**Original Message**-----
From: Dave.Shack@Ononon.co.uk
Sent: 06 January 2003 12:12
To: 'Russell Wood'
Subject: RE: Now they know how last January was!

Yeah Russ - what price Cardiff (if they win the replay) in the draw?

-----**Original Message**-----
From: Wathen, Dorian, The Peacocks
Sent: 06 January 2003 12:12
To: Shack, Dave, Ononon
Subject: RE: Take a bow, Bowyer!

I'll second that good riddance sentiment - Repka's there too. Would make a midfield of Sinclair - Cole - Carrick - Bowyer - not bad for the First division - and one can only hope he joins a relegated side - not a hint of bitterness there...

wouldn't mind Brighton away - would fancy a trip there.

-----**Original Message**-----
From: Shack, Dave, Ononon
Sent: 06 January 2003 12:15
To: Wathen, Dorian, The Peacocks
Subject: RE: Take a bow, Bowyer!

Repka - that's the thug I meant not Rieper! - cheers son!

-----**Original Message**-----
From: Dave.Shack@Ononon.co.uk
Sent: 06 January 2003 13:10
To: TheWhites, all 02/03 User group
Subject: The 4th Round of the FA Cup brings us....

The Gills away. C'mon...let's do City & then go down to Kent for some Shepeard Neame beer!

-----*Original Message*-----
From: Russ@Vivaleedspana.spa
Sent: 13 January 2003 13:40
To: TheWhites, all 02/03 User group
Subject: whereyagonedavid?

It seems by lack of communication that dave's on the missing list! here's my list of possibilitys.

1) Driven on by depression dave slices wrists.

2) Nicky arranged for dave to meet his pop idol Gareth for an autograph, in doing so missed the match and result and is now desparately trying to find a friend to tell him the result, before conecting

3) He's on yet another exotic holiday island sunning his big arse a giving all the natives a eye full either side of his very sexy thong

For all that were there or saw the highlights, did you think it was a case of us not wanting it as much or as el tel says just plain old bad luck that we never scored before them!!

Yet again we have a stunning goal put past Englands N°1 Come in dave we miss ya!

-----Original Message-----
From: Wathen, Dorian, The Peacocks
Sent: 13 January 2003 14:24
To: TheWhites, all 02/03 User group
Subject: RE: whereyagonedavid

just to diffuse the speculation - I received a missive from Shack this morning ...bet you have by now too Russ! E:me if you haven't.
Dorian

-----Original Message-----
From: Shack, Dave, Ononon
Sent: 13 January 2003 13:46
To: TheWhites, all 02/03 User group
Subject: Harry saves our real blushes!

Defeat to Man City - and by all accounts we were poor - but at least we didn't give up & WE got a late goal. Sounds like Robbo played out of his skin again & they just caught us on the break. In all honesty they are not a bad side when their backs are against the wall - & the scabby defeat last week fired 'em up!

Elland Road E:males   Chapter: 13 New Year: New found resolution.

Verdana ⌄ 10 ⌄ B *I* U A ...

The Gills didn't lose again (7 matches - we just ended on 6!) and so they will be looking forward to the Cup game. Let's hope next week brings a player in just for morale & we can get back to winning ways.

Cheers to Bow (for the good times) & Olly (a few less - but not quite the lows) and may they never forget what Leeds United did for them both.

We'll be back - you just watch! Because we are Leeds!

```
-----Original Message-----
From: Firhad, Mohd, Eltelasia
Sent: 13 January 2003 03:46
To: Shack, Dave, Ononon
Subject: FW: Harry saves our real blushes!

Lose again.........But at least to a good side and fighting. All the best
to Bow and Olly.
```

-----Original Message-----
From: Wathen, Dorian, The Peacocks
Sent: 13 January 2003 11:21
To: Shack, Dave, Ononon
Subject: RE: Harry saves our real blushes!

I have the feeling by the time we sell Fowler, Johnson (to Boro ?), we're going to be too late to get anyone - looks like Toon Army are in for Kleberson ahead of us - and all we'll end with is Stan Lazaridis !

```
-----Original Message-----
From: chris@noredscum.co.uk
Sent: 13 January 2003 12:04
To: TheWhites, all 02/03 User group
Subject: Re: Harry saves our real blushes!

Well after a long train journey starting at some ungodly hour
of the morning I finally got to Maine Road.
What can I say about the game - we were quite unlucky - Viduka
should have had a penalty and we did press for most of the
match  and lets face it one of their goals was the best goal
I have ever seen scored!!
The journey back was a laugh though - a carriage full of City
and Leeds fans just discussing how much beating Manure had
made them happy and annoyed the plastic prawn munchers!
```

Courier New   ☑ 10 ☑   ≣▾ **B** *I* U A̲ ≣ ≣ ≔ ≔ ≣ ≣ ≣ ≣ — 🔊 🖼

Lets just hope we get back on track against the Baggies on
Saturday - anything less than 3 points would be a disaster!

-----**Original Message**-----
From: nelly@whitellie-phant.co.uk
Sent: 13 January 2003 12:17
To: Dave.Shack@Ononon.co.uk
Subject: Re: FW: Harry saves our real blushes!

Rhys and i left the ground thinking we were worth a draw - genius save from
Schemiecehleshlcccmeghead - old red nose- plus a once-in-a-career goal
from Jensen. But thinking about it later I realised we would only have scored
one more even if old red nose had been leaning on his post.
Apart from Harry's goal only his first half shot (cue: the wonder save)and
Wilcox's lame header of the parry were on target. This was the most shot-shy
I've ever seen Leeds. Highlight of the day? Penalty shoot-out at half time
when some mini manc scally had to be restrained from over-celebrating in
front of us... and the reception Fowler got when he came on - from the City
fans.

----Original Message-----
From: Davidharveysmonkey@aol.com
Sent: 13 January 2003 14:42
To: Dorian. Wathen @ The Peacocks.co.uk
Cc: TheWhites, all 02/03 User group
Subject: RE: Re: Harry saves our real blushes!

I hope Fowler doesn't go, he has a cutting edge and commitment that we
rarely see from Viduka. Big Mark just seems to drift in and out of form
when he should be belting them in like that one against Chelsea a couple
of seasons ago. DH'sM

-----**Original Message**-----
From: russ@Vivaleedspana.esp
Sent: 13 January 2003 14:34
To: Davidharveysmonkey; thePeacock
Cc: TheWhites, all 02/03 User group
Subject: RE: Re: Harry saves our real blushes!

ere ere, monkey boy
but don't you think we seem to have lost all our strength going from the middle
of the park to the forward line? i mean has anyone seen wilcox or mills shoot
since those spectalular goals at bolton??

141

Century Gothic   10   B *I* U A,   ≡ ≔ ⇥ ⇤   ≣ ≡ ≡ ≣   — 🔲 🖼

-----Original Message-----
From: Wathen, Dorian, The Peacocks
Sent: 13 January 2003 14:52
To: TheWhites, all 02/03 User group
Subject: RE: RE: Harry saves our real blushes!

Let's face facts, midfield has been lacking in pace and creativity for the last year - now that Bow, Olly have gone and Harry has been promoted to attack, it's hardly threatening ... Wilcox - Okon - Bakke (with McFail and Burns in reserve - oooooh...) is hardly enough to strike fear into Prem sides. Look at West Ham - Sinclair - Cole - Carrick and now Bow...

-----Original Message-----
From: Shack, Dave, Ononon.co.uk
Sent: 13 January 2003 15:04
To: Wathen, Dorian, ThePeacocks; 'Russell Wood'; 'DH's Monkey
Cc: TheWhites, all 02/03 User group
Subject: RE: Re: Harry saves our real blushes!

Unbelivable - you have been mentioning West Ham's midfield for months - do you like young men in shorts or what?

-----Original Message-----
From: russ@Vivaleedspana.esp
Sent: 13 January 2003 15:08
To: TheWhites, all 02/03 User group
Subject: RE: Re: Re: Harry saves our real blushes!

DAVE AT LAST YOU HAVE TYPED SOMTHING FUNNY!!! BUT HOW DO YOU SPELL UNBELEVEiBLE?

-----Original Message-----
From: Shack, Dave, Ononon.co.uk
Sent: 13 January 2003 15:21
To: 'Russell Wood' TheWhites, all 02/03 User group
Subject: RE: RE: Re: Harry saves our real blushes!

Not like that! Don't fucking get me started with your spelling mate - I have to improve it just so it's readable. I then leave some of the funny mistakes in there just for colour...

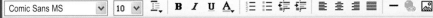

Comic Sans MS   10   B *I* U A

-----Original Message-----
From: russ@Vivaleedspana.esp
Sent: 13 January 2003 15:23
To: Dave.Shack@Ononon.co.uk
Subject: RE: RE: Re: Harry saves our real blushes!

mmmmmmmmmmmmmm gotcha swearing again...........colourful i must say

-----Original Message-----
From: chris@noredscum.co.uk
Sent: 13 January 2003 14:53
To: Dave.shack@Ononon.co.uk
Cc: TheWhites, all 02/03 User group
Subject: Re: RE: Re: Harry saves our real blushes!

I think Fowler will stay based on the following logic...
On this years team photo look at the middle row - Keane,
Bowyer and Dacourt were on that row and have left the club.
Batty is also on that row and looks very unlikely ever to
figure in TV's plans. On a lighter note both Harte and Kelly
are on that row so every cloud has a silver lining.

-----Original Message-----
From: russ@Vivaleedspana.esp
Sent: 13 January 2003 14:56
To: Tamsy; cc: TheWhites, all 02/03 User group
Subject: Re: RE: Re: Harry saves our real blushes!

top spot on the team photo son!

-----Original Message-----
From: Wathen, Dorian, The Peacocks
Sent: 14 January 2003 10:27
To: TheWhites, all 02/03 User group
Subject: Fowler Gone

a resignation is needed over this - we have sold Keane, Bow, Olly and Fowler
for £14 mill and some spare change. We bought for a combined fee of £34
million approx. That's the Rio profit down the drain.

-----Original Message-----
From: Nelly@whitellie-phant.co.uk

Century Gothic   10   **B** *I* <u>U</u> <u>A</u>

Sent: 14 January 2003 10:47
To: TheWhites, all 02/03 User group
Subject:Re: Fowler Gone

It's not about cash anymore - selling Rio for £30 million was the last really big money deal and nobody is going to spend even a third of that on a footballer again... even if they were valued as highly just six months ago. Now it's about cutting the salary bill. Bowyer's wages till the end of the season were £0.75million. Dacourt's maybe more. Fowler's £1m at least.

Although I'm sorry to see him go because of the signals it sends out, I never really thought of Fowler as a Leeds player and he hasn't been the same since his injury. Keane is the one we should have kept. But they're both gone so forget them.

Now it's all about the next crop of youngsters - we're backto where we were when O'Leary took over. Decent squad, potential, chasing Europe. them's the breaks. It could be worse, we could have lost to Bolton and be staring the Nationwide in the face!

-----Original Message-----
From: Shack, Dave, Ononon.co.uk
Sent: 14 January 2003 10:44
To: TheWhites, all 02/03 User group
Subject: RE: Fowler Gone

You're right - and Venables is meant to be the master (market) trader - with these deals he looks like bloody Del & Rodney!
I think that the board must know that a big name like Kleberson will be the only kind that will pacify the fans! If we end up keeping shite (on big wages) like Duberry then we are still in a right mess. Watch now how quickly Viduka either gets hurt or again realises that there is no competition for his place & stop trying.
If/when Kewell goes in the summer then where are we? We need to start seeing Hackwork & Singh blooded in for next season or we are gonna be in trouble again. Bridges could still be out for ever - at least the guy will be a nervous wreck on the pitch & no one will blame him!

-----Original Message-----
From: Jeremy@Donsgloryears.co.uk
Sent: 14 January 2003 11:24
To:TheWhites, all 02/03 User group
Subject: RE:Fowler Gone

Seaman
Maybury, Ferdinand, Wetherall, Irwin
Bowyer, Dacourt, Speed, Keane
Fowler, Hasselbaink
Subs: Huckerby, Haaland, Jones, McAllister.

Not a bad team, eh? And most of them sold recently from Elland Road.

Maybe this is all just a reality check. The fantasy of the last 3 or 4 years is now clearly over, and we are back to having a pretty ordinary, and fairly threadbare, squad. Yes, I am worried particularly about the midfield (or lack of) and who - if anyone - we get in before the end of the month is absolutely crucial. But maybe the future is going to be about the kids again - Milner we now know about, and if any of Richardson, Kilgallon, McMaster, Singh or Cansdell-Sherrif come through we'll be made up.

-----Original Message-----
From: Chris@Noredscum.co.uk
Sent: 14 January 2003 10:49
To: TheWhites, all 02/03 User group
Subject: Re: Fowler Gone

Who next? Why don't we just go the full hog and sell of our whole club? Sheffield United will need a bigger ground when they get in to the Premiership, Chelsea definitely need a new pitch, Huddersfield could do with a new kit and Fulham could do with some fans to liven up the graveyard atmosphere at their ground.

-----Original Message-----
From: Wathen, Dorian, The Peacocks
Sent: 14 January 2003 12:31
To: TheWhites, all 02/03 User group
Subject: Oh you won't believe this...

and to cap it all Bakke's been arrested and detained for drink driving ...

-----Original Message-----
From: Russ@VivaLeedspana.spa
Sent: 14 January 2003 13:10
To: TheWhites, all 02/03 User group
Subject: RE: Oh you won't believe this...

what an effect lufc have on our players!!!

-----Original Message-----
From: Nelly@whitellie-phant.co.uk
Sent: 14 January 2003 13:44
To:TheWhites, all 02/03 User group
Subject: Re: Oh you won't believe this...

Twenty grand a week and he can't afford a cab home?

-----Original Message-----
From: Shack, Dave, Ononon.co.uk
Sent: 14 January 2003 13:44
To: TheWhites, all 02/03 User group
Subject: RE: Oh you won't believe this...

Call Dorian and I a cab...**we** need a drink!

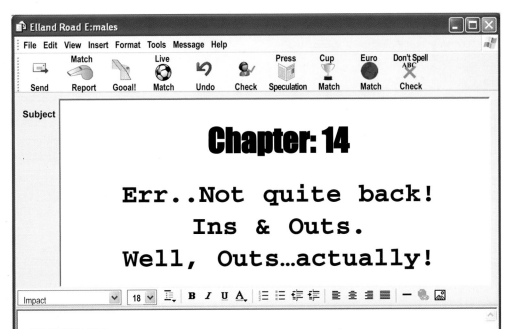

Elland Road E:males

File   Edit   View   Insert   Format   Tools   Message   Help

Match   Live   Press   Cup   Euro   Don't Spell
                                                                                                 ABC
Send   Report   Gooal!   Match   Undo   Check   Speculation   Match   Match   Check

Subject

Chapter: 14

Err..Not quite back!
Ins & Outs.
Well, Outs...actually!

Impact   18   B *I* U A

PREFACE:

Shut that transfer window! - it's not drafty it's bloody lethal. More Leeds market than Elland Road, the PLC seems to be flogging our best players at knock-down car boot sale prices. The natives are restless and not even the news that Kewell's set to re-sign until 2008 (What's a contract? just ask Rio!) can stop everyone asking what the hell is going on. One bit of good news is the 'in' of Leeds author Rob Bagchi to join this team on loan from his own amazing book, The Unforgiven - The Story of Don Revie's Leeds United. Rob@The-unforgiven.com was pitched straight into the melee of Fowler, Johnson & God knows who else...on the pitch it's... well, you know by now...

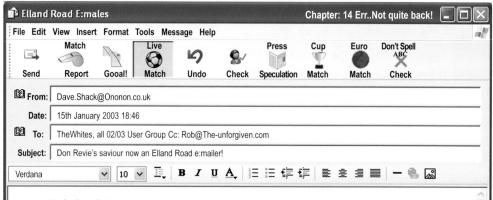

	Match		Live			Press	Cup	Euro	Don't Spell
Send	Report	Gooal!	Match	Undo	Check	Speculation	Match	Match	Check

From: Dave.Shack@Ononon.co.uk

Date: 15th January 2003 18:46

To: TheWhites, all 02/03 User Group Cc: Rob@The-unforgiven.com

Subject: Don Revie's saviour now an Elland Road e:mailer!

Verdana   10   B   *I*   U   A

-----Original Message-----
From: Shack, Dave, Ononon.co.uk
Sent: 15th January 2003 18:46
To: TheWhites, all 02/03 User group
Cc: Rob@The-unforgiven.com
Subject: Don Revie's saviour now an Elland Road e:mailer!

Lads, please all join me in welcoming our replacement for Robbie Fowler - Mr Rob Bagchi - the co-author of one of the best books I have ever read about Leeds United (including Motorways, Madness & LUFC!) - "The Unforgiven" The Story of Don Revie's Leeds United. I got this off my Mum for Christmas & had read it by New Years Day to the exclusion of everything (except the Chelsea game of course) so gripped was I by the style of writing and the story that he & co-author, Paul Rogerson, told about our crucial era. I thought I knew a lot of it, but I did not realise just how shafted we really were & before Revie came just how close we were to never, ever making the grade as a football club. In fact I would probably have been watching Bradford Park Avenue if the great man had not done all that I thought he'd done & a whole lot more. It's an awesome read - well worth £10 of anyone's money - and I'll even get him to sign it for you if you buy it. Now let's get down to business shall we? There's West Brom & half a team to talk about...

-----Original Message-----
From: rob@the-unforgiven.com
Sent: 15 January 2003 23:46
To: TheWhites, all 02/03 User Group
Subject: Re: Don Revie's saviour now an Elland Road e:mailer!

Lads
Sorry to start on such a negative note but is it time to drag out the Joy Division albums? Has Fowler gone or not? He's been having this medical now for 36 hours and City seem no further to stumping up the cash.

Georgia   10   B *I* U A

Even better, if you've seen the press release on PA News, is that Kleberson's "15 yr old fiancee" has given the go ahead to a move to Leeds. As Tony Hancock's suicide note went "too many things seem to go wrong too many times." We're in Jerry Leeds Lewis territory now...

-----Original Message-----
From: Firhad, Mohd, Eltelasia.ma
Sent: 16 January 2003 02:23
To: TheWhites, all 02/03 User Group
Subject: FW: Don Revie's saviour now an Elland Road e:mailer!

Welcome aboard.........Fowler's departure will allow Kleberson in. What a talent. Need sublime, skills and control in midfield. Strikers need ammo to pump in the goals and Kleberson with Okon and Bakke may be the answer.

Have faith in El tel. Must see that he came in with an instruction not to buy and as we sell he is shorhanded. 2 strikers and a natural winger as stikers speaks for itself.

On you Leeds Firhad

-----Original Message-----
From: chris@noredscum.co.uk
Sent: 16 January 2003 10:39
To: TheWhites, all 02/03 User Group
Subject: Re: Don Revie's saviour now an Elland Road e:mailer!

Technically though he still hasn't gone as Rob mentioned. I recon that medical at Maine Road will last about a week - it needs to just to make sure that we've not off-loaded a cripple. Is their any truth in the rumour that Fowler actually only cost £7m and the figure of £11m quoted was only if we got into the Champions League? If so we might have actually made some money on Fowler reversing our recent trait of selling players for bargain basement prices. Is this Kleberson deal actually going to come off or is it just fantasy football?

Bring on the Baggies - we could do with a goal fest!!!

Chris

PS Has anyone got a spare ticket for Gillingham? The ticket office have let me down again!!!

149

-----Original Message-----
From: russ@vivaleedspana.esp
Sent: 16 January 2003 11:59
To: TheWhites, all 02/03 User Group
Subject: Re: Don Revie's saviour now an Elland Road e:mailer!

Hello Rob, nice to have a proffesional on board, daves spelling is shite!!!
I wonder if el tel is listening, you know the manager that has not allowed nige or batty back in the team since telling him "no wer'e not" going to auss in the summer!!
Talking of aussies why are we going to buy another one that was'nt good enough for the hammers and is not in the brum team??
marching on
rtb

-----Original Message-----
From: Chris@noredscum.co.uk
Sent: 16 January 2003 16:39
To: TheWhites, all 02/03 User Group
Subject: Re: Don Revie's saviour now an Elland Road e:mailer!

Apparently the Fowler move is now off and the club deny approaching Kleberson

-----Original Message-----
From: Wathen, Dorian, The Peacocks
Sent: 16 January 2003 16:53
To: TheWhites, all 02/03 User Group
Subject: RE: Don Revie's saviour now an Elland Road e:mailer!

Looks like the Dacourt situation all over again.

-----Original Message-----
From: Davidharveysmonkey@aol.com
Sent: 16 January 2003 17:11
To: TheWhites, all 02/03 User Group
Subject: Re(2): Don Revie's saviour now an Elland Road e:mailer!

The bring and buy sale has been halted while we get ready to give another of our best players to man United

Verdana   10   **B** *I* U A

-----**Original Message**-----
From: Shack, Dave, Ononon.co.uk
Sent: 19th January 2003 13:00
To: TheWhites, all 02/03 User group
Cc: Rob@The-unforgiven.com
Subject: Baggies,baggage & bag o'shite?

In fairness, Russ' 4-0 was a bit optimistic, but with 10 men, four strikers &
a full house we really should have completed a double over them. Hoult was
outstanding (in saying that - aaway fans must say that every week about
Robbo!) and we were bloody lucky over the penalty. It was bag o'shite that
neither the premiership nor Goals on Sunday had decent highlights of the
game - not a glimpse of Fowlers reaction - nor the alleged Viduka fan
incident (Rob did you see it?) to help me write this mail.
So this week is all about Klebers -on or Klebers-off? It's about Fowlers
new found 'love' for Leeds, it's about re-surgent Gillingham getting ready
for the cup tie next week (anyone fancy picking me up at Heathrow - 9am
arrival from New York) and, I guess, about re-buffing the bids for Woody
& Johnson whilst making Dubes look as attractive as possible...

-----Original Message-----
From: rob@the-unforgiven.com
Sent: 19 January 2003 17:53
To: Dave.Shack@Ononon.co.uk
Subject: Re: Baggies,baggage & bag o'shite?

Didn't catch the Viduka incident at all. I could have been asleep. It was the most dull
match of the season. Shades of the depths of last Spring or (even worse) 1996/97.
Still a clean sheet's a clean sheet, I suppose and that's how Venables saved 'Boro.
The only funny thing was Gary Megson's performance - I've never seen anything like
it. He was like someone's dad on the touchline at a school game, shouting and
screaming at his players all the time, kicking every ball for them as the cliche goes. I
thought he was going to have a heart attack.
The money thing still doesn't add up - there's all sorts of insinuations about
'malpractice' concerning some of O'Leary's deals in today's tabloids - the team that
played yesterday cost fuck all , only Viduka was more than £5m and Robinson, Kelly,
Kewell and Smith didn't cost a penny.
Did anyone else think that Danny Mills' relegation to the bench was a bit fishy. A
sign that he might be next in the shop window?
Rob

-----**Original Message**-----
From: Andy@whitetoreply.com
Sent: 19 January 2003 13:07

To: Dave.Shack@Ononon.co.uk
Subject: Re: Baggies,baggage & bag o'shite?

What another dull and dreary affair. We looked back to our clueless selves. Smith's left foot effort was about the highlight of the match, and I would say that Viduka's touches were still pretty impressive.
Can we afford Kleberson now? It's not just the sign on fee, the wages are going to be a killer. We don't want another geedy Hasselbank, Yeboah, or that Swedish git whose name escapes me at the moment.
At some point I will wake up and realise it was all a bad dream and that the season is only 2 games old and we have six points out of six.
Andy

-----Original Message-----
From: Firhad, Mohd, Eltelasia.ma
Sent: 20 January 2003 02:13
To: Thewhites,all 02/03 User group
Subject: Baggies,baggage & bag o'shite?

Fowler:
Belief that he wants to stay and work with El Tel..........Its just in the business sense we need to offload him to buy. Hard for us to re built with this limitations imposed over El Tel.

WBA:
A Draws a draw............With the current limitations it is commendable. Still think Kleb will make da difference.Risdale give El Tel the $$$$$$$$$$$$ and we shall wait for wedding boy even if its March.

Restructuring has a limit, To let Woody go ??!!!

-----Original Message-----
From: Nelly@Whitellie-phant.co.uk
Sent: 20 January 2003 12:40
To: TheWhites, all 02/03 User group
Subject: Re(2): Baggies,baggage & bag o'shite?

Ridsdale just turned me down for an interview - again

-----Original Message-----
From: Andy Lawson [mailto:Andy@whitetoreply.co.uk]
Sent: 20 January 2003 13:41
To: TheWhites, all 02/03 User group
Subject: RE: Re(2): Baggies,baggage & bag o'shite?

Tahoma　　　10　B *I* U A

Concerning the cost of the team yesterday, does that mean that the bench cost more than the starting eleven? Concerning "malpractice", is he a forward or a midfielder.

-----Original Message-----
From: russ@vivaleedspana.esp
Sent: 20 January 2003 18:24
To: Dave.Shack@Ononon.co.uk
Subject: Re: Baggies,baggage & bag o'shite?

Guys Hola
Just back into office after a strenous day on the golf course 5 and a half hours! hitting the fuck out of that little fucker of a ball (dave 300 yards straight and becoming regular) and i think a little bit of elland rd frustration coming out. Dave i agree with you totally about the comments made by el tel about quote "yes we expected this with wba they always give 100% and make it difficult for teams and as we have seen they normally only lose 1-0", great tel but why is it okay for us to draw and not beat them 1-0 like everyone else!!!! R T B

-----Original Message-----
From: Shack, Dave, Ononon.co.uk
Sent: 20 January 2003 14:15
To: TheWhites, all 02/03 User group
Subject: Elland Rd Exodus!

Lads - expect another player to be out of the door by the end of this week.
Clue: He might be found in Emmerdale
Clue: He has a skinhead
Clue: We'll lose on the deal - oops that's not much of a clue is it!!

-----Original Message-----
From: Nelly@thewhitellie-phant.co.uk
Sent: 20 January 2003 14:31
To: Dave.Shack@Ononon.co.uk
Subject: Re: Elland Rd Exodus!

£4 million, prob

-----Original Message-----
From: russ@vivaleedspana.esp
Sent: 20 January 2003 18:37

Comic Sans MS | 10 | B *I* U A

To: Dave.shack@Ononon.co.uk
Subject: Re: Elland Rd Exodus!

What's emmerdale dave?

-----Original Message-----
From: Wathen, Dorian, The Peacocks
Sent: 21 January 2003 10:52
To: TheWhites, all 02/03 User group
Subject: RE: Elland Rd Exodus!

Speculation that TV is in for Upson, which would indicate ...

-----Original Message-----
From: Andy Lawson@whitetoreply.co.uk
Sent: 21 January 2003 13:34
To: Dave.Shack@Ononon.co.uk
Subject: Re: Elland Rd Exodus!

Why the last clue. How can we lose?

-----Original Message-----
From: rob@the-unforgiven.com
Sent: 21 January 2003 14:51
To: Dave.Shack@Ononon.co.uk
Subject: RE: Elland Rd Exodus!

I know how we lose! Sell for less than we bought him for, right? Looking at the share
price, the whole fucking club's only worth £11m now.
Time for a crusade? Are you going to lead it Shacky?

-----Original Message-----
From: Firhad, Mohd, Eltelasia.ma
Sent: 23 January 2003 05:35
To: Shack, Dave, On on on, London
Cc: Wathen, Dorian, Peacocks, London
Subject: Oh my God! What's happening?

Its about time that we gave our thoughts on this ridiculous going ons that
may push our team back 10 years. All the great work started via Wilko will
go to waste. Lets not look at Division One all over gain. Long years of
the 80's in the wildersness is torture enuff'. If we dont address it than
we may be on to that era all ovber again.

154

Woody is our asset and a true trooper. Leeds should be built around him, Robbo and Smithy with Milener of coz. Come on chairman, the debtors can wait can;t they ??!!! El tel and Peter has tried their best but lets hope the debtors will ease up and get us to have a really decent team to rise up the standings.

Forever leed no matter What. Firhad (LUFC 1973 - 4ever)

-----Original Message-----
From: Chris@noredscum.co.uk
Sent: 24 January 2003 16:41
To: TheWhites, all 02/03 User group
Subject: Re:

He's in the States coming back tomorrow - well I hope he is he has my ticket and lift for Gillingham!!
Anyone else going?

-----Original Message-----
From: Shack, Dave, Ononon.co.uk
Sent: 26 January 2003 11:47
To: TheWhites, all 02/03 User group
Subject: No surprise -We give the Gills(or is it us?)an extra pay day!

Well lads, it was a nice enough day - no aggro, a great goal, nice to stand on a terrace - great to see Jeremy, Chris, DH's Monkey, Nelly the Elliephant & Radio Rhys as well as my mate (& full on Norwich fan) Paul in full riot gear directing the Kent police in their exertions to stop the Leeds fans clobbering either Venable or Ridsdale never mind the Gills fans! The banter was actually brilliant - as it always is when things are, shall we say, tough! There were quite a few banners & photocopied 'Tell Us the Truth' or 'Sack the board' leaflets - on red paper, I ask you? We are not at that stage yet where we have to rely on bloody red paper for our protests!
The side was pretty predictable, Hartey was on the bench & apart from that it was West Brom again. Kewell should have made it 2-0 to kill the game off & then ball #13 would have been all ours. Frighteningly, Duberry was about to come on before 'dukes got sent off (so that did us a favour then!) instead of Fowler. Why couldn't we think about really winning the match than sitting back with another bad defender?
Fear & self-doubt crept back in & they equalised. They nearly won it too if the big Fiji-an could head straight, but fortunately he missed & whilst I'm

Verdana | 10 | B *I* U A

sure we'll easily beat them at home, we could have done with the result
to take us into Chelsea which I'm really not looking forward to now.
I wonder if I won 'furthest distance travelled' for the match? 70 miles
from Chiswick & 3500 miles from New York? Arrived at 8.55, met Tamsy
& drove to Gillingham. I'm staying here for Chelsea & then back to NY at
8.30 am Wednesday morning.
In adversity, we will support them! Wish the transfer window would hurry
up & close - why don't we kidnap Woody & then he can't move.

-----Original Message-----
From: Andy@Whitetoreply.co.uk
Sent: 26 January 2003 21:51
To: Dave.Shack@On on on
Subject: Re: No surprise - We give the Gills (or is it us?) an extra pay day!

Nice thought on the kidnap Woody idea.

Another lack lustre result will have the fans wakening up if we're not too
careful. Gillingham! I ask you. Mind you, it's very much what we have some
to expect over the last several years, ie can be great against the better
sides and then bring on the likes of Cardiff and we're pap. Ah well, the
Leeds City 5 a side is still open as a competition to get some silverware
this season.

Well done for travelling such a long distance to support the boys.

-----Original Message-----
From: Jeremy@Donsgloryears. Co.uk
Sent: 27 January 2003 10:03
To: Dave.Shack @ Ononon.co.uk
Subject: Re: No surprise - We give the Gills (our is it us?) an extra pay day!

I've never seen anyone sent off before for "hitting" someone with his
armpit. Watch it again on TV and you'll see that's the part of his body that makes contact. If
Big Mark had wanted to take Hassenthaler out with his elbow, the little dwarf would still be
laying spark out on the pitch. Nice to see managers setting such a good sportsmanlike
example for his team.

-----Original Message-----
From: Davidharveysmonkey@ aol .com
Sent: 27 January 2003 11:00
To: TheWhites, all 02/03 User group
Subject: Re: No surprise - We give the Gills (our is it us?) an extra pay day!

I feel the best thing that came out of this game- apart from the joy of standing- was the realisation of exactly who Lucic is. Caveman, as I said at the time, has only recently joined Leeds from FC Piltdown Man, and is only just coming to terms with being this side of the soil. You'll know some of his relatives like Stig of The Dump, Fred Flintstone, and Zola. Unlike them Our Cavey is a one club man - it's about two feet long and made of dinosaur bone.

His earliest games were at Jurassic Park, the home of Piltdown, but you may also have seen him third from the right on the Ascent of Man monkeys to businessmen silouette poster that exists in all Biology labs.

Since joining Leeds Cavey has slowly been acclimitising to the wooden goalposts, at Piltodown the posts were made of the long teeth of a giant woolly elephant, as he attacked there was always a massive tusk ahead of him.

It's a tribute to his work ethic that Cavey is known to stay out on the pitch for hours after a game, though some believe this is just to stare in awe at the floodlights. he is an ardent trainer and often joins a run round Otley Chevin chased by raptors.

His factfile includes: Favourite Car: ?? Favourite Food: T-Rex Steak and chips

feel free to add to it. Yours David Harvey's Monkey

-----Original Message-----
From: Wathen, Dorian, The Peacocks
Sent: 27 January 2003 11:04
To: TheWhites, all 02/03 User group
Subject: RE: No surprise - We give the Gills (or is it us?) an extra pay day!

What about:
Hobbies: Cave painting (fave gallery - Lascaux, France), making fire, shouting, waving fist.
Favourite wo-man: Raquel Welch
Fave film: Anything by Oliver Stone and Chris Rock.
Fave Music: Rock and Rock.
Sorry about that...

-----Original Message-----
From: Davidharveysmonkey@ aol. com
Sent: 27 January 2003 11:34
To: Dave.Shack @ On on on
Subject: Re: RE: No surprise - We give the Gills (or is it us?) an extra pay day!

That's true, to clarify, caveman had a horrible experience with Charlton Heston, every time he gets too close to the net he starts worrying about Apes getting him.
I really wish all games could be like saturday - I'm talking crowd not pitch. The banter was great as was the celebration - just like being thirteen again down the front at The jam at the Queens Hall. Shacky for you and nelly just add Thin Lizzy or Black Sabbath to the end of the last line.

Verdana | 10 | B *I* U A

-----Original Message-----
From: Shack, Dave, Ononon.co.uk
Sent: Monday, January 27, 2003 7:18 PM
To: 'TheWhites, all 02/03 User group
Subject: RE: No surprise - We give the Gills (our is it us?)...

Wow! Yeah - have you noticed that he never stands on the goal-line for corners - or goes too far up front? He's scared of the net things. He once lost his family; they were captured in a big net and is (rightly) fearful of them! You may also notice him crowd staring from time to time - which is when he spots someone lighting a fag - it's the fire! But it goes so quickly he soon forgets about it.
The other big problem he has is the team coach - the lads cover his eyes to get him on there because, of course, the wheel so has not been invented yet!
Cavey - we love him!

-----Original Message-----
From: Chris@noredscum.co.uk
Sent: 27 January 2003 16:15
To: TheWhites, all 02/03 User group
Subject: Re: No surprise - We give the Gills (our is it us?)...

Dave - no complaints with me regarding the super fan travel - you neglected to add on the 3 miles we must have walked trying to remember where we'd parked the car after the game!
The banter on the terraces was great - Also we should give the lads who'd spent loads of money photocopying signs for people to hold up and show the telly cameras a bit of advice - use your spell check - black type on red is not very easy to read from far away - neither is font size 14.
Roll on Chelsea should be a giggle now that Shacky has decided to sit with us mere mortals rather than use the corporate box - expect the roof to leak and you not to be able to see half the pitch and don't even get me started with Chelsea's stewards should you dare to stand up to try and see better. Well worth the £40 if you ask me!!!

-----Original Message-----
From: Murphy, Mark, @blue=thecolour.co.uk
Sent: 28 January 2003 11:33
To: Shack, Dave, On on on
Subject: Revenge time at the Bridge!

Times New Roman   10   **B** *I* U A   ≡ ≔ ⫶≡ ⫶≡   ≣ ≣ ≣ ≣   — 🖳 🖾

We all fucking hate Leeds. We all hate Leeds & Leeds & Leeds, Leeds & Leeds & Leeds & Leeds, Leeds & Leeds & Leeds & Leeds. We are the Leeds haters.

-----Original Message-----
From: Shack, Dave, Ononon.co.uk
Sent: 28 January 2003 11:41
To: Murphy, Mark, Blue=the colour
Subject: RE: Revenge time at the Bridge!

If you hate Leeds Utd have a go, if you hate Leeds united ave a go...if you hate Leeds United, hate Leeds united, hate Leeds united, 'ave a go!

We hate Chelsea.

-----Original Message-----
From: Murphy, Mark, Blue=the colour
Sent: 28 January 2003 11:43
To: Shack, Dave, On on on
Subject: RE: Revenge time at the Bridge!

Don't tempt me

-----Original Message-----
From: Shack, Dave, Ononon.co.uk
Sent: 28 January 2003 11:44
To: Murphy, Mark @ Blue=thecolour.co.uk
Subject: RE:RE Revenge time at the Bridge!

Will (Did)you come to Leeds? Will (did)you fuck, will (did) you fuck...

P.S. You didn't 'cos you were in Australia hiding...

-----Original Message-----
From: Russ@Vivaleedspana.co.uk
Sent: 29 January 2003 16:13
To: TheWhites, all 02/03 User group
Subject: Chelsea wankers SILENCE! was it that bad?

I thought they had lost all idea of how to beat us until that piece of brilliance and then the deflection and then the own goal!

It was nice to see some unity and grit out there.

How many times have we played against teams, where after their player has come to the interview and admitted "yes that was the best goal i have ever scored"?

Sheff utd 90th min 45 yard screamer from a player that has not scored since!!

So much for fowler staying for the cause!

-----Original Message-----
From: Shack, Dave, Ononon.co.uk
Sent: 29 January 2003 16.14
To: Russ@ Vivaleedspana.spa
Subject: Out of Office AutoReply: Hope we beat Chelsea!

Wed(29th)/Thurs/Fri I'm in New York on business followed by a LARO conference in Cancun. E:mail will be only occasionally monitored.

I'm back in the UK on Feb.7th 2003.

e:you then! Dave Shack

P.S. Hopefully Everton will have their youngster up-staged by ours too!

```
-----Original Message-----
From: Chris@noredscum.co.uk
Sent: 30 January 2003 11:21
To: TheWhites, all 02/03 User group
Subject: Re: chelsea


Well if we set out our stall to defend we are going to get
more results like this.
We continue to put all eleven men defending in the box at
corners so when the ball is cleared there is no-one to fight
for possession. We were unlucky to lose on Tuesday but once
they went infront we never even got the ball past the halfway
line.
At last Caveman could put his fear of the net to one side for
a moment to score - I think personally he was looking at the
Shed end and recognised some cousins amongst the many knuckle
dragging neanderthals there - he started doing a caveman dance
and the ball hit him and flew in to the net.
We battled well and the desire and commitment were there
```

unfortunately our tactics leave a lot to be desired -
England's future opponents will have to look forward to
Michael Owen playing as a centre back under Brian Kidd's
"everyone behind the ball at all times" school of football.
World football domination surely is just around the corner.
So Fowler's unfinished business at Leeds took all of three
days to complete. Its £3 million now and then £500,000 every
15 games he plays up to £6 million - so we'll have al our
money in about 20 years then!
Apparently also today the board are considering a
"substantial" offer for Woodgate - given the poor state of the
transfer market and our club's inability to negotiate we will
probably sell him for a couple of million with a crate of
Newcastle Brown ale thrown in.
Not a good week at all...

-----Original Message-----
From: Russ@Vivaleedspana.spa
Sent: 05 February 2003 16:05
To: TheWhites, all 02/03 User group
Subject: Am I the only one left?

Fucking el, everyone's off including 'our' leader...
Wheres dave? has he decided to quit on he's own book!
Probably on that bleeding beach again.
RTB

-----Original Message-----
From: Wathen, Dorian, The Peacocks
Sent: 05 February 2003 16:08
To: Russ@Vivaleedspana.spa
Subject: RE: RE: What is happening?

Correct.
He's in Cancun, Mexico (at a conference) playing golf.
It's tough at the top.

-----Original Message-----
From: Shack, Dave, On on on
Sent: 05 February 2003 16:16
To: TheWhites, all 02/03 User group
Subject: 10 minutes on line for 800 mexican shitters! Bye Bye
Gills!

Just logged on & Russ is slagging me off! DON'T YOU READ THE AUTO-REPLY YOU APE? Anyway, returned from the meeting last night to find on lufc.co.uk that Peter is going to meet the fans, Smithy has signed a new cointract from his sick-bed & we only had half a team out last night. But Dukes answered the critics & shut that little maning twat Hessenthaler up in the best way. I'm sure it was tight & nervy at the end, but we did it so come on Palace tonight eh? Fat chance I think... What's happened to Villa? Wow! Let's hope West Ham are no problemo for us next (bet they are!) & this new Roberto Carlos -esque player is as good as they say.

Russ, I could do with a few Spanish transalations like - "No, you Mexican twat, we're not shite we're just going through a bad patch" and "Yes, we did get to a Champions league semi by beating loads of Spanish teams only a couple of years ago!"

Back to London for Thursday afternoon!

-----Original Message-----
From: Russ@ Vivaleedspana.esp
Sent: 05 February 2003 17:02
To: Dave.Shack@ Ononon.co.uk
Subject: Re: 10 minutes on line for 800 mexican shitters! Bye Bye Gills!

Ehhhhhhhhhhhhhh Shagger!
Lovely to ere from you again!
Just correct me if i am wrong dave but should it be contract not cointract? and moaning not maning? just to help the book you understand!
Ok that your spelling lesson over with now lets see if i can help you with the Spanish/Mexican.
1. No cabrón, no somos malos solo estamos pasando un bache. (note: always laugh when you say cabrón to a mexican, if you say it siriously they'll take it the wrong way)
2. Sí llegamos a la semifinal de la liga de Campeones ganandole a un montón de equipos españoles hace apenas dos años.

From your lovable Ape
R.T.B

162

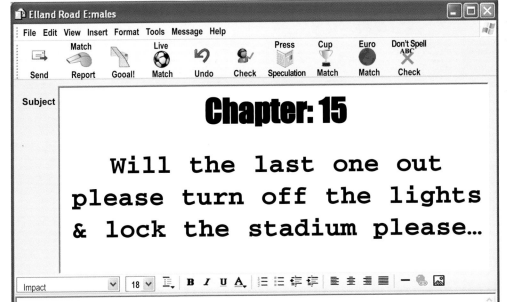

PREFACE:

True to his name - (Get) Rid, Sale! Is flogging the crown jewels - or so we think. The straw that broke the camel's back is Woody (who may be daft as a brush and therefore completing the camel metaphor perfectly!), but has proven that he is a far better natural centre-half than Rio. Sold to a 'loadsamoney' Newcastle, we're now really in the doldrums. El Tel hasn't a clue what's going on - and neither have we.

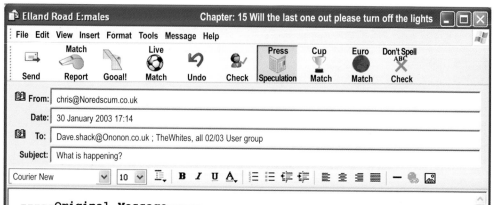

File   Edit   View   Insert   Format   Tools   Message   Help

Match   Live   Press   Cup   Euro   Don't Spell

Send   Report   Gooal!   Match   Undo   Check   Speculation   Match   Match   Check

From: chris@Noredscum.co.uk

Date: 30 January 2003 17:14

To: Dave.shack@Ononon.co.uk ; TheWhites, all 02/03 User group

Subject: What is happening?

Courier New   10   **B** *I* U A

-----Original Message-----
From: chris@noredscum.co.uk
Sent: 30 January 2003 17:14
To: Dave.Shack@Ononon.co.uk ; TheWhites, all 02/03 User group
Subject: What is happening?

So one of the "Crown Jewels" and the player that Rio was cover for has been sold. Why don't we just sell Smithy, Robinson and Kewell and then we can just speed up the inevitable.

We are currently the laughing stock of English football - every fan of every other Premiership club is pissing themselves laughing at us. We have a board who are utterly without any scruples and who are clearly just concentrating on a very short term view. If we manage to survive in top flight football then I for one will be amazed.

Our back four will most likely be centred around Michael Duberry - a player who has never impressed. Even Radebe doesn't look like he is going to last much longer. Give me a couple of months to sweat off my beer belly and I'm going to ask for a trial.

Does this now mean that Venables will resign?

-----Original Message-----
From: Russ@Vivaleedspana.spa
Sent: 30 January 2003 17:40
To: TheWhites, all 02/03 user group
Subject: Re: What is happening?

Chris, your dead right pal, they are lying fuckers and ridsdale should fuck off now.

-----Original Message-----
From: rob@the-unforgiven.com
Sent: 30 January 2003 17:57
To: TheWhites, all 02/03 user group
Subject: Re: What is happening?

Ever get the feeling you've been cheated?

Why do we have to keep taking this crap? These carpet-bagging scumbag financiers
who only ever invested in the club so as not to miss out on football's boom have bled
the heart out of it. Zippy Ridsdale has had his gob shut but not by the method we'd
all choose for him.

So O' Leary spends 100 million and recoups 25 (Hasselbaink, Molenaar, Hopkin,
Haaland, Wethers etc.) This poor bastard Venables spends 3 million and recoups 48
million. Net loss over 5 years trading - 30 million and we still can't sustain that.
We've fucking had it!

If Venables did resign I'd think a hell of a lot more of him than I ever have before.

-----Original Message-----
From: Andy@Whitetoreply.co.uk
Sent: 30 January 2003 18:16
To: TheWhites, all 02/03 user group
Subject: Re: What is happening?

Plc's have no right to be in football. What happened to Football as a game.
It shouldn't be about the money, it should be about playing and spectating.
Even if money has to be involved, why are all these tossers in charge in big
business. They obviously have no fucking clue how to run a business. They seem to
be big gamblers who have no bleedin' idea.

I'm with the luddite faction. Burn it down and let's have Leeds Pheonix United (and
no effin' business in charge).

-----Original Message-----
From: Shack, Dave, On on on
Sent: 31 January 2003 00:32
To: TheWhites, all 02/03 user group
Subject: RE: What is happening?

Imagine being in an all day meeting whilst this is going on in New York.
Imagine trying to ring the missus at the end of the day & having your

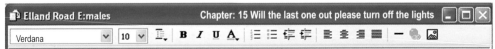

phone jammed with texts & voice messages & then having 2 minutes to shower, shit & shave before going out to a dinner.

Well, how ever bad it is for you lot there where it's going on - it's FUCKING 10 times worse being here.

Fuck it. I've said it before - Leeds United is not just about now - it's about the next 100 years - it's about us all taking our kids or our grandchildren to see them. (I promised my nephews, Christopher & Dougal they could go when they are 7 - and they're only 5 at the moment!)At least we've all seen some unbelievable times personally. If we have a nightmare for a while now (which looks pretty likely) maybe we just have to face up to the fact that someone, somewhere has looked at Leeds & said - if serious shit does not happen now (ie write off £20k, 50k or 100k)then it's going to disappear - then , tough as it it is today, we should all be thankful that someone has been that bold.

Lads, if writing this book has shown me anything -it's that Leeds United part defines who I am - who all of us are & without it I'd be less of the man I think I am. I hope you all will feel this way too & we can carry on with a club who is purging the past - the shit, the wrong hidelines & can go forward like we did until that fateful night in Leeds City Centre - fully proud to be a fan of Leeds United Football Club & everyone involved in it.

Being away from it, bizarrely has given be this objectivity. Bye Woody, Bye Bowyer, bye Fowler, maybe Bye Tel, now let's get on with rebuilding on a very solid foundation that can take us into the next 100 years without the inevitable collapse that some clubs will face in the not too distant future.

I'm Leeds & I'm proud of it.

-----Original Message-----
From: Russ@Vivaleedspana.spa
Sent: 31 January 2003 09:24
To: TheWhites, all 02/03 User group
Subject: RE: What is happening?

Yeh Yeh great dave, now come down off that fucking soap box and tell us what you really think!
nice speech darling!

Arial   ⌄   10 ⌄   ≡↴ **B** *I* U A̲   ≣ ≔ ⇤ ⇥ ≣ ≣ ≣ ≣ — ● ▨

-----Original Message-----
From: Chris@Captdom.co.uk
Sent: 04 February 2003 20:16
To: Dave.Shack@Ononon.co.uk
Subject: Re: What is happening?
Know it's late ... been living in builders hell in my flat all year.

I think you're right Shack old son.

If you ever had to prove that your not a glory hunter, this is the test. Support Leeds
cos you love 'em, not cos they win all the time.

Moylesy

-----Original Message-----
From: Jeremy@Donsgloryears.co.uk
Sent: 02 February 2003 19:00
To: TheWhites, all 02/03 user group
Subject: RE: What is happening?

Like Shacky I have been away in the States during this traumatic week. Every time I switch
on my laptop there's more bad news on the website,followed by screen after screen of e-mails
from you lot.

I think if I'd had the time to reply at any time over the past few days I would have echoed
everyone's feelings of anger and bitterness, but maybe by being several thousand miles away
(and not being exposed to the British media and the childish taunts of non LUFC so-called
friends) a degree of perspective has kicked in.

Every thing in football goes in cycles. We had the great Revie-era from 65-74, followed by
mediocrity from the mid-70's to the early 80's, followed by 8 years of nightmare 2nd Division
horrors, followed by Wilko leading us to 2nd Div and then Championship triumphs, then
another dull going-nowhere period until O'Leary. That era brought us 4 years of amazing
excitement, European adventures, great football, heightened expectations etc. Sadly it is now
over and I think we all have to brace ourselves for another spell of mid-table mediocrity (or
re-building as it is euphomistically called).

At the time, I couldn't figure out how we had the money to buy thelikes of Rio, Keano,
Fowler, Ollie etc. Now we know - we didn't andwe're paying the price. But what would we
rather have had? The unambitious policy adopted by similar sized clubs to us like Aston
Villa, Tottenham, Everton? At least we had a go. We took a gamble, borrowed big, bought
bigger, and for a while genuinely threatened to break the monopoly of M** U, Arsenal etc.
Personally, I'd take the adventurous route any time. Better to have loved and lost than to have
never loved at all (as someone a lot more learned than I once said).

Times New Roman   10   B *I* U A

One last point - we can only guess what the club might have achieved without that mad drunken night in Leeds city centre three years ago. The 2 players at the centre of it, and therefore the cause of all the ensuing trauma, have now gone. Maybe we shouldn't be too sad about that. Roll on the new era!

-----Original Message-----
From: Russ@VivaLeedspana.spa
Sent: 03 February 2003 09:24
To: TheWhites, all 02/03 User group
Subject: RE: What is happening?

Well i don't know about everyone else, but what Jeremy has just said explains exactly how i feel, wer'e Leeds and proud of it and i for one would not have wanted to miss out on the european tours experienced by all of us in the last 5 years.
Risdale gave us that chance and we should not forget that.
There is not a manager in the world that given the chance wouldn't want to take on the opportunity that Risdale gave O'leary and whilst he did a great job, how many other managers would have won a trophy? just one trophy in 4 years, no matter how small would, no could have changed everything.
I don't think you can blame Ridsdale for that, maybe we should all be man enough to just accept that the crop of players that we all raved about were not good enough!
Mid table this season and fuck all else, so lets just relax and see where the milners of our world will take us.

-----Original Message-----
From: Firhad, Mohd, Eltelasia.ma
Sent: 06 February 2003 02:16
To: Shack, Dave, Ononon.co.uk
Cc: TheWhites, all 02/03 User group
Subject: What is happening? Viva Leeds

Despite what has happened, will happen and ro happen will forever remain a true Leeds fan. 1973 till now have endured it all. Survived the Div 2 wilderness years and the latest storm is part of transition.

On El Tel, we cannot blame him too as he has a certain way of playing soccer and the players tyhat can execute it has to be brought in. Alas instead he had a major blow. One by one they leave.

Batang   10   B *I* U A

Newcastle is heading that way. Champions League beckon but as we experienced the minute we are out of it $$$$ creeps in. Risdale, angry I may be but in a business sense he has to do what he has to do.

We shall overcome. Look forward to a grand finish in the last few months of season 02/03. Leeds 4Ever - Firhad

-----Original Message-----
From: Shack, Dave, Ononon.co.uk
Sent: 07 February 2003 18:13
To: TheWhites, all 02/03 User group
Subject: Torres Torres! Our new Spanish wunderkid...

Hi Lads,
Just spoke to Mr Steve Mcmanaman (de der de de de!) who had just spoken to Raul Bravo. He's been asked (by Venables) if he wants to play against West Ham or be on the bench tomorrow. He said I'll play in spanish (doesn't speak a word of English!), but according to Steve is excellent. I hope they use Hartey on the left of midfield now...? Looks like we'll have less than half a team to play their full strength squad (Kanoute & Di Canio are back! -typical!) So at best a draw...

As I said at the start of the cup campaign that is where all our eggs should be. Save players this weekend with a view to getting into the last 8! A Uefa spot would be a total laugh if we were to get to a final - where even a draw against Man U or Arse would see us gain the Euro spot!!

I don't think Bowyer should be booed - but I'm glad he's gone. I hope Johnson can step up to the plate & bull-fighter can protect us from the inevitable Duberry-isms...

Cheers & did you hear Moyles with Gareth this afternoon? Great....

-----Original Message-----
From: Wathen, Dorian, The Peacocks
Sent: 08 February 2003 17:45
To: Shack, Dave, On on on
Subject: RE: Torres Torres! Our new Spanish wunderkid...

am I missing something on this torres business - or is it a rioja, no ?

-----Original Message-----
From: Shack, Dave, On on on
Sent: 08 February 2003 19:49

Verdana · 10 · B *I* U A · lists · align · — · image

To: Wathen, Dorian, The Peacocks
Subject: RE: Torres Torres! Our new Spanish wunderkid...

Just a phrase - when a bull charges? Is a nice spanish wine though!

-----Original Message-----
From: Wathen, Dorian, The Peacocks
Sent: 08 February 2003 19:55
To: Shack, Dave, On on on
Subject: RE: Torres Torres! Our new Spanish wunderkid...

Is a cracker - though not quite as good as marques de riscal or caceres. er.. OK - torres means towers I reckon. degree in Spanish don't you know...

-----Original Message-----
From: Shack, Dave, On on on
Sent: 08 February 2003 19:57
To: Wathen, Dorian, The Peacocks
Subject: RE: Torres Torres! Our new Spanish wunderkid...

put yourself forward for transalater on match days?

-----Original Message-----
From: Wathen, Dorian, The Peacocks
Sent: 08 February 2003 20:02
To: Shack, Dave, On on on
Subject: RE: Torres Torres! Our new Spanish wunderkid...

think el tel has that one nailed for himself to make a bit more dinero on the side ...

-----Original Message-----
From: Shack, Dave, On on on
Sent: 08 February 2003 20:07
To: Wathen, Dorian, The Peacocks
Subject: RE: Torres Torres! Our new Spanish wunderkid...

Euro - you twat - and before that pesetas...

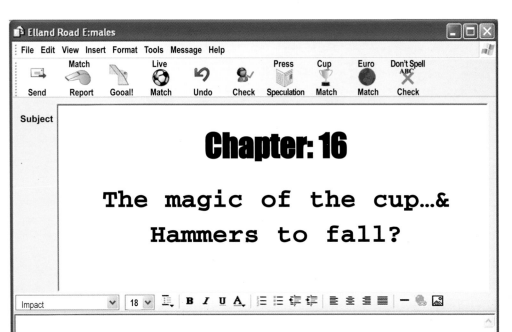

Chapter: 16

The magic of the cup...& Hammers to fall?

PREFACE:

So, despite the fears of all, Leeds gain a pretty comfortable win against a hapless West Ham - a team clearly in the spot-light that week as England play host to Australia at Upton Park. The fact that the Leeds team contributes almost 25% to the Aussies makes it a real them vs us - except for the fact that Robbo didn't get to take his rightful place in goal & Millsy didn't even get a look in. Don't even mention Woody or Smith. The plaudits were all Kewell & Viduka. Okon played well too and speculative Leeds target Stan Lazaridis had a stormer...

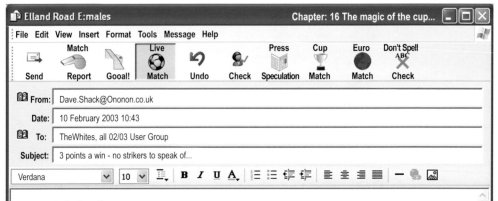

File   Edit   View   Insert   Format   Tools   Message   Help

Match   Live   Press   Cup   Euro   Don't Spell
                                                   ABC

Send   Report   Gooal!   Match   Undo   Check   Speculation   Match   Match   Check

From: Dave.Shack@Ononon.co.uk

Date: 10 February 2003 10:43

To: TheWhites, all 02/03 User Group

Subject: 3 points a win - no strikers to speak of...

Verdana   10   **B** *I* U A   ≡ ≡ 譚 譚   ≡ ≡ ≡ ≡   — ● 🖼

-----**Original Message**-----
From: Shack, Dave, Ononon.co.uk
Sent: 10 February 2003 10:43
To: TheWhites, all 02/03 User Group
Subject: 3 points a win - no strikers to speak of...

Well lads, WH was another bananna skin we managed to avoid (Gillingham being the other most recent one) and , most importantly, rested all our best players for the cup game! Let's pray that Kewell doesn't get kicked on Wednesday! So without a recognized striker we won at home - we kept a clean sheet (how could anyone other than Robbo be in goal for England?) and Senor Bravo got stuck in - well, at least I think he did, but The Premiership as usual didn't show us fuck all...

As for Johnson - I'm delighted for him to do well, because he is quality & I remember sitting with Ridsdale & the other directors for the last game against 'Boro last season & PR was absolutely purring about him & his potential. Maybe he'll be a bit of a shining light for us for the rest of the season. Bow seemed quite quiet & whilst the crowd were against him it wasn't unanimous - which is how it should be, I guess.

Palace lost so we could be going into Sunday in a great frame of mind. C'mon Leeds let's get into Europe via the FA Cup! Terry get all those eggs in that one basket...

-----Original Message-----
From: rob@the-unforgiven.com
Sent: 09 February 2003 23:35
To: TheWhites, all 02/03 User group
Subject: Re: 3 points a win - no strikers to speak of...

Did anyone go yesterday? I did and was pleasantly surprised after driving up with a vague sense of looming despondency. Torres doesn't look as though he can defend

Georgia   10   **B** *I* U A ≡ ≡ ≡ ≡ ≡ ≡ ≡ ≡ —

any better than Hartey but oozes quality. Wilcox and Kelly on the flanks were fantastic. We all know their limitations but Gaz, particularly, was in storming form. Having thought him finished six months ago, it's great to see a man who loves the club as much as he does back to running his arse off and playing so well. Jesus, even Dubes put in a competent performance making you think that PR's next boast will be "Of course Woodgate was only ever drafted in while Duberry was injured...." Anyway, it looked as though there was going to be a bit of aggro at the end on the West Stand concourse but after hanging around for half an hour, I buggered off as it was pretty clear that the Board weren't going to make an appearance until the crowd had frozen to death or sodded off. All in all, some signs for optimism given that Bakke and Milnerinho were the front two and Seth finally showed the rest of us what O'Leary must have seen in him. The only down side is the vantage I get from my seat this season (having missed the dealine for renewal in the West Stand Upper - I'm now right between the two dugouts) - was that Kidd and Venables were constantly urging the defenders to welly the ball into the corners and waste time from about the 70th minute onwards. Shades of Gerard Houffier...

-----Original Message-----
From: Andy@whitetoreply.co.uk
Sent: 09 February 2003 11:51
To: Dave.Shack@Ononon.co.uk
Subject: Re: 3 points a win - no strikers to speak of...

I thought that the standby team that played were full value for the money yesterday. West Ham didn't look particularly threatening apart from Joe Cole and when they had a corner. Duberry was in fine form and justified his place (albeit as we didn't have anyone else). Seth Johnson was totally up for it. Bakke was great up front and was knackered by the time he was stretchered off.
With all the injuries now, the public address asked for supporters to bring their kits for the next match in case we have to draft someone in.

-----Original Message-----
From: Firhad, Mohd, Eltelasia.ma
Sent: 11 February 2003 01:51
To: TheWhites, all 02/03 user group
Subject: 3 points a win - no strikers to speak of...

Gillingham: Yep banana skin alright. Shades of last FA Cup do come to mind when its all square. Again with a stand in striker in Bakke we seem to hold on fine. Most important to clear and re build from it all.

West Ham: Bow- its fine to see him playing again and we should remain "light" on him as it is him that wants out. This applies to Fowler and Woody in my opinion.Rio ???? A Scum is a scum.

Seth Johnson: In my earlier notes mentioned that he is potential Brooking.
Need more exposure and with experience he will be the force that he is
poised to be. He will the turing point for us. Imagine Milner - dinho on
the flanks. Okon holding the fort with Simthy upfront the future holds
good for us all. Trust the future.

FA Cup: A good run is possible. Palace is a better prospect than The
Kops. I hope its a sign for a great c'ship run.

El Tel you re the man. Steer us to Europe and a good final rum and you
will enhance your legacy. With adversities and scarce resources he can
kame us a winner.

-----Original Message-----
From: Russ@Vivaleedspana.spa
Sent: 11 February 2003 14:37
To: TheWhites, all 02/03 user group
Subject: Re: 3 points a win - no strikers to speak of...

It was great to see us claim two wins on the trot again, lets hope this is the
start of something!
Although i think someone up there does not want to see that, can you believe
our bad injury luck?
Now Mattio and Bakke just when they were both showing tremendous form.
And just wait till tomorrow with Kewell!
Could someone tell me if it really is a case of bring on the Eagles? or should i
not be getting that exicted yet? RTB

-----Original Message-----
From: Shack, Dave, Ononon.co.uk
Sent: 14 February 2003 18:35
To: TheWhites, all 02/03 user group
Subject: Aussie Rules! Best possible result really eh?

So - what did that prove? Rio's dodgy? Kewell is back to his very best?
Robbo should be #1? Even Okon has a role in midfield? Apart from pretyy
much vindicating all of the above, that was a nightmare. Poor old West
Ham fans - another defeat at home! Shocker. Great that Kewell, Okon,
Robbo & Millsy didn't get injured. Great that Popovitch (or whatever) did!
 I can't wait for Sunday I've got a good feeling about it. Look forward to
seeing quite a lot of you again for this cup run.

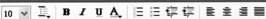
Verdana   10   B *I* U A

C'mon Leeds! The last 8!!

-----**Original Message**-----
From: Shack, Dave, Ononon.co.uk
Sent: 17 February 2003 10:07
To: TheWhites, all 02/03 user group
Subject: Lucky Leeds rob the Palace!

Another great Cup day out! From the concourse at Victoria it was a blast to see DH's Monkey, Tamsy, Jeremy, Nelly, Dorian & Moylesy. Andy you've got to make the next game! Rob were you there?

Well, at last our luck has changed - let's pray it lasts into the draw today (Watford away please!) and we can all dream of getting to Cardiff to play Arsenal knowing that even a defeat will put us into Europe. Talk about Houdini - that will make the final chapter of El Tel's new, updated biography! Forget saving 'Boro - getting Leeds into Europe would be the story of the year.

What about Scum? Ha Ha - great that Tamsy started his "Who put Rio on his arse? Harry, Harry Kewell" chant on Sunday and eveyone followed. Nice one.

Off to a meeting now so got to dash. Come on the draw! Fingers crossed.

PS Check out www.Ononon.co.uk for a few early chapters!

-----Original Message-----
From: Jeremy@Donsgloryears.co.uk
Sent: 17 February 2003 10:51
To: Dave.Shack@Ononon.co.uk
Subject: Re: Lucky Leeds rob the Palace!

Whoever complains about luck when it's going your way? But there was nothing lucky about Harry's wonder goal. The last time I got that
excited at Selhurst Pasrk was Yeboah's amazing strike against Wimbledon in 1995 when I celebrated so vigourously that I ended up 3 rows back from where I was sitting.
Leeds fans in fine voice/humour yesterday too. Good new chant for Harry (to the tune of "Daddy Cool" - I've been wanting us to adopt that since that car ad started using it); and the one about "putting Rio on his arse" - nice one, Tamsy if it was you that started it! Also when Neil Morrissey did his celebrity penalty shoot-our at half time, very amusing chant of "One Les Dennis, there's only one Les Dennis..."

-----Original Message-----
From: Nelly@thewhitellie-phant.co.uk
Sent: 17 February 2003 12:31
To: Dave.Shack@Ononon.co.uk
Subject: Re: Lucky Leeds rob the Palace!

Most fun I've had all season. Especially after seeing replays of the goal that wasn't. Tip to the palace: if you want your goals to count, hit the ball so hard it reaches the back of the net. then the referee will notice it. Kelly and kewell managed it from about five times further out.

-----Original Message-----
From: Russ@Vivaleedspana.spa
Sent: 17 February 2003 17:47
To: TheWhites, all 02/03 user group
Subject: Re: Lucky Leeds rob the Palace!

eh that looked and sounded fantastic, god i miss that.
anyway lets hope we can hang on this time at bramell lane and i will be on my way home for the semi's
mind you lets not get carried away!
wheres all the quality in our team gone?
we really do look like a team of reserves.
although we deserve what were getting in the cup run because of those players working their balls off and their desire to win is fantastic, but can we really go another round just on that?
we still failed to get in enough shots on goal for me, from anywhere or anyone.
still lets enjoy some lighter relief from the doldrums of recently.
Rio, Keano, Dacourt, Bow, Woody and Folwer, where are they now? well there not in the quarter final of the fa cup, so fuck em all !!

-----Original Message-----
From: Firhad, Mohd, Eltelasia
Sent: 18 February 2003 02:44
To: Shack, Dave, Ononon
Cc: Whites,all User Group 02/03
Subject: Lucky Leeds rob the Palace!

Team Of Destiny ?????????? Spurs used to claim that. Now itis us ???? !!!!
Why ? The luck of the draw syas it all. Arse vs Chelsea. We are on for a
"rematch" wid Sheffield Utd.
Luck is a luck. We had our fair share of bad ones earlier.Now we need to

Batang   10   **B** *I* U A

live up to that Team Of destiny tag.Scums!!!! Now you know. Fergie kick up
Becks.....in da eye. Bet Becks will be off soon. Italy / Spain's a bet.
Rio ha ha ha !!!!!!!!! Edu's thru' ball made us see his limitations plus
Kewell's masterful side step.
FA Cup On we go !!!!!!!!

-----Original Message-----
From: Chris@noredscum.co.uk
Sent: 18 February 2003 12:38
To: TheWhites, all 02/03 user group
Subject: Re: Lucky Leeds rob the Palace!

Well as I told you as soon as we knew that Dermott Gallagher
was the ref we were through. Its now 18 games unbeaten with
him as a ref.

My next song? "Dermot is a Leeds fan!!!"

-----Original Message-----
From: Russ@Vivaleedspana.spa
Sent: 18 February 2003 13:57
To: TheWhites, all 02/03 user group
Subject: Re: Lucky Leeds rob the Palace!

Impressive facts, any chance of signing him up for the Sheffield quarters, semis
and final!

-----Original Message-----
From: Davidharveysmonkey@aol.com
Sent: 19 February 2003 12:19
To: Dave.Shack@Ononon.co.uk
Subject: Re: Lucky Leeds rob the Palace!

Phrases you never hear at a Leeds game:

"And Leeds have just shut up shop now"

"That's put it beyond Palace's reach"

"That goals allows Terry the opportunity to rest the big guns for the
Champions :League."

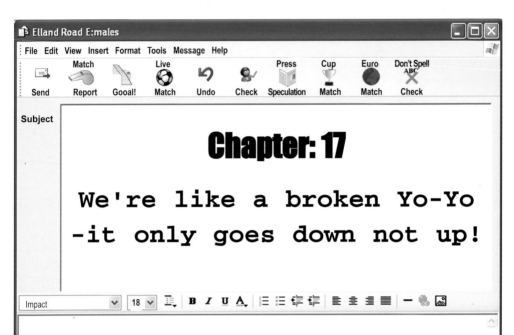

Chapter: 17

We're like a broken Yo-Yo -it only goes down not up!

Impact   18

PREFACE:

Star defender Woody has gone to Newcastle United. Leeds have endured & lost a 'boardroom' battle with them all season - over Kleberson, over Kieron Dyer (last season) & now over Woody. They have flashed loadsamoney & become everyone's favourite 2nd team - an accolade that under O' Leary's fledgling reign was ours. The two clubs couldn't look any more chalk & cheese this week. All that was left was for us to play them at home. Guess what? A 3-0 Defeat.

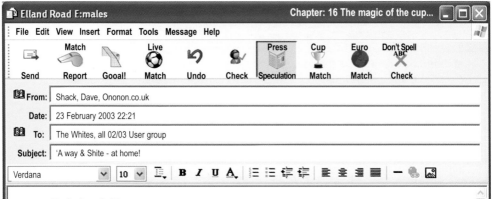

File   Edit   View   Insert   Format   Tools   Message   Help

| Match | Live | | | Press | Cup | Euro | Don't Spell |
| Send | Report | Gooal! | Match | Undo | Check | Speculation | Match | Match | Check |

From: Shack, Dave, Ononon.co.uk

Date: 23 February 2003 22:21

To: The Whites, all 02/03 User group

Subject: 'A way & Shite - at home!

Verdana   10

-----Original Message-----
From: Shack, Dave, Ononon.co.uk
Sent: 23 February 2003 22:21
To: TheWhites, all 02/03 User group
Subject: 'A way & Shite - at home!

Singing: Oh Woody, woody!
               Gone to N'castle & left fuck all!
               Repeat to fade...

(c) Dave Shack, Elland Road e:males, Feb 2003... but probably heard on the terrace on Saturday.

-----Original Message-----
From: Firhad, Mohd, Eltelasia
Sent: 24 February 2003 10:00
To: Shack, Dave, Ononon.co.uk
Subject: 'A way & Shite - at home!

What was it all about. 3-0.........Risdale !!!! Risdale !!!! Whats the score ????? The stand was singing. Gosh !!! When would the nightmare be over???!!!

-----Original Message-----
From: Chris@Captdom.co.uk
Sent: 26 February 2003 12:51
To: TheWhites, all 02/03 user group
Subject: RE: 'A way & Shite - at home!

So it was my birthday on Saturday (thanks for all the cards) and a trip to ER was one of my presents.

179

Arial   10   B *I* U A

I ended up watching the game up in the gantry with Braders from Radio Aire, doing the commentary next to us - very surreal, and Mr. Matteo. Great view. It was like the biggest widescreen tv ever.

90 minutes later and my thoughts. Just a better view to witness Leeds get stuffed by the bar codes ... happy birthday!!!

One thing did make me smile. I got an e-mail from a listner who said he saw Dyer getting in his car after the game. He shouted over to him 'Why can't you play like that for England you twat'. Dyer closed the window and left!!
   Got a little look in the dressing rooms just at that start of the second half, only to see wilCOX coming out of the shower. Now that was a birthday surprise I wasn't expecting...not!

```
-----Original Message-----
From: Chris@Noredscum.co.uk
Sent: 26 February 2003 13:00
To: TheWhites, all 02/03 user group
Subject: Re: 'A way & Shite - at home!

I've lost count of the times Newcastle have beaten us now
- admittedly I've not seen us play that badly in a long
long time.

It's nice to see that Ridsdale has accepted the inevitable
and is going to apply for the Inter To-To cup. Now all we
need to do is finish 12th or above in the League - based
on Saturday's performance I'm not going to dust off my
passport just yet.
```

-----Original Message-----
From: Russ@Vivaleedspana.spa
Sent: 27 February 2003 09:24
To: TheWhites, all 02/03 user group
Subject: Re: 'A way & Shite - at home!

If we can win the next two cup matches, we won't have to worry about the intoe toe-to crapy cup!
Mind you it may get us back on, a european tour european tour european tour wer'e all going on a lalalalalalalalal

Verdana   10   **B** *I* U A

-----Original Message-----
From: Shack, Dave, Ononon.co.uk
Sent: 05 March 2003 09:37
To: TheWhites, all 02/03 user group
Subject: It's tought now innit? United against the 'uniteds';
white/yellow & blue versus red/white & black - twice.

Well lads, I can't say I blame us all for going a bit quiet. It's tough
being a Leeds fan right now - especially after seeing Woody play at
the weekend. Hey! At leat Man U were done at Cardiff & Jimmy scored
a great own goal - & Spurs lost. Hey in fact it was a great weekend
last weekend - and we didn't lose! (natch).

So, Tonight. Kewell out (that'll save him getting injured their by some
sneaky off the ball incident, as usual) and Batty has been training
with the first team squad! Dom might be back miraculously - but let's
say a random drug test might be a bit of a problem for him after all
his treatments!!

Truth be told I really don't give a shit about tonight (well, I do) but I
just want a full (in Leeds terms) squad fit to face Sheff on Sunday. We
all know what the European 'tour' means to the club & the fans so to
get in the back door (ie coming second to Arsenal in the final will do)
would surely keep a few players at Leeds & help us buy a couple
more.

So - utilitarianism (never thought that word would be in the book!) -
which means (Tamsy & Jeremy know!) the greatest good for the
greatest number. Yep, sod the league & the indignity of coming in
12th or something this season - let's get to an FA CUP Final & play
without fear of defeat. (Unless we play Southampton!) - but whatever
that would be a great story & Venables would complete his
rehabilitation (& some) with the fans.

That would be nice & we can start to build again next year & watch a
couple of other clubs have a problem or too...
One final push - to finish the book & get us in the final. It's not much
to ask is it?

On, on, ON!

Shacky

PS. Tamsy's got my ticket for Sheff Utd - I'm in Amsterdam with Will Young at the bloody Pop Idol Dutch final...

-----Original Message-----
From: Jeremy@Donsgloryears.co.uk
Sent: 05 March 2003 10:32
To: Dave.Shack@Ononon.co.uk; TheWhites, all 02/03 user group
Subject: Re: It's tought now innit? United against the 'uniteds'; white/yellow& blue versus red/white & black - twice.

The best I can hope for tonight is not losing too heavily - I'd actually settle for a by-no-more-than-two-goals defeat. Now that says something about how low my expectations have sunk to this season.

I agree with you Shacky, it's more important not to risk players tonight if they might not be fit for Sunday. So please rest Dom and the Chief and (I thought I'd never hear myself say this) play Dubes the Clown!

Having said that, the league table makes pretty depressing reading at present - I doubt if it'll look any better tomorrow morning.

-----Original Message-----
From: Wathen, Dorian, The Peacocks
Sent: 05 March 2003 11:57
To: TheWhites, all 02/03 user group
Subject: RE: It's tought now innit? United against the 'uniteds'; white/yellow & blue versus red/white & black - twice.

can't quite believe you're giving up your ticket for the weekend - am impressed (or dumbfounded) ... all signs point to us getting hammered this evening with the injuries and suspensions - have a funny feeling we could get a point though and put Man U out of title race.

-----Original Message-----
From: Chris@Noredscum.co.uk
Sent: 05 March 2003 12:22
To: Dave.Shack@Ononon.co.uk
Subject: Re: It's tought now innit? United against the

Courier New ∨ | 10 ∨ | B *I* U A, | ≡ ≡ 譚 譚 | ≣ ≣ ≣ ≣ | — 🍥 🖼

'uniteds'; white/yellow & blue versus red/white & black -
twice.

I know what you mean - I have never approached a Leeds vs.
Scum game with so much apathy. I actually think we will do
OK tonight - we wont win but I don't think we are going to
get battered 5 or 6 nil either.

I too would sacrifice 3 points from tonight for a full
team on Sunday - we have not had a better chance of
securing an FA Cup final place in years - if we get
through Sunday then we only have to raise our game once
more in the semis to ensure a nice day out in Cardiff.

Well I have a night out in Sheffield on Saturday which
should be fun - thanks very much for the ticket mate (I
got it in the post from Nelly today), our ticket office
are the pits.

Enjoy Amsterdam at the weekend and I'll text you the
scores.

On on on Tamsy

-----Original Message-----
From: Shack, Dave, Ononon.co.uk
Sent: 05 March 2003 22:00
To: TheWhites, all 02/03 user group
Subject: LUFC Reserves vs Scum First XI

Game just finished. 1-2. Unlucky. Not bad for the 'b' team. Was sure
it was on Sky...Well done Dukes, Hartey & Smiffy. Wanker Beckham.
Bring on Sunday...

Cheers Shacky

-----Original Message-----
From: Chris@Noredscum.co.uk
Sent: 06 March 2003 10:25
To: TheWhites, all 02/03 user group
Subject: Re: LUFC Reserves vs Scum First XI

Courier New   10   **B** *I* U A

It was funny watching the replays of the Viduka "hand ball" incident - either biology's changed since I was at school or he hit the ball with his shoulder.

However what was Mark thinking? A penalty at Old Trafford - surely not sir! They only give those away once in a blue moon, I think the next one is due in 2037.

Anyway on reflection 2 - 2 on aggregate and we win on away goals!!!
See you all (except Dave - I'd rather be mincing with Will in Amsterdam - Shack) on Sunday

On on on

Chris

-----Original Message-----
From: Jeremy@Donsgloryears.co.uk
Sent: 06 March 2003 10:41
To: TheWhites, all 02/03 user group
Subject: Re: LUFC Reserves vs Scum First XI

Closer than I thought it would be considering that a) we're not very good when all the players left at the club are available, and b) we're even worse when half of them are out injured or suspended. If we've slipped in standards dramatically this season, then so have M** U** who would have murdered the side we put out last night a couple of years ago.

And what a cop out by Graham "Asshole" Poll. To get out of giving a dead cert penalty for that foul on Dukes he contrives to give a totally spurious handball against him. Probably the worst referee in England (but accredited with being our top international referee - who decides these things?)

-----Original Message-----
From: Andy@Whitetoreply.co.uk
Sent: 06 March 2003 12:33
To: Dave.Shack@Ononon.co.uk
Subject: Re: LUFC Reserves vs Scum First XI

Tahoma   10   B *I* U A

If we don't beat the blades, game over for the season. All we will have to look forward to is next season, no new players, a squad depleted by injuries from pre season friendlies because we have foregone the Inter Toto, and possibly a new manager with a new way of playing that gets us off to another slow start. Hey, but look on the brightside - at least season ticket prices will drop!!!

Andy

-----Original Message-----
From: Shack, Dave, Ononon.co.uk
Sent: 06 March 2003 12:40
To: TheWhites, all 02/03 user group
Subject: LUFC Reserves vs Scum First XI

has this season taught you nowt lad? Season tickets are not going down or even staying frozen....

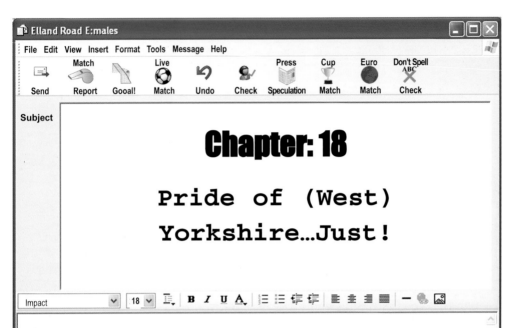

Chapter: 18

Pride of (West) Yorkshire...Just!

PREFACE:

The FA Cup defeat effectively finished our season. The team didn't perform (again) and our last chance of anything like glory (or Europe) went out the window. To add insult to injury, the spectre of relegation is entering stage...left.

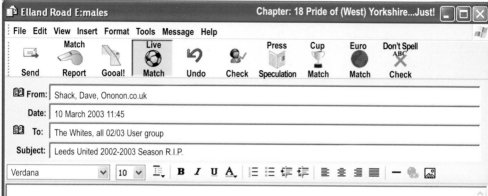

File   Edit   View   Insert   Format   Tools   Message   Help

| Send | Report | Gooal! | Match | Undo | Check | Speculation | Match | Match | Check |

From: Shack, Dave, Ononon.co.uk

Date: 10 March 2003 11:45

To: The Whites, all 02/03 User group

Subject: Leeds United 2002-2003 Season R.I.P.

Verdana   10   B   I   U   A

-----Original Message-----
From: Shack, Dave, Ononon.co.uk
Sent: 10 March 2003 11:45
To: TheWhites, all 02/03 User group
Subject: Leeds United 2002-2003 Season R.I.P

Sat embarrassed in a bar in Amsterdam in a shirt & scarf. Everyone else in that place fucking cheered for Sheffield. How embarrassing was that 2nd half - did Viduka touch it once? Total fucking shite out there. See ya players, see ya dreams for the next couple of seasons, see ya crowds, see ya Ridsdale. - see the only thing to cheer about will be avoiding relegation in a months time.

The players let themselves, Venables & ourselves down yesterday. It was fucking awful & I don't even want to discuss it. You watch   - it'll be Watford vs Sheff Utd semi today. Bollocks.

P.S. Don't expect a happy ending to this book. There isn't one.

-----Original Message-----
From: Russ@VivaLeedspana.spa
Sent: 10 March 2003 11:53
To: TheWhites, all 02/03 User group
Subject: Re: Leeds United 2002-2003 Season R.I.P

WHAT MAKES YOU THINK THAT PILE OF SHITE WILL AVOID RELEGATION?

-----Original Message-----
From: Wathen, Dorian, The Peacocks
Sent: 10 March 2003 12:06
To: TheWhites, all 02/03 User group
Subject: RE: Leeds United 2002-2003 Season R.I.P

I find it incredible that a team of international players - and they all play or have played for their country - are unable to pass the ball to feet - how many times did we lose possession when in acres of space to a sloppy misguided pass or a hoof upfield - it was all ugly and embarrassing stuff.

Comedy moment - when Teddy tried to hoof the ball upfield, hopelessy miscued the ball and sliced it, only for Chief to do the same trick immediately afterwards - desperate stuff.

-----Original Message-----
From: Nelly@thewhitellie-phant.co.uk
Sent: 10 March 2003 12:46
To: Dave.Shack@Ononon.co.uk
Subject: Re: Leeds United 2002-2003 Season R.I.P

The gallow's humour is back. (Chants of "Wilkinson out!", Tony Yeboah and Arthur Graham - I kid you not.) But we aren't laughing. We're dying. We're a first division club now.

-----Original Message-----
From: Shack, Dave, On on on
Sent: 10 March 2003 12:39
To: 'Nelly the Ellie'
Subject: RE: Leeds United 2002-2003 Season R.I.P

yeah Nelly. You're right. Great Pretenders.

-----Original Message-----
From: Chris@Captdom.co.uk
Sent: 10 March 2003 13:05
To: Dave.Shack@Ononon.co.uk
Subject: RE: Leeds United 2002-2003 Season R.I.P

A friend of mine asked me if I wanted a seat for the Sheffield United v Leeds game, but I told him I picked one up off the pitch last time we were there!

I must admit, I was very excited about the game. And after watching the Arsenal V Chelsea match, I was even more so.

Got up at 9AM just cos didn't want to miss any of it.

WHAT A FUCKING PILE OF SHITE

I was so embarrassed. Players that I love, dying on their arse, and worse, not even trying that hard.

Tahoma   10   **B** *I* <u>U</u> A

-----**Original Message**-----
From: Andy@Whitetoreply.co.uk
Sent: 10 March 2003 13:40
To: Dave.Shack@Ononon.co.uk
Subject: Re: Leeds United 2002-2003 Season R.I.P

What a load of shite. I really can't believe they have done us twice. Where is the passion? Where is the skill? Why are they paid so much to underperform. The whole thing is so diabolical, I'm thinking of going back to being an armchair supporter.

How Ridsdale could ever say we have had a glory ride and now we must pay for it is disgraceful. Selling your "best" players is not the answer. Where did it all go wrong?

Had a look at the website and the entries. Can't wait for the final book. You could publish it through Mills & Boon as a weepy love story - a man and his club - the journey through good and bad times.

-----Original Message-----
From: Chris@Noredscum.co.uk
Sent: 10 March 2003 13:58
To: TheWhites, all 02/03 User group
Subject: Re: Leeds United 2002-2003 Season R.I.P

Cost of train fare to Sheffield - £29 Hotel - £40 Ticket to game - £20 Programme - £4
Watching the worst game of football you've ever seen in your life - Priceless

-----Original Message-----
From: Russ@VivaLeedspana.spa
Sent: 10 March 2003 14:06
To: TheWhites, all 02/03 User group
Subject: Re: Leeds United 2002-2003 Season R.I.P

God to i feel sorry for everone of you that did the same as chris or even the day trip, at least i have an excuse not to have had to make that journey!

-----Original Message-----
From: Jeremy @ Donsgloryears.co.uk
Sent: 10 March 2003 14:10
To: TheWhites, all 02/03 User group
Subject: Re: Leeds United 2002-2003 Season R.I.P

Oh what a mess we are in. Yesterday's performance and result were not really that surprising. If you want to know the reasons just look back at the e-mails we were all sending each other in October and November.

For my part, I do still find it hard to believe that Venables could have sent out a team as unmotivated and passionless for any game, let alone an F.A.Cup quarter final and Yorkshire derby.

No, Shacky you're wrong. The players didn't let Venables down - he has let the club down. He has to go - the only question is whether it should be now or at the end of the season.

-----Original Message-----
From: Rob@The-unforgiven.com
Sent: 10 March 2003 18:03
To: TheWhites, all 02/03 User group
Subject: Re: Leeds United 2002-2003 Season R.I.P

Too true, Jeremy. The Emperor has no clothes and stark bollock naked, he had his arse whipped yesterday. "Major reassessment at the end of the season", he demands today. He's got a nerve. From a midfield of Bow, Ollie, Batts and H last year to Smith, Okon, Johnson and Bravo this, it makes you want to cry + the bleating on Sunday morning - "it's gonna be tough, we're missing Kelly, Wilcox & Duberry." They wouldn't get a game for 90% of other Prem clubs.

Let's face facts. It's over. We're fucked.

-----Original Message-----
From: Shack, Dave, On on on
Sent: 13 March 2003 13:21
To: TheWhites, all 02/03 User group
Subject: Sulking

Just so you know - I turned down a free box at Elland Road this Saturday. I'm not going to waste the afternoon. I have, for the first time in about 5 years refused to look at the LUFC web site this week since the match because I just cannot bear to read any of the bollocks they print on there when we've lost.

So that's my protest. Silent as it may be - but it's a protest & it makes me feel bloody righteous. Yeah.

PS Shame McCarthy has gone to Sunderland - I left him a message last night saying if he'd waited until June he could have had the Leeds job...

Tahoma   10   **B** *I* U A̲

-----Original Message-----
From: Andy@Whitetoreply.co.uk
Sent: 13 March 2003 15:45
To: Dave.Shack@Ononon.co.uk
Subject: Re: Sulking

I guess we're all in the same boat. I feel totally deflated and unenthusiastic. I've heard that Leeds have put a team into the National Watch Paint Dry competition...and they lost.

-----Original Message-----
From: Russ@VivaLeedspana.spa
Sent: 18 March 2003 13:50
To: TheWhites, all 02/03 User group
Subject: Re: Sulking

Bring back D.O. At least he had motivation and we had a lot of spirit and commitment then. He will not have any money this time and will have to use the full squad which in hindsite he probably wishes he did before. Haveing seen the run in, i can't see how we will avoid the drop. The hammers and bolton are on the ascendency picking up points now and we are doing the opposite!!!

-----Original Message-----
From: Russ@VivaLeedspana.spa
Sent: 18 March 2003 14:28
To: TheWhites, all 02/03 User group
Subject: Re: Sulking

Hola lads - another bit! This is a quote from the first supporters v P.R. and i would like to know if P.R. thinks he did not give D.O. ENOUGH!!!!!!
"What we have to do is to make sure the manager has the resources, both in the existing playing squad and in the players that he wishes to recruit to be able to challenge the teams at the top of the Premiership".
Sounds like dejavoo to me Peter (even if i can`t spell it)

-----Original Message-----
From: Shack, Dave, On on on
Sent: 19 March 2003 12:16
To: TheWhites, all 02/03 User group
Subject: Lucky Pub - any port in a storm - whatever...

Verdana   10   **B** *I* U A

Lads, How about trying to get together to watch us get done by Liverpool on Sunday? I'm heading up to that Beacon of hope - The Haverstock Arms. Come & join me & who knows what might happen...

-----Original Message-----
From: Wathen, Dorian, The Peacocks
Sent: 19 March 2003 12:21
To: Shack, Dave, On on on
Subject: RE: Lucky Pub - any port in a storm - whatever...

maybe - am really struggling to get excited though. hopefully H will be back for some inspiration.

-----Original Message-----
From: Shack, Dave, On on on
Sent: 19 March 2003 04:22
To: Wathen, Dorian, The Peacocks
Subject: RE: Lucky Pub - any port in a storm - whatever...

c'mon! The lights, the crowd...the smell of the greasepaint. Oops sorry wrong thing...

-----Original Message-----
From: Wathen, Dorian, The Peacocks
Sent: 19 March 2003 12:28
To: Shack, Dave, On on on
Subject: RE: Lucky Pub - any port in a storm - whatever...

yes indeed ... at least Kelly and Dubes are back from injury - look what it's come to - we're grateful that they're back - 6 months ago we couldn't wait to get rid of them...

-----Original Message-----
From: Nelly@thewhitellie-phant.co.uk
Sent: 20 March 2003 11:37
To: Dave.Shack@Ononon.co.uk
Subject: Re: Lucky Pub - any port in a storm - whatever...

Is there a match on? I couldn't care less.

Did you want those two Charlton tickets?

192

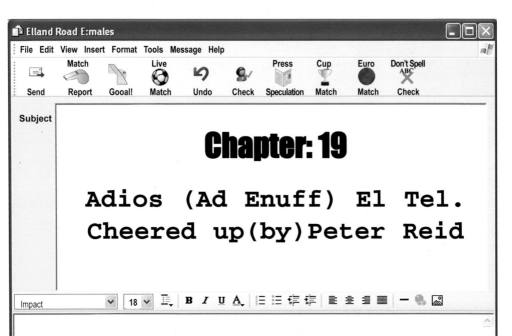

Elland Road E:males

File   Edit   View   Insert   Format   Tools   Message   Help

Match   Live   Press   Cup   Euro   Don't Spell
                                                                                                    ABC
Send   Report   Gooal!   Match   Undo   Check   Speculation   Match   Match   Check

Subject

Chapter: 19

Adios (Ad Enuff) El Tel. Cheered up(by)Peter Reid

Impact   18   B *I* U A

PREFACE:

It had to happen. El Tel didn't last the season & we all pretty much breathed a sigh of relief. Inconsistency was his legacy as was a stubborn streak that alienated not just the likes of Batty & Dacourt - but with it 1000's of fans who looked at a midfield that was about as powerful as an energy drink without its lid on... As usual, cue speculation...

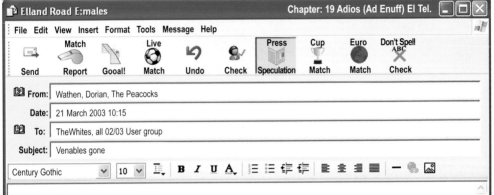

-----Original Message-----
From: Wathen, Dorian, The Peacocks
Sent: 21 March 2003 10:15
To: TheWhites, all 02/03 User group
Subject: Venables Gone ...

where's the e-mail or are you still in shock or maybe just partying...

-----Original Message-----
From: Shack, Dave, Ononon.co.uk
Sent: 21 March 2003 10:28
To: TheWhites, all 02/03 User group
Subject: Venables out - Batty in?

Well, I suppose it's well done Peter this time. No point in waiting until the summer. get the kids in , get batty back & win a couple of games.
Forget Europe next season & have a cosolidation period. Offload the big wage earners & promote the youth. Eddie must know the kids who can...& who can't.
Less than a year in the job - more than Wilko up the road, more than Jock or Cloughie.
Please let someone see this book for the invaluable document of the season annus horriblus in our history.

Court case - can't even remember it now...Shacky

PS Hartey & Laura had a baby girl. Top man!

-----Original Message-----
From: Chris@NoRedscum.com
Sent: 21 March 2003 10:36
To: TheWhites, all 02/03 User group
Subject: Re: Venables out - Batty in?

Courier New   10   B *I* U A

This is the best news we've had in years. Is that useless twat
Kidd going as well?

I presume Eddie is the caretaker until the end of the season?
If so I hope he's on the phone to Olly this morning getting
him back in time for Sunday, and is telling Batty that he has
an opportunity to show El Tel how wrong he was.

Lets hope Notts Forest don't get promoted then we can have
Paul Hart, because lets face it we are hardly an attractive
prospect for any big incoming manager.

-----Original Message-----
From: Russ@Vivaleedspana.spa
Sent: 21 March 2003 12:01
To: TheWhites, all 02/03 User group
Subject: Re: Venables out - Batty in?

Congrats to hartey. Adios El Tel.

-----Original Message-----
From: Wathen, Dorian, The Peacocks
Sent: 21 March 2003 10:57
To: TheWhites, all 02/03 User group
Subject: RE: Venables out - Batty in?

It's a sigh of relief all round ...only downside is that H has gone on record as
saying if he goes ...
Choices ? I'd have to say Strachan and/or cheap and cheerful McAllister -
we can even draft them into central midfield - sign Speed and we can have
our old midfield back with Batts - I saw that Sheridan scored a great free kick
in that charity friendly recently as well - think I'm losing the plot now..

-----Original Message-----
From: Nelly@thewhitellie-phant.co.uk
To: Dave.Shack@Ononon.co.uk
TheWhites, all 02/03 User group
Subject: Re: Venables out - Batty in?

Dave.Shack@Ononon.co.uk writes:
Well, I suppose it's well done Peter.

well done nothing - it's rotten timing like it's rotten chairmanship. Made 17

Century Gothic ▾ |10 ▾| ☰▾ **B** *I* U A̲▾ | ☰ ☰ ☰ ☰ | ☰ ☰ ☰ ☰ | — ◉ 🖼

more office staff redundant this month. More good people gone. Forget Batty - he's history, Check out the reserves this week. If Aitken didn't pick him, I doubt if Gray will.

Forget Europe next season surely you mean next PRE-season?

Please let someone see this book for the invaluable document of the season annus horriblus in our history.

another one (season I mean!)

-----Original Message-----
From: Andy@Whitetoreply.co.uk
Sent: 22 March 2003 13:45
To: TheWhites, all 02/03 User group
Subject: Re: Venables out - Batty in?

You couldn't have picked a better year to do this book could you!?

Just what is the story at Leeds. How much in debt are we still and how did we get there after the huge offloads and the millions we got from sponsership and European games? What is going on?

At least we're rid of Venebles but Ridsdale has a lot to answer for and should do the decent thing. Him and the consortium are responsible for the utter turmoil and they should stand up and be judged.

I am ashamed to be associated with this whole fiasco.

Revolution here I come!

-----Original Message-----
From: Wathen, Dorian, The Peacocks
Sent: 21 March 2003 11:33
To: Shack, Dave, On on on
Subject: RE: Venables out - Batty in?

Peter fucking Reid !!!!!!!!!!!!!!!!!!!

-----Original Message-----
From: Shack, Dave, On on on
Sent: 21 March 2003 13:00
To: TheWhites, all 02/03 User group
Subject: Cheer up ...it's Peter Reid!

Verdana | 10 |

Does anyone really know what to make of this - how do you react to him? I think he has some great attributes - honest (won't get far at Leeds), workhorse, still a get stuck in guy, but what's he ever done - and do we have a right to expect some who has done anything?

Leeds - god we love it don't we? It's a fuckin' soap opera (Ellandale Farm?) without the weddings every month.

-----Original Message-----
From: Russ@Vivaleedspana.spa
Sent: 21 March 2003 13:06
To: TheWhites, all 02/03 User group
Subject: Re: Cheer up ...it's Peter Reid!

i don't see the point in the move until summer! or is he that good at motivation that pr thinks he can get us out of trouble?

-----Original Message-----
From: Chris@Noredscum.com
Sent: 21 March 2003 13:14
To: TheWhites, all 02/03 User group
Subject: Re: Cheer up ...it's Peter Reid!

Shacky - are you sure that you didn't bung Ridsdale a few thousand at the start of this season to make things a bit exciting for the duration of your book?

Peter F**king Reid - jesus even I'm a better manager than he is. Why not just let Eddie finish the season and then appoint someone in the summer.

If Leeds Utd were a soap opera - I'd suggest that serial killer from Coronation street popped over the pennines for a while

Cue Sunday and 40,000 Scousers "Cheer up Peter Reid etc etc"

-----Original Message-----
From: Nelly@thewhitellie-phant.co.uk
Sent: 21 March 2003 13:29
To: Dave.Shack@Ononon.co.uk
Subject: Re: Cheer up ...it's Peter Reid!

Verdana   10   B *I* U A

Dave.Shack@Ononon.co.uk writes:
>but what's he ever done?

he's got Sunderland relegated a couple of times! But how many more times will LUFC shit on Eddie Gray?????

-----Original Message-----
From: Chris@Captdom.co.uk
Sent: 21 March 2003 13:37
To: TheWhites, all 02/03 User group
Subject: RE: Cheer up ...it's Peter Reid!

Lessons in Football #125

So remind me, as I'm still learning about the beautiful game;
O'Leary went.
Leeds brought in a football pundit.
He's gone
Leeds bring in ANOTHER football pundit.

Shouldn't we just go straight for the kill and give the job to Des Lynam!!

-----Original Message-----
From: Andy@Whitetoreply.co.uk
Sent: 22 March 2003 13:48
To: TheWhites, all 02/03 User group
Subject: Re: Cheer up ...it's Peter Reid!

At least I like the guy, scouser or not. However not sure whether he will do the job.

Is it time Leeds properly set out it's stall and honestly said where it is, what it wants to do, and how it sees achievement of this. Do we have to suffer the crap of politics and lies!

Just saw Peter on Football Focus and he is struggling with what day it is. However, I would like to see him achieve his first goal and put one over the Liverpool. Revenge would be sweet.

-----Original Message-----
From: Firhad@Fareastreid.ma
Sent: 01 April 2003 12:45
To: TheWhites, all 02/03 User group
Subject: Re: Cheer up ...it's Peter Reid!

Batang   10   B   *I*   U   A

Well bye, bye El Tel. Sure is sad but its the best way for us to move
forward. Reid ???? Right attributes but results ???? Do we have a choice
???

I got my new address again today - am hopeing that it lasts longer than
Eltelasia!!

-----Original Message-----
From: Jeremy@Donsgloryears.co.uk
Sent: 24 March 2003 12:12
To: TheWhites, all 02/03 User group
Subject: Re: Cheer up ...it's Peter Reid!

Oh the joys of following LUFC from abroad.
Here in S.Africa watching the cricket World Cup Final (what a pleasure to see some world-
class sporting action after the torture of watching Leeds this season).

Even with the benefit of being several thousand miles away from home,
it does seem as if our club had gone completely fucking mad. I got the call on Friday with the
good news (Venables out) only to be followed by the bad (Reid in). As you all have said -
why? A caretaker manager should be someone from within (Eddie Gray) and then take stock
in the summer when the most suitable/available/affordable candidates can be assessed.

We have become a complete laughing stock of a football club.

-----Original Message-----
From: Shack, Dave, On on on
Sent: 24 March 2003 12:22
To: TheWhites, all 02/03 User group
Subject: Well at least Reidy can deliver a half-time team talk!

First 20 minutes I thought we were gonna lose 5-0, end of first half we
had a stab at it & well battled Viduka for that goal. Then the start of the
second half we looked like a different team - the midfield worked (Barmby
was pointless)& they got worried. Only that goal killed us. Why o why
doesn't Milner start? He's hardly gonna get tired out with 7 games to go -
blood him now!

On hols now for a couple of weeks - Tamsy boy - don't let me down
again.

Shacky (Caribbean bound...) C U in two weeks!

Arial 10 **B** *I* U A

-----Original Message-----
From: Chris@Captdom.co.uk
Sent: 24 March 2003 12:30
To: TheWhites, all 02/03 User group
Subject: RE: Cheer up ...it's Peter Reid!

It was my girlfriend's birthday on Sunday.
She had arranged lunch with the family for 3.00 o'clock
Meeting at 2 in a pub with no television ....
THANK FUCK FOR THAT. I NEVER SAW A THING
Thanks to Shack for the updates. 3 too many really

-----Original Message-----
From: Davidharveysmonkey@aol.com
Sent: 24 March 2003 22:36
To: Chris Moyles
Bcc: Dave.Shack@Ononon.co.uk
Subject: Re: Cheer up ...it's Peter Reid!

Re: Sunday - Unbelievable, you having a girlfriend and all that.

-----Original Message-----
From: Chris@Captdom.co.uk
Sent: 25 March 2003 12:53
To: Davidharveysmonkey.co.uk
Subject: RE: Cheer up ...it's Peter Reid!

Yeah, she's your mother : o)

-----Original Message-----
From: Chris@NoRedscum.com
Sent: 24 March 2003 12:52
To: TheWhites, all 02/03 User group
Subject: Re: Well at least Reidy can deliver...

Well I think we were always going to lose that game - we were
generally awful at defending on the left hand side in the
first half - Bravo should be sent back to Spain asap - I'll
personally stump up the £80 to send him home on Gippo jet.
How good was it to see Batty on the bench? Its a shame that
he didn't play but I'd rather have him play in our crunch
relegation battles to come where he could make a difference.
Lets hope Peter Reid bucks a few of the players ideas up

200

because if we play like that for the rest of the season we
will go down - end of story.
Lets hope the time off for internationals gives everyone a
chance to re-group for the next match against Charlton. Chris

PS - Shacky some 100% proof rum would be great mate!!!

-----Original Message-----
From: Russ@Vivaleedspana.co.uk
Sent: 24 March 2003 13:04
To: Dave.Shack@Ononon.co.uk; TheWhites, all 02/03 User group
Subject: Re: Well at least Reidy can deliver a half-time team talk!

i can`t comment on the game. Off to get bollocksed on cheap spanish beer.
Laters

-----Original Message-----
From: Wathen, Dorian, The Peacocks
Sent: 24 March 2003 13:09
To: TheWhites, all 02/03 User group
Subject: RE: Well at least Reidy can deliver a half-time team talk!

Am sure Bravo wishes he was back in Madrid as well - can't really load the
blame all on him (however tempting) - he was hardly given any defensive
help by Wilcox (he did play didn't he ?) and Caveman...
You're right Mills is playing as he was a few years ago and lumping the ball
down the touchline again - the amount of times he's giving the ball away is a
liability. The ball was a hot potato for us yesterday, no-one wanted it and if
they did it was soon got rid of, usually backwards and to Robbo.

-----Original Message-----
From: Andy@Whitetoreply.co.uk
Sent: 24 March 2003 17:39
To: Dave.Shack@Ononon.co.uk; Chris@Noredscum.co.uk
Subject: Re: Well at least Reidy can deliver a half-time team talk!

It's all Doom and Gloom. I'd rather watch the Gulf War. At least we have a team out
there worth supporting.

Have a Rum Punch for me you lucky devil.

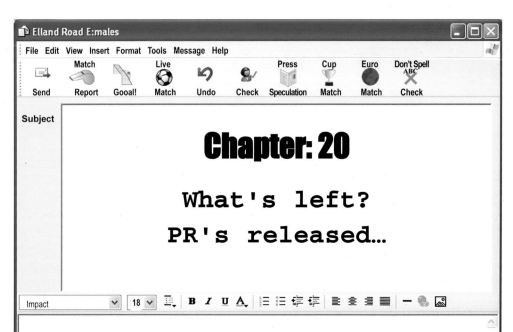

Chapter: 20

What's left?
PR's released...

PREFACE:

It's not just players & the manager that are on their way - it's now the Chairman, Peter Ridsdale. His last throes changed nothing with the fans & he was gone. Talk about a clearout - Elland Road's security guards must have escorted more people out of the building than the stewards do in the South Stand on match day! But was it getting better on the pitch? For a moment...

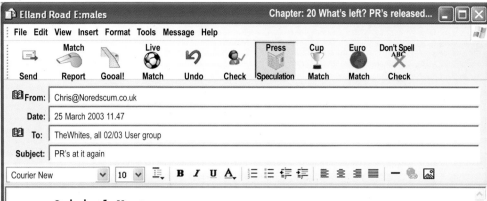

File   Edit   View   Insert   Format   Tools   Message   Help

| Send | Match Report | Live Gooal! | Match | Undo | Check | Press Speculation | Cup Match | Euro Match | Don't Spell Check |

From: Chris@Noredscum.co.uk

Date: 25 March 2003 11.47

To: TheWhites, all 02/03 User group

Subject: PR's at it again

Courier New   10   **B** *I* U A

-----Original Message-----
From: Chris@Noredscum.co.uk
Sent: 25 March 2003 11:47
To: TheWhites, all 02/03 User group
Subject: PR's at it again

Apparently Peter Ridsdale has been quoted as saying that Alan
Smith is not for sale.
Translated into English - "we've had an approach for Smithy
and we are currently trying to whip up interest in the press
to make sure he goes to one of our biggest rivals for a
fraction of his true value".
So my guess is £6 million to Liverpool.
Anyone else to like to hazard a guess? - bag of sweets or
Jacob Burns to the winner.

-----Original Message-----
From: Russ@Vivaleedspana.spa
Sent: 25 March 2003 11:58
To: TheWhites, all 02/03 User group
Subject: Re: PR's at it again

Arsenal want a straight swap for Henri! dream on dream on! I hear you all say,
err yes I have woken up now!
So Smithy to Man u to partner van the man 8.000mil

-----Original Message-----
From: chris@noredscum.co.uk
Sent: 31 March 2003 10:15
To: TheWhites, all 02/03 User group
Subject: PR's final Press Release. He's resigned & we're
resigned to a tough time.

Peter Ridsdale has resigned.

I for one will not miss him but I'm slightly worried about the
mad Professor John McKenzie - who is he? Can we expect more of
the same since we have also announced a £17 million plus for
the six months ending in December? Can we now expect a little
bit of the truth from our board? Are the sales of Smith,
Robinson and Mills around the corner? Ridsdale mentioned
further cuts were needed so I'm not really looking forward to
the transfer window opening again.

However I feel we should try and see this as a new starting
point - we have seven games left to determine the future of
this club. Forget Europe, forget
away trips to Milan and Barcelona - we have to make sure our
away trips next year are still in Manchester and Liverpool
rather than Preston and Burnley. On on on

-----Original Message-----
From: russ@vivaleedspana.esp
Sent: 31 March 2003 12:51
To: Chris @ Noredscum.co.uk; TheWhites, all 02/03 user group
Subject: Re:PR's final Press Release. He's resigned.

Totally agree with that Chris, thats the most important thing now, the points, no
matter how they come. on on on

-----Original Message-----
From: Shack, Dave, Caribsurf.com
Sent: 2 April 2003 19:05
To: TheWhites, all 02/03 User group
Subject: Ridsdale - rid of the sale more like!

A Nutty professor? - he must be! You don't have to be an academic to
work out what has been going wrong at least - but someone has to do
something about it. You're right a couple of wins & then start re-building
for the future. Let's hope it's not last game of the season & we need a
result to go our way elsewhere or that will be a disaster.

Here on line at Harold's Bar, Barbados we are a laughing stock & almost a
sympathy case. I hate that. Cheers. Shacky - mine's a Banks with a rum
sour chaser!

Batang   10   B *I* U A ≡ ≡ ≡ ≡ ≡ ≡ ≡ ≡ —

-----Original Message-----
From: Firhad@ Fareastreid.ma
Sent: 01 April 2003 12:49
To: TheWhites, all 02/03 User group
Subject: Re: PR's final Press Release. He's resigned.

Bye Bye Risdale !!!!!!! After the Liverpoll match, it sure does reflect
the state we were in. Remember where we were after beating MU early of the
season and where we are today.

Reid.....be the saviour. Just get us the ponits to keep us up and we shall
re think our way next season. Let the points come from no matter where.

-----Original Message-----
From: russ@vivaleedspana.esp
Sent: 02 April 2003 16:21
To: TheWhites, all 02/03 User group
Subject: Marion

Lads, A prayer for Marion:

Marching on together   forever in our memories.

For any of you who knew her - she was a special girl who followed the whites
everywhere home & abroad from london to every part of the globe and will be
missed big time.

-----Original Message-----
From: Chris@Noredscum.co.uk
Sent: 03 April 2003 12:21
To: TheWhites, all 02/03 User group
Subject: A welcome break. England expects...nowt from Leeds!

How we have faltered so badly this season amazes me - I find
myself actually worrying about losing to Charlton - even last
season you'd have put Charlton vs. Leeds as an away win
without hesitation. This season I'm thinking a draw wouldn't
be a bad result.

Seven games left to stay up. That's a maximum of 21 points
available. Before this season we would have looked at these
last seven games and thought that only Arsenal Away would be

205

any problem and we would have allowed one slip up result
giving us fifteen points.

This season I think it will be a miracle if we get six. Am I
alone in these thoughts? What does everyone else think?

The entire club must rally together for these games - give our
all as players, fans, directors and prey that all the other
teams in our immediate area suffer the voodoo curse we've had
all season. Shacky - while you're on holiday have a word with
a Witch Doctor or two mate.
See you at Charlton on Saturday...
On on on

-----Original Message-----
From: Wathen, Dorian, The Peacocks
Sent: 03 April 2003 16:44
To: TheWhites, all 02/03 User group
Subject: RE: A welcome break. England expects...nowt from Leeds!

For no sound or logical reason whatsoever, I for one reckon we'll win on
Saturday - prediction 2-1 - good news he's left Okon, Teddy and Bravo at
home and H, Kells and most important Dom Matteo back. Robbo, Mills,
Matteo, Lucas, Harte, - Kells, Bakke, Barmby, Kewell - Dukes, Smith.

-----Original Message-----
From: Shack, Dave, Caribsurf.com
Sent: 03 April 2003 19:08
To: Wathen, Dorian, The Peacocks
Subject: RE: Cheer up ...it's Peter Reid!

Objective opinion from Reidy! (dropping journeymen) Thank god someone
is able to see the shite from the trees (sorry to mix a metaphor).
Hot here - fingers crossed for Charlton. can watch it delayed as live out
here. Nerves on holiday - nightmare...

-----Original Message-----
From: Davidharveysmonkey@aol.com
Sent: 03 April 2003 19:50
To: TheWhites, all 02/03 User group
Subject: Re: A welcome break. England expects...nowt from Leeds!

a little bird told me the team for charlton

Garamond   10

Robbo
Mills, Lucas, Dubes, Matteo
kelly, bakke, ?? (Batts not match fit yet but on the bench), Kewell (left midfield)
Smith, Viduka
Okon, Lukic, Bravo all binned.

DH'sM

-----Original Message-----
From: Russ@Vivaleedspana.spa
Sent: 03 April 2003 13:48
To: TheWhites, all 02/03 User group
Subject: Re: A welcome break. England expects...nowt from Leeds!

The 1st problem we have in our fight for survival is, every team we have to play
is involved in the race for europe, and when you look at those teams who would
have thought that.
The second is Arsenal, will know we will get nothing, so that leaves only six
matches to survive.
The third is that while we are picking up no points at all every week, bolton,
west ham and birmingham are!
There is probably a 4th but i am to depressed to find it.

-----Original Message-----
From: Andy@Whitetoreply.co.uk
Sent: 03 April 2003 22:14
To: TheWhites, all 02/03 User group
Subject: RE: A welcome break. England expects...nowt from Leeds!

Glad to see some non Vulcan philosophy being used. Illogical we should win, but we
have a gut feeling!
Team mentioned does look good on paper.
Here's to PR (that's Reidy not Ridsdale). Let's hope he weaves some scouser magic.

-----Original Message-----
From: Wathen, Dorian, The Peacocks
Sent: 04 April 2003 11:15
To: TheWhites, all 02/03 User group
Subject: RE: A welcome break. England expects...nowt from Leeds!

or should that be Monkey Magic...

Courier New ▼　10 ▼　▤▾　**B** *I* U A▾　☰ ☷ ⯮ ⯮　▤ ▤ ▤ ▤　— ◉ ▨

```
-----Original Message-----
From: Chris@Noredscum.co.uk
Sent: 04 April 2003 10:18
To: TheWhites, all 02/03 User group
Subject: Three Years Ago tomorrow.
```

As we again prepare to go to match this weekend my thoughts
are drawn to events that happened in Istanbul 3 years ago. Two
ordinary football fans, Kevin Speight and Chris Loftus, were
stabbed and suffered fatal injuries.

I for one will be having a quiet moment of reflection at the
Charlton game to remember two guys I never even knew but who
could have been any one of us.No one should ever have to
through what they and their families subsequently have
endured. Never let them be forgotten

-----Original Message-----
From: Shack, Dave, Caribsurf.ca
Sent: 04 April 2003 19:09
To: 'Chris Tams'
Subject: RE: Cheer up ...it's Peter Reid!

Here here mate - never let them be forgotten. I'll never forget being
turned back at Heathrow with DH'sM, Jeremy & Nelly - and then calling
Russ who was already out there...

-----Original Message-----
From: Russ@Vivaleedspana.spa
Sent: 04 April 2003 19:53
To: chris@collective.mu; TheWhites, all 02/03 User group
Subject: Re: Three Years Ago tomorrow.

Well i will never forget what i saw out there and will never forget the two lads
and i hope the the fans remember them too. Have a good un everybody

```
-----Original Message-----
From: Chris@Noredscum.co.uk
Sent: 07 April 2003 17:22
To: TheWhites, all 02/03 User group
Subject: Sunshine - 6 Goals - is it still August? Was it all a
nightmare?
```

Courier New ▾ 10 ▾ ≡▾ **B** *I* U A▾ ☰ ☰ ☵ ☶ ☰ ☰ ☰ ☰ — ● ▣

Sorry I was meaning to write something earlier today but I've had one of those busy days and I'm still recovering from the celebrations that stared on Saturday afternoon and finally finished on Sunday evening.

How good were we on Saturday - back to the old Leeds that just dominated the entire game and hardly let Charlton have a touch. How good was it to see us even at 6-1 up still chase for every ball? I watched in amazement as Viduka was still running after long balls when he'd got his hat-trick.

Six matches to go and we play like that in all of them six wins!!!!!!!!!!!!!!

-----Original Message-----
From: Jeremy@Donsgloryears.co.uk
Sent: 07 April 2003 23:43
To: TheWhites, all 02/03 User group
Subject: Re: Sunshine - 6 Goals - is it still August? Was it all a nightmare?

Shacky and I found ourselves by complete coincidence on holiday in Barbados at the same time and of course also found ourselves in front of a big screen that was showing the whole game as live (but a few hours after it had finished). We both tried not to find out the score beforehand, but kept overhearing people saying things like "did you hear the Leeds result? amazing!" and being told that we "would enjoy what we are going to see" as we set off. Along with the 2 other Leeds fans watching, we celebrated each goal as if we had no idea what had actually happened, and for one and half hours could forget about the misery of the past 7 months.

So what went right? Smart team selection, great start to the game with lots of good early possession, and a tempo and - above all - a passion that we haven't seen for quite some time. In short, all the things that Very Terribles so miserably failed to bring to our club. So is Peter Reid the right man for the job long term? Right now, I don't care, but as long as he steers us through the next 6 games with similar performances, I suspect we might all love him that little bit more by the end of the season.

-----Original Message-----
From: Wathen, Dorian, The Peacocks
Sent: 07 April 2003 17:33
To: TheWhites, all 02/03 User group
Subject: RE: Sunshine - 6 Goals - is it still August? Was it all a nightmare?

inspirational positional selection - Dom Matteo in the middle and Smith and H returned to their rightful positions, both looked far better players for it. Kells was inspirational and Viduka looks better with a partner taking the share of being target man. Best performance by a mile I've seen this year.

Only downside is I've lost my voice as a result... and Shack, I've recorded the chanting on my phone for you!

-----Original Message-----
From: Russ@Vivaleedspana.spa
Sent: 07 April 2003 18:10
To: TheWhites, all 02/03 User group
Subject: RE: Sunshine - 6 Goals - is it still August? Was it all a nightmare?

slow down lads, while it was fantastic and i am still in shock, we still have a way to go although looking at the other teams run in's i am a lot happier than i was before sat.
but then for it all to be dragged down by the slags in the press and suggest that h is off to s for a meagre 6.000mil.
Dave fancy driving me up for the spurs game on sat?

-----Original Message-----
From: davidharveysmonkey@aol.com
Sent: 08 April 2003 23:01
To: TheWhites, all 02/03 User group
Subject: Re: Cheer up ...it's Peter Reid!

I THINK VIDUKA MADE A VERY CANDID POINT ON TV WHEN HE RESPONDED TO THE QUESTION WHAT'S PETER REID DONE DIFFERENTLY ?
with'carefull pause to think and then:

"He's encouraged ALL of us"

-----Original Message-----
From: Nelly@thewhitellie-phant.co.uk
Sent: 07 April 2003 17:37
To: Dave.shack@Ononon.co.uk
Subject: six bloody one

Explain to me again why I sold my bastard ticket?

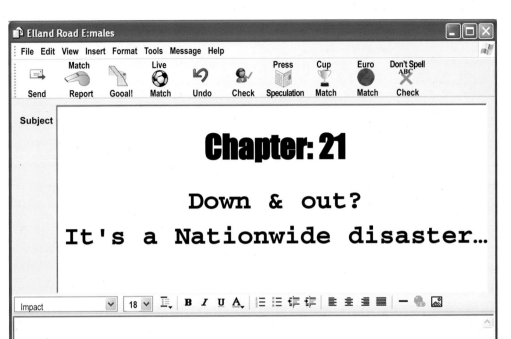

Elland Road E:males

File   Edit   View   Insert   Format   Tools   Message   Help

Match   Live   Press   Cup   Euro   Don't Spell
                                                                  ABC

Send   Report   Gooal!   Match   Undo   Check   Speculation   Match   Match   Check

Subject

Chapter: 21

Down & out?
It's a Nationwide disaster...

Impact   18

PREFACE:

Southampton 3-2 (Lost), Fulham 2-0 (Won), Blackburn 2-3 (Lost)... Leeds are right in the thick of the relegation battle and the whole season, maybe the club's whole future revolves around the last couple of games of the season. Our rivals have form with them - we're as mercurial as ever - watch the temperature - it's rising...

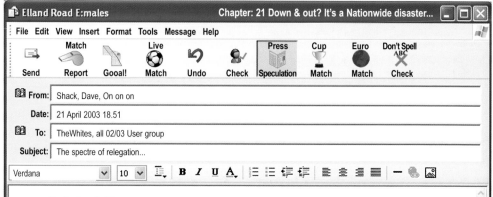

-----Original Message-----
From: Shack, Dave, Ononon.co.uk
Sent: 21 April 2003 18:51
To: TheWhites, all 02/03 User group
Subject: The spectre of relegation...

So -Southampton was a horror show right? Tamsy gave me the result over the phone & didn't even tell me Smith was sent off so I can guess how bad he felt about the game. Today, back from Madrid, I saw bloody West Ham get a win that really puts us back in the mixer. If we don't beat Fulham tomorrow then I think we are really 50/50 to go down. Arsenal - no chance, Blackburn - draw at best & then Villa - who knows actually?
Bolton got a win on Saturday & a decent draw today so we're really looking dodgy. I was with Steve Mcmanaman most of the weekend & he was pretty much of the opinion that we would be OK, but only just. He rates Reidy, but talking as Fowler's mate he believes there is a lot wrong (no shit sherlock!) and that we are not gonna figure as a force in the premiership for a few years at least now. Hey we might not even be in it...
How's everyone else feeling? Rob/ Moylesy - you've been quiet for a while...? I still cannot believe that the season started with so much hope & is now almost over with complete despair.

Believe you me this book is incredible - when I look back at some of the matches & events, no matter what, I'm so glad we've done it. Never has a season been quite like this - and let's hope it never f*cking is again!
How can teams like 'Boro not beat West Ham? How could Fulham beat Newcastle? What a nightmare...

-----Original Message-----
From: mohd@Fareastreid.ma
Sent: 22 April 2003 03:03
To: TheWhites, all 02/03 User group
Subject: Re: The spectre of relegation...

Batang   10   **B** *I* U A

Ouch ....Just when we thought it was safe we are hit by bad defensive jobs. The goals by Spurs and also Soton are unlike the Leeds of the past. If only we have tightened it up we may be in a much stronger position but all now boils down to the last stretch.

Shacky, it is great that we document our excitement, anguish, fears and anger this time around. These are moments we Leeds United fans rally around and share our emotions and with this book it will reveal to all at Elland Road and anyone reading the book that we are what keps the club going. This season all has happened that owuld never ever be experienced by Leeds or any other club. I am all for the 'sequel' next season as we pull back trying to get back into the pole positions that we have become accustomed to in the last 3 - 4 years.

We shall be back. Fulham, move aside in our survival battle.

Firhad

-----Original Message-----
From: russ@vivaleedspana.esp
Sent: 22 April 2003 09:45
To: TheWhites, all 02/03 User Group
Subject: Re: The spectre of relegation...

fantastic words Firhad, but i don't think you will get many backers for the sequel!

It would help if we had a team that wasn't just full of words, unfortunately we have and their performances have been proof of this.

This one tonight will be the biggest game this season because its the only one i can see us having a chance in!!

My stomach aches for what could be just around the corner, i just pray the players have the same feeling.

r t b

-----Original Message-----
From: Jeremy@Donsgloryears.co.uk
Sent: 22 April 2003 10:42
To: TheWhites, all 02/03 User Group
Subject: Re: The spectre of relegation...

If I was Peter Reid (not a particularly enticing prospect I must admit!)I would get 16 enlarged photocopies of the league table this morning and pin one up above every player and substitute's peg in the changing room!

Times New Roman   10   **B** *I* U A

If seeing the name "Leeds United" one place above the relegation zone with only 3 points more than W.Ham doesn't motivate the players than nothing will.

We've got to do it tonight and on Saturday against Blackburn. Smith, Viduka and Bakke are all suspended for the last 2 games. What's going to be our striking pair against Arsenal? Milner and Simon Johnson?

Onefirst team start between the two of them.....?

-----Original Message-----
From: Chris@Noredscum.co.uk
Sent: 22 April 2003 11:05
To: TheWhites, all 02/03 User group
Subject: Re: The spectre of relegation...

How bad is it that we are needing a win against Fulham to stay up and we are all nervous about it? We were shit on Saturday despite some of the best away support Southampton have ever seen.

Sorry about the phonecall Shacky - I wasn't really in the mood to speak after watching that shower of shite.

I think we will survive this season by the skin of our teeth.

-----Original Message-----
From: Andy@whitetoreply.co.uk
Sent: 22 April 2003 17:58
To: TheWhites, all 02/03 User Group
Subject: Re: The spectre of relegation...

I wanted to put my thoughts into song, so to the tune of Bad Moon Rising........

I feel the Storm Clouds are a-gathering
I feel the drop is getting near
I hope we get our shit together
Caus I don't want to experience my fear

So let's sort things out tonight
If we win we may be allright
I don't want to be in Division One
If for once we could play as a team
We could realise our dream

Any all those Storm Clouds would soon be gone.

Oh well, I have to have some pleasure in life if Football's failing.

Good luck to the Whites (that would be the total whites and not the white tops and black shorts!).

-----Original Message-----
From: Shack, Dave, Ononon.co.uk
Sent: 22 April 2003 18:47
To: TheWhites, all 02/03 User Group
Subject: Tonight is a night of Destiny! Come on Leeds one win should do it!

Jees - how nerve racking (sp?) is this? I'm gonna stay here in the office & listen to it online for the partisan approach.
C'mon Leeds, us fans don't deserve this.

-----Original Message-----
From: Shack, Dave, Ononon.co.uk
Sent: 22 April 2003 19:52
To: TheWhites, all 02/03 User Group
Subject: RE: Tonight is a night of Destiny! Come on Leeds one win should do it!

Yeeeessssssssssss!!!!!!!!!! 3 chances & then Vidukas in there!! a couple of minutes in. Dorigo summarising on Aire FM. Love it!

-----Original Message-----
From: Shack, Dave, Ononon.co.uk
Sent: 22 April 2003 20:54
To: TheWhites, all 02/03 User Group
Subject: RE: Tonight is a night of Destiny! Come on Leeds one win should do it!

YEEEEEEEEEEEEEESSSSSSSSSSSSSSSSSSSSSSSSS!!!!!!!!!!! 2-0 Viduka is gonna win the bloody golden boot if he isn't careful.

-----Original Message-----
From: Shack, Dave, Ononon.co.uk
Sent: 22 April 2003 21:37
To: TheWhites, all 02/03 User Group
Subject: Logging off & Going home happy!

Verdana   10   **B** *I* U A

2-0. Lads - we've all but done it! Great goal difference. One more point will do it. Thank God.

Cheers to you all& Reidy for motivating this team! Viduka on fire & solid defending. A bit of hope...

Shack

-----Original Message-----
From: Andy@whitetoreply.co.uk
Sent: 23 April 2003 08:24
To: Dave.Shack@Ononon.co.uk
Subject: Re: Logging off & Going home happy!

The boys are back in tow-wow-wow-wown!!! Marvellous. Enjoy your day. Andy

-----Original Message-----
From: russ@vivaleedspana.esp
Sent: 23 April 2003 09:54
To: TheWhites, all 02/03 User Group
Subject: Re: Logging off & Going home happy!

Yesssssssssssssssss get in there with that header vid.
Great result, just what everyone deserves, a lift.
Is everyone going up for the Villa game it would be good to meet some of you guys before the game?

-----Original Message-----
From: Jeremy@Donsgloryears.co.uk
Sent: 23 April 2003 10:15
To: Dave.Shack@Ononon.co.uk
Subject: Re: Logging off & Going home happy!

I think relief is the word. But it's qualification for Europe we should be fretting on, not bloody relegation!

Interesting thought - every one of the players who started last night
(and against Southampton on Saturday) featured heavily during our
Champions League adventure 2 years ago. How the mighty have fallen. And 10 of them are internationals, and it surely can't be long before
Duberry joins them (only joking....)

Batang | 10

-----Original Message-----
From: mohd@FareastReid.ma
Sent: 23 April 2003 12:54
To: TheWhites, all 02/03 User Group
Subject: Win Win Win !!!!!!

Great result y'all........Told that we shall prevail. Shacky....sequel on
for next season.We shall landmark this season as a transitional period for
a better Leeds. reid-sy for da job !!!!! 1 mo' ponit and we shall be
alright. If only we tighten the defense as of yesterday we shall be
alright. Reid has learnt well after just a handful and to have Viduks on
fire again speaks volume of what El tel have not been able to do. We need
ammo form midfield and with that the goals will come.

-----Original Message-----
Chris@Captaindom.co.uk
Sent: 23 April 2003 13:59
To: TheWhites, all 02/03 User Group
Subject: RE: Win Win Win !!!!!!

Heard that Viduka turned up at ER late before the game. Reid got him in the office
and instead of shouting at him and then handing him a fine, Reid said; "You know
I've got to fine you and all that, but just go out there and get me 2 goals"!!!!
Here's to Smudger running late on Saturday!!

-----Original Message-----
From: rob@the-unforgiven.com
Sent: 23 April 2003 23:46
To: TheWhites, all 02/03 User Group
Subject: Re: Win Win Win !!!!!!

Happy days are here again? Back to the future and all that? Not sure. Peter Reid
can certainly motivate the players (as well as being able to eat bananas with his feet)
and has saved our season from that madcap interlude with the Cockernee hasbeen
but will he take us any further next year? Who cares for now I suppose. The Mad
Prof is rumoured not to want any further sales and will do some sort of rights issue
with the shares to pull that off - that's why Peter and the Dreamers has left one
supposes. It's possible but how many city institutions are going to stump up more?
It'll be us, the fans, who pull them out of this one.

Anyway Vidukes has been sensational, Kewell working, Kelly magnificent in the Reid
games I've seen. Good joke about Smith, Chris. He'll never score again! More cards
than goals. I know he cares and loves playing for Leeds but could someone show him

how to put the ball in the fucking net every once in a while? Here's to Mickey Bridges
and a full recovery starting today. Nothing could be better than seeing this truly
great player getting back to the form he showed in 1999/2000. Sorry to rant on, it's
late. Good night

-----Original Message-----
From: Chris@Noredscum.co.uk
Sent: 24 April 2003 13:20
To: TheWhites, all 02/03 User Group
Subject: Re: Win Win Win !!!!!!

I read this morning that Reid has given Viduka lots of
positive motivation - ie he stuck his size tens up his lazy
arse. Now if we can only keep hold of him and a few other
players this summer we should have a better season next time.

I still don't feel that Reid is the right man for the job full
time but I think we owe him a great deal of thanks for the
rescue job that he has all but finished.

Apparently Paul Hart was at the Fulham game - If Notts Forest
don't come up then I think he is the right man for us.

Leeds are a top six club and should be embarrassed about
finishing even lower than that. We can excuse this season as
an "annus horribilious" just like the one after we won the
championship - we need to start from scratch and get people in
our team who are 100% focussed on playing their hearts out for
the team every week.

Anyway only three games left - I'm missing Blackburn but will
be at Arsenal (pub-crawl up Upper Street if anyone's
interested - the day after is a Bank holiday so there are no
excuses really) and maybe at Villa. Three more games until
Saturdays are no longer important for a few weeks.

Another three points on Saturday will make things even better

-----Original Message-----
From: DavidHarveysmonkey@aol.com
Sent: 24 April 2003 20:19
To: TheWhites, all 02/03 User Group
Subject: Re: Win Win Win !!!!!!

Tamsy I agree Paul hart would be an interesting choice because of his
history of developing homegrown talent but let me get this right, your current logic is: If he fails
to get promoted he'll be good enough for us?

Not arguing with your choice of man, he'd be on my shortlist if we're
looking to raise funds and cut costs by growing and keeping or selling all future teams. Just the
logic. Does that also mean Nigel Worthington might be in the frame?

On that point have you noticed how many ex leeds players are currently managing in the first
division: Nigel Worthington, McAllister, Mickey Adams,
Paul Hart, anyone else?

-----Original Message-----
From: Jeremy@Donsgloryears.co.uk
Sent: 24 April 2003 15:16
To: TheWhites, all 02/03 User Group
Subject: Re: Win Win Win !!!!!!

I wish I could share the optimism for next season. Yes it would be great if Paul Hart (or
Martin O'Neill - remember him?) comes, Robbo Harry Dukes Smithy all stay, Batty and
Bridges get fit, and we bring in a couple of central defenders and midfielders.

But what about the £90m debt? How can we keep our top players and bring in new quality
players with that looming over us? I'm hoping and praying that the Prof will come up with
some great financial solution -
otherwise I can see the next few years being grim relegation fights.
Someone please tell me I'm wrong...

-----Original Message-----
From: Shack, Dave, Ononon.co.uk
Sent: 27 April 2003 21:54
To: TheWhites, all 02/03 User Group
Subject: What a Black(burn) of a weekend!

Leeds Rhinos get conned by the Bulls (& the ref)...Arsenal draw...Scum
win...Hammers win...Bolton get a point...Fulham get a point...Birmingham
win...ahhh at least Villa lose...oh and we lost again. There's no doubt that
we are gonna need to win against Villa in the last game of the season is
there?

Hey Smithy! perfect time to remember where the net is. Jeez. Welcome to
2003! Robbo too - you may be going to Arsenal, but right now we don't
need even one mistake from you. We've all come to accept shite from
pretty much everyone else on the pitch - but not you, the most consistent

player of this whole nightmare of a season.It's between the 2 of them for Player of the Season apparently - it has to be Robbo as Smith's in-discipline should not be seen as something to be voted for. It's a huge negative. Personally, I'd give Gary Kelly it.

God, I just feel sick writing this. We really are courting disaster here and I don't sense we've got the guts for it - especially without Viduka & Smith.

There's much more to write about - but I honestly cannot face it. We're gonna need a small miracle to survive the drop without help from the other clubs and that is just too awful to contemplate. Christ! Even the wife knows we're in trouble and that means the rest of the country must too.

Aaaaaaaaaaarrrrrrrrrrggggggggggggggghhhhhhhhhhhhhh!
Shakey (sic)

-----Original Message-----
From: Andy@whitetoreply.co.uk
Sent: 28 April 2003 07:26
To: Dave.Shack@Ononon.co.uk
Subject: Re: What a Black(burn) of a weekend!

Let's be positive.3-1 win over a rapidly degrading Arsenal and we're safe.

Come on the boys.

-----Original Message-----
From: Shack, Dave, Ononon.co.uk
Sent: 28 April 2003 09:20
To: Andy@whitetoreply.co.uk
Subject: RE: What a Black(burn) of a weekend!

Great attitude Laws, that's the spirit, yes we can do it.   Shit , I just woke up... Bollocks.

-----Original Message-----
From: Chris @ Noredscum.co.uk
Sent: 28 April 2003 11:02
To: TheWhites, all 02/03 User group
Subject: Re: What a Black(burn) of a weekend!

I really don't know what to say - our defence couldn't stop a team from the Sunday pub leagues at the moment.

Courier New   10

We have a game on Sunday at Highbury where Arsenal will be chasing three points in the faint hope that Manure will slip up - West Ham play Chelsea and Bolton play at Southampton. Normally I'd say no problems for Arsenal, Chelsea and Southampton however the way things have been going this season who knows?

We still could go down and we really wont know until the final whistle on the final day of the season - I'm not confident whereas every Hammers and Bolton fan I know are on a roll and are so confident it's sickening.

Is Uncle Shacky organising a "celebrate the relegate" coach tour to Elland rd for the Villa game?

-----Original Message-----
From: Nelly@whitellie-phant.co.uk
Sent: 28 April 2003 10:06
To: Dave.Shack @ Ononon
Subject: Re: What a Black(burn) of a weekend!

You're right. It's very grim. When West Ham scored I got a horrible sick feeling in the pit of my stomach.
It's still there. And will be until at least 5pm on Saturday. Jeezus, how could it come to this?

-----Original Message-----
From: Chris@Captaindom.co.uk
Sent: 28 April 2003 12:55
To: TheWhites, all 02/03 User Group
Subject: RE: What a Black(burn) of a weekend!

My girlfriend is beautiful. She's smart, intelligent and funny; and makes me feel like the luckiest man alive. She is, however, a massive Arsenal fan!!!!! This weekend, she came with me to watch the Blackburn game. OH JOY I swear she thinks that Leeds just don't win ever; and she'd almost be right I was out of my seat when we scored. I actually thought that we were going to win. Luckily I didn't see the Dubs incident. My pal said it was like watching basketball. I have no idea about Arsenal next week. Half of me knows that they will kill us, the half believes that we'll actually win, thus giving Man U the title. SO here's the thing, I would gladly give Man U the title, if it meant Leeds stay up. I'm not bothered about 1st, 2nd, 3rd ...... Only LUFC playing in the premiership next season......

Comic Sans MS   10   B I U A

-----Original Message-----
From: Russ@Vivaleedspana.esp
Sent: 28 April 2003 16:28
To: TheWhites, all 02/03 User group
Subject: RE: What a Black(burn) of a weekend!

Chris i havent seen Leeds win in over 2 years! and fuck off dave! You can not class me as the jynx anymore due to the amount of games we lose when i am not there!!!

-----Original Message-----
From: Davidharveysmonkey@aol.com
Sent: 28 April 2003 09:06
To: TheWhites, all 02/03 User group
Subject: Re: What a Black(burn) of a weekend!

If we're selling Robbo they should just give Nige his job back, we had a much better record with him in goals and I know Robbo's great but you have to wonder if he really commands the defence in the style Nige did.

-----Original Message-----
From: Shack, Dave, On on on
Sent: 29 April 2003 09:29
To: TheWhites, all 02/03 User group
Subject: RE: What a Black(burn) of a weekend!

We'll need his experience & composure in the Nationwide...

-----Original Message-----
From: russ@Vivaleedspana.esp
Sent: 29 April 2003 09:30
To: Dave.Shack@Ononon.
Subject: RE: What a Black(burn) of a weekend!

nice one dave, where did that sense of humor come from???

-----Original Message-----
From: Shack, Dave, Ononon
Sent: 29 April 2003 09:33
To: russ@vivaleedspana.esp
Subject: RE: What a Black(burn) of a weekend!

Verdana | 10 | B *I* U A

I was born with it - yorkshire sarcasm & all that. Fuck! this is a nightmare...

-----Original Message-----
From: russ@vivaleedspana.esp
Sent: 29 April 2003 09:37
To: Dave.Shack@Ononon.
Subject: RE: What a Black(burn) of a weekend!

more for you than me at least i have an excuse not to have to travel everyweek to places like burnley, stoke or Grimsby.

-----Original Message-----
From: Shack, Dave, On on on
Sent: 29 April 2003 12:36
To: Thewhites, all 02/03 User group
Subject: Villa game - Photo opp!

I'm aiming to get a group photo at the Billy statue at about 12 noon. Please can you all try & make it - preferably in some Leeds tops or similar.

I have tickets for Dorian, DH'sM, Chris & Jeremy - my treat. I'd like to buy everyone else beer/lunch as close to the ground as possible - any suggestions? What about the Commercial? Mal Maison?

I'll be driving up about 8.30 that morning if anyone wants a lift. Tamsy is already on board - 2/3 more spaces left...

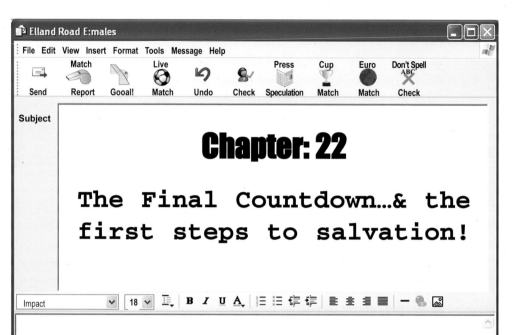

Chapter: 22

The Final Countdown...& the first steps to salvation!

PREFACE:

Not often a team to make it easy on their fans - the performance of the season came against Arsenal away. Relegation was avoided, some degree of pride was restored & the final home game became a party not a wake. Leeds United, we hope, go On, on, on!

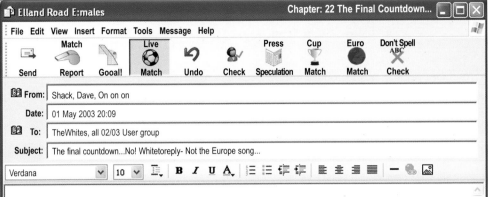

File Edit View Insert Format Tools Message Help

Send   Report   Gooal!   Match   Undo   Check   Speculation   Match   Match   Check

From: Shack, Dave, On on on

Date: 01 May 2003 20:09

To: TheWhites, all 02/03 User group

Subject: The final countdown...No! Whitetoreply- Not the Europe song...

Verdana   10   B I U A

-----Original Message-----
From: Shack, Dave, On on on
Sent: 01 May 2003 20:09
To: TheWhites, all 02/03 User group
Subject: The final countdown...No! Whitetoreply- Not the Europe song...

Sunday - 4pm GMT Arsenal vs Leeds. Next Sunday 3pm Leeds vs Aston Villa. In the meantime Villa have Sunderland, Fulham have Everton & Charlton, Bolton have Southampton & 'Boro & most importantly West Ham have Chelsea & Birmingham.
Despite everything I have got this mad feeling that we will draw or beat Arsenal on Sunday. I think their season is over (bar the FA Cup) and just like that fateful night when Jimmy nailed their premiership dreams in a coffin at Elland Road, I think we'll do it again.
I'm in sodding Munich this weekend (the real one Tamsy!)with Westlife so I'm gonna watch the game on Sky. I hope that Chelsea can do us a favour and that the similar blue of Everton gets back on track too. Shit, it's come to this.
Last weekend's results were so bad we deserve a break when we aren't even playing... don't we? Don't we...?
Get ready for the last ride on this rollercoaster lads - the biggest thrill (if you can call it that) starts this weekend! Ononon.

-----Original Message-----
From: Russ@Vivaleedspana.esp
Sent: 02 May 2003 09:21
To: TheWhites, all 02/03 User group
Subject: Re: The final countdown...No! Whitetoreply- Not the Europe song...

Im only sorry that we havent got Jimmy playing on Sunday!
Sorry lads but i said it some 4/5 matches back that all the other clubs somehow are picking up points and we are not.

225

Comic Sans MS   10   **B** *I* U A

That was when birmingham were behind us! Their now safe. I really do have a bad bad feeling, but eh i have always been a pessimist.
Ononon

-----Original Message-----
From: Jeremy@Donsgloryears
Sent: 02 May 2003 10:05
To: Dave.shack@Ononon.co.uk
Subject: Re: The final countdown...

It was a different sort of excitement and tension that I anticipated for the end of a Leeds United season!

-----Original Message-----
From: Chris@ No Red Scum
Sent: 02 May 2003 11:11
To: TheWhites, all 02/03 User Group
Subject: Re: The final countdown...

I never thought I'd say this but "Come On Chelsea!!"

-----Original Message-----
From: Nelly@Whitellie-phant.co.uk
Sent: 02 May 2003 11:26
To: chris@Noredscum.co.uk
Cc:Dave.Shack @Ononon.co.uk
Subject: Re(2): The final countdown...

I've been checking and I think it's OK to say that if you keep your fingers crossed on one hand.

-----Original Message-----
From: Mohd@FareastReid.ma
Sent: 02 May 2003 11:29
To: TheWhites, all 02/03 User group
Subject: Re: The final countdown...

Have to agree with Dave on a surprise for Arsenal.....Too bad it will make Scums champ but got to help ourselves to it though !!!!! 2-1 for us. Dave, regards to the Westlife boys.......memories of October 2002 still remains where I became Ian Harte for a few minutes. And having you play in my Leeds kit for the practise. On On On leeds !!!!

Batang   10   ≣▾ B I U A̲, ≣ ≣ 堂 堂 ≣ ≣ ≣ ≣ ━ ◉ ▨

-----Original Message-----
From: Shack, Dave, On on on
Sent: 02 May 2003 11:32
To: Mohd Firhad, Leeds4Ever
Subject: Re: The final countdown...

Great memories my friend. You'll see this pic in the book!

-----Original Message-----
From: Andy@Whitetoreply.co.uk
Sent: 02 May 2003 18:00
To: Dave.Shack@Ononon.co.uk
Subject: Re: The final countdown...

I have the same sneaky feeeling about getting something at Highbury. But my
hopes will be pinned more on Chelsea anihilating West Ham.
Have a good Umpah! Andy P.S. Europe who? (Ha!)

-----Original Message-----
From: Shack, Dave, On on on
Sent: 05 May 2003 14:26
To: TheWhites, all 02/03 User group
Subject: Highbury Heaven!

Never on the field of football conflict have so many owed so much to so
few... - Elland Road E:males 2002-2003
12 players forgot about the reputations of their opposition; they forgot
about their own short-comings & they worked like a team to clear their
own names of being complicit in one of the biggest shock's of the club's
84 year history. Broad shoulders faced the brick-bats from everywhere -
and the senior players were the rock that everyone else leaned on. From
Lucas's faultless tackle on Henri to Harry's intuitive wunder-goal; from
Kelly's tire-less running to nephew Harte's confident free-kick; to Matteo's
visionary ball & Viduka's seamless flick & shot to foil England's #1 keeper.
It was manna from heaven for the fans that have followed this team
through thick & thicker shit this season.
Self-preservation washed away any care of that other race going on - that
of the title race. Our interest in that was the same as Grimsby's was in
Beckham's possible availability this summer: Cursory & abstract.
But what is now quite special, quite perverse is that the Man United
players & more importantly, the fans owe us. Hell, we've given Rio his
first major honour after he left us. Man United did not step off a field to
receive the cup, Leeds United handed it to them whilst they were all sat
at home. Smile knowingly lads every time someone from Surrey mentions

the 8th title; the most special one - because just like before we gave it to them.
What a day! It was great to hear you all in the crowd on Tamsy's mobile - I'm just glad you could use my ticket. I sat exhausted from the rigours of Munich with my Dad & saw this great game of football. My dad even half volleyed an empty bottle of pepsi when Dukes scored that goal - it just missing the Tv set by inches and putting a dent in the side cupboard an indelible mark of this great day when we salvaged pride and hinted at we're anything but down & out!
To see the reactions of the players was awesome - I just wish I could have seen Smithy's & Batty's face on that bench -supporting their colleagues. Amazing.

-----Original Message-----
From: mohd@FareastReid.ma
Sent: 06 May 2003 06:22
To: TheWhites, all 02/03 user group
Subject: Re: Highbury Heaven!

What a welcome performance..........My mail said we shall win 2-1 but instead rewarded with a 5 goal thriller. We now have beaten the top 3 teams this season Scums, Arse and Newcastle.This proves that we indeed have materials that can redeem us next season.Hence my excitement for a sequel of our book.
After what has happened nothing beats the past 10 months communicating with my fellow Leed buddies (thats you guys) and sharing our thoughts, 1973 - Eternity 30th Anniversary. ON On On.................E males Rulez !!!!!!!!!
From Firhad 'Clarke'

-----Original Message-----
From: chris@Noredscum.co.uk
Sent: 06 May 2003 11:33
To: TheWhites, all 02/03 User group
Subject: Re: Highbury Heaven!

Well I knew it was going to be one of those great days as soon as I'd seen a tube full of Jimmy Saville look-alikes at 11.30 in the morning!
Leeds seem to be able to turn on the style when we need to and boy did we need to on Sunday. Dave you missed one of the gutsiest performances I've ever seen Leeds pull off this season - I don't know what it is about Leeds and sunshine but we always seem to play well on very sunny days. Kewell

Courier New   10   B *I* U A

terrorised Arsenal's defence and scored the goal of the
season, christ even Wilcox and Duberry looked good.
The twenty minutes or so of non stop chanting at the end of
the game was awesome its just a shame that the players
couldn't come out back on to the pitch to share in our sense
of relief.
My head still hurts I'm covered in bruises and I've lost my
voice, however I'm happy for the moment.
This season has been a roller coaster ride with very little to
smile about - we have at times played excellent football
(Sunday at Arsenal, away at Charlton and at home to Chelsea)
but mostly this season we have been very poor and not
performed to our potential. Sure there have been far too many
distractions off the pitch but at the end of the day we've
consistently had eleven players who haven't performed.
We've escaped just - lets hope this is the start of our return
back to the top

-----Original Message-----
From: Jeremy@Donsgloryears
Sent: 06 May 2003 12:01
To: TheWhites, all 02/03 user group
Subject: Re: Highbury Heavan

Cometh the hour cometh the men! And all 12 of them (including Simon Johnson who managed in 10 minutes on the pitch to get up the noses of both Bergkamp and Keown - a star in the making?) were magnificent on Sunday. Harry's goal has to one of the Goals of the Season, and Dukes' performance hopefully once and for all will silence those moaning idiots who say he's lazy and want him out of the club. The central midfield and defence for once looked strong (hell, even Dubes had a blinder!), and no one can say that we didn't deserve a couple of lucky breaks and the victory.
All of which begs the obvious question - why couldn't we have played like that for the rest of the season? We all know we're capable - I mean we've beaten (convinvingly) the Top 3 teams in the Division. Once the euphoria dies down, let's not forget it was an escape from relegation we were celebrating , not the fucking Championship!
OK, so let's enjoy the last week of the season, before - I fear - a very tough summer. Who knows who, out of the playing and coaching staff, will be around when next season starts. And I think we'll all have to prepare ourselves for a few years of midtable mediocrity while we rebuild a club for the future, based this time on reality not flights of fancy.
Keep on believing.

------Original Message-----
From: chris@Captaindom.co.uk
Sent: 06 May 2003 14:13
To: TheWhites, all 02/03 User group

Arial   10   B *I* U A

Subject: RE: Highbury Heaven! (via manchester!!)

I, like Mister Shack was away working this weekend ... in Manchester!!
A tent with 10,000 people, (as it turned out, lots of them Man U fans!), in Heaton park to watch White Stripes, Feeder, Badly Drawn Boy, Stereophonics etc.
I had asked for, and was granted, a dish from SKY and a box to watch the game. The screen was set up for me, mum and dad, my cousin, my girlfriend (t'other team) and a few pals that might have been interested in watching the game. During the day, the word spread that there was a screen on site. Everybody from a Man U supporting security guy(who was like a giant) to the drummer with feeder and Kelly, the lead singer with the phonics, all asked where it was and if they could sit and watch.
I missed the White Stripes perform as I wanted to get the table right in front of the screen. I have never been so anxious in all my months of supporting football!
I leapt out of my seat when H belted that blinder into the net. My heart racing at the thought that we might just pull off one of the greatest games of the season. I then had to go on stage with mark, Feeders drummer. I was introducing them, but we both would've stayed, not missing a second. (He even asked Kelly if they could swap sets so he could stay and watch .. Kelly said no chance)
I told the 10,000 audience the score (we were leading at that point) and they went mental. Introduced the boys, ran off stage to be told by my girlfriend it was 1-1. I stayed and watched 4 of the songs, but had to go back to the tent to see the second half.
I'm not going to write much more because my emotions are probably the same as everybody else's. The highlights being;
1)	Every time Leeds scored, the man u supporting security guy shook my hand, then after Viduka's winner, lifted me up in the air and hugged me till I almost passed out.
2)	Mark the drummer, and my new best pal that day, looking sick as a dog for the last 20 mins. Despite just playing a fucking ace set in front of 10,000 fans.
3)	My phone beeping after every goal with about 6 messages each time from mates all watching the match. All pretty much just saying "FUCKING COME ON" etc
4)	Me jumping in the air and shouting so loudly after Viduka's goal that I went very dizzy for 10 seconds and thought I was gonna collapse.
5)	Watching The Stereophonics at the side of the stage knowing we had survived. Kelly then looking over and asking me the score. Then saying to the audience;
"I'm a Leeds fan and we just beat Arsenal 3 -2."
The audience booed to which Kelly replied;
"Don't boo me, we just won you the league you fuckers!!"

What a great fucking day. Thank you boys. I was proud to be a Leeds fan.

-----Original Message-----
From: Wathen, Dorian, The Peacocks
Sent: 06 May 2003 14:24
To: TheWhites, all 02/03 user group

Century Gothic | 10 | B *I* U A | ☰ ☰ ☰ ☰ | ☰ ☰ ☰ ☰ | — 🌐 🖼

Subject: RE: Highbury Heaven!

Hungover from release of tension the night before, arrived at Highbury on a glorious day alone, Eden's flash car having broken down - what a game to miss - trying not to rub it in Shack, and not a little stressed - how stressed we'd be with 5 mins of extra time was no comparison though... Great seat 3 rows from the front - Kewell was absolutely magnificent, skinning Arsenal players for fun as Big Ron would say - that first strike was world class - unbelievable - hope above hope that we can keep him for another season at least. Crowd went ballistic - Arsenal tried to respond with the one song in their repertoire (Vieira wasn't playing which fucked up their second choice) - god they have shit fans - you'd have thought it was us needing a win to keep in the race for the title. Backs to the wall for the majority of the first half, I said to Nick Rowe at half time that Hartey was due a free kick and he soon delivered! Wicked!

-----Original Message-----
From: russ@Vivaleedspana.esp
Sent: 07 May 2003 11:27
To: TheWhites, all 02/03 User group
Subject: RE: Highbury Heaven!

All of a sudden i feel a great calm in myself which has spread to my mind and now in my office and so much so i think i will take the afternoon off and go and play golf in the glorious sunshine of the costa del sol..........
Anybody else experiancing the same calm.
Could it have anything to do with our club? ahahahahahah i am so happy!
Looking forward to seeing you all Sunday. R.T.B

-----Original Message-----
From: Andy@whitetoreply.co.uk
Sent: 09 May 2003 04:50
To: Dave.Shack@Ononon.co.uk
Subject: Re: Highbury Heaven!

What a fantastic performance. It's days like that that remind me why I love the game so much. A great gutsy performance, full of thrills and spills and the right result to boot.
Two "triffic" goals as Reidy would say. Even Dubes did well and the Chief was magnificent.
I was on the edge of my seat round, at a neighbours, and was glad of the inch of malt whisky that he poured me prior to the start.
We can now go to Villa on Sunday without fear and enjoy what could be a great game as long as the boys put in the same type of performance.

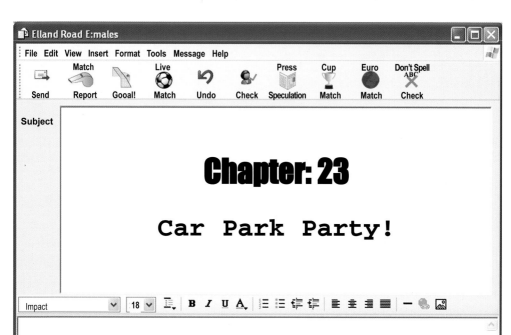

Chapter: 23

Car Park Party!

PREFACE:

Not even a rainstorm could dampen the spirits on the last day of the season. A home win, the end of the season & with Mrs Shack's car boot picnic all was good.Even Eddie Gray wandered past our little gathering - but what was he doing in the bloody Fullerton car park?

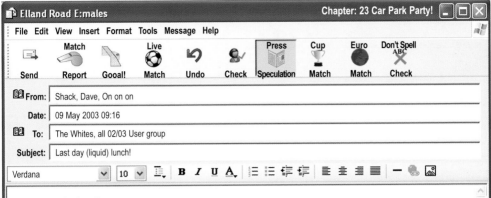

| | Match | | Live | | | Press | Cup | Euro | Don't Spell |
| Send | Report | Gooal! | Match | Undo | Check | Speculation | Match | Match | Check |

From: Shack, Dave, On on on

Date: 09 May 2003 09:16

To: The Whites, all 02/03 User group

Subject: Last day (liquid) lunch!

Verdana   10   B *I* U A | ≣ ≣ ⧉ ⧉ | ≣ ≣ ≣ ≣ | — 🔗 🖼

-----Original Message-----
From: Shack, Dave, On on on
Sent: 09 May 2003 09:16
To: The Whites, all 02/03 User group
Subject: Last day (liquid) lunch!

Ok lads - here's the plan - we all meet at about 12.15 at Billy. Hopefully a photographer (nelly?) will be there to take the shots of us all grouped around my laptop in Leeds regalia. After that I've got me mum & I parked in the Fullerton car park (behind the West Stand) and we've prepared a 'picnic' lunch for us all plus some beers (natch). You're all invited, plus any +1s you have as a thank you from me.
Guys, I look forward to seeing you (except poor Firhad) on Sunday. Dorian, Nelly & Chris (DH'sM?) - see you at mine 8.45 - 9.00 am Sunday. Cheers & here's to Reidy saying to the players - "Lads - you're the only C.V. I've got so whoop those brummie tossers & we'll have a crack in the summer & next season."
Shacky P.S. Mum - get buttering those rolls...

-----Original Message-----
From: chris@Noredscum.co.uk
Sent: 09 May 2003 10:52
To: Dave.Shack@Ononon.co.uk
Subject: Re: Last day (liquid) lunch!

Top banana - I'll bring some Midget Gems for the car journey! See you Sunday am

-----Original Message-----
From: Andy@whitetoreply.co.uk
Sent: 09 May 2003 15:31
To: Dave.Shak@Ononon.co.uk
Subject: Re: Last day (liquid) lunch!

I can't believe you're exploiting your mum this way. See you Sunday. Cheers

-----Original Message-----
From: chris@Noredscum.co.uk
Sent: 09 May 2003 14:14
To: TheWhites, all 02/03 user group
Subject: Re: Last day (liquid) lunch!

Well its officially Peter Reid as our new manager - anyone got
any details?

-----Original Message-----
From: Wathen, Dorian, The Peacocks
Sent: 09 May 2003 14:58
To: TheWhites, all 02/03 User group
Subject: RE: Last day (liquid) lunch!

Yeah - Average midfielder for Everton and England, famous for Maradona leaving him in his wake for "that" goal. Became average manager sacked by Man City and Sunderland...does the disappointment show ? At least he isn't a former player, coach, manager, cleaner ... here's hoping Willie Donachie doesn't replace Eddie Gray.

-----Original Message-----
From: Shack, Dave, On on on
Sent: 09 May 2003 16:04
To: TheWhites, all 02/03 User group
Subject: Wow man! like...Symmetry!

Freaky...the book starts with speculation & then a new manager. The book all but ends with speculation & then a new manager...Cosmic maan!

Let's hope it ends with a win like it started too!

-----Original Message-----
From: Andy@ Whitetoreply.co.uk
Sent: 09 May 2003 17:56
To: Dave Shack, On on on
Subject: Re: Wow man! like...Symmetry!

Sod it! A win. I'm going for 7-2 to Leeds. Our strikers are on fire and our defenders should be set on fire.

Verdana   10   B *I* U A

-----Original Message-----
From: Shack, Dave, Ononon
Sent: 09 May 2003 16:04
To: Andy@whitetoreply.co.uk
Subject: Wow man! like...Symmetry!

That's the funniest thing you've said all season - what took you so long?
Were you saving the best 'til last?

-----Original Message-----
From: Nelly@ Whitellie-phant.co.uk
Sent: 12 May 2003 10:17
To: Dave.Shack@Onon on.co.uk
Subject: Re: CarPark (Pork Pie) Picnic

Do you know what? I actually went to a Leeds match and enjoyed myself -
all day! Good company, good result despite a rotten season... Thanks toyou
and your mum for laying on the car park picnic of the season. And thanks
also to the very nice man from the AA who handed the car keys I'd left in
hanging the boot of my car into the Travelodge's reception. I wouldn't have
minded having the car nicked if we'd just won the title, but it would have
been a bit of a bummer after just scraping into 15th!

-----Original Message-----
From: Davidharveysmonkey@aol.com
Sent: 13 May 2003 20:38
To: TheWhites, all 02/03 User group
Subject: Re: Car Park (Pork Pie) Party

Great yesterday Shack - car park a top idea - but did anyone notice any of the following?
1) The Villa Elvises?
2) The Villa Gorilla which the Villa fans chanted 'One Karen Brady!' at?
3) A decent Leeds set piece, free kick I think.

-----Original Message-----
From: Nelly@whitelliphant.co.uk
Sent: 12 May 2003 14:24
To: Thewhites, all 02/03 User group
Subject: a trainspotter writes

Did you notice that at one point yesterday (26 past 4, according to my
paper), with Bolton 2-1 up a West Ham taking the lead at Birmingham - at 1-1,
we'd have been there if not for the win at Arsenal... (15 mins later Horsfield
then equalised the same minute Barmby scored for us). Thank god for Mark

235

Century Gothic | 10 | B *I* U A | lists | align | — 🖼

Viduka and an iffy offside decision at Highbury!

Nelly (in the style of Statto....)

-----Original Message-----
From: Russ @ Vivaleedspana.spa
Sent: 14 May 2003 09:51
To: Dave.Shack@On, On on
Subject: Re: Wow man! like...Symmetry!

Well it did and fuck it felt great to see the team win, and although it was not that convincing in parts, it really was a case of who fucking cares.
We were safe and so we could relax and have a good old beer and porky pie! (thanks for the spread Joyce!)
It was great to meet everyone from the next best swearer to me in the group in Tammzi, to the man who needs to ask for a pay rise (i think not) to replace his life long favourite holey shirt 'DH's monkey!
Dave, it was great to see you looking much calmer and less stressed than usual but i was a little bit dissapointed at the lack of name dropping, you know the type: "i need to get annie lennox on air" & "sorry lads can't see you at Arsenal because i am with Westlife" or "I'd rather be at the game than in Amsterdam with Will judging their pop idol".(thanks for the top pal)
I still think you need to spend a few more holidays with Jeremy though because he always seems to be super cool and who wouldn't be with a son who is nearly twice his size!!
To Dorian who looks as young as in the picture i have in my office of us lot in Barcelona clinging on to his beer!
And to the rest of you it was a pleasure in conversing and laughing and joking and swearing and taking the general piss out of each other and mainly slagging off our team!!
Final word goes out to Firhad on missing out...It must be difficult to follow a teams fortunes when you are so far away, but the enthusiam you have shown has been applaudable and i am sure when you have the ways of getting over for a game, the lads will look after you and show you a great time, i just hope the team put on a show worth while, just like all the effort put in by you into daves book, you know like a "Scum 1-0" or a Charlton 1-6 or "or especially and "Arsenal 2-3 but not under those circumstances! and of coures theres always next year.................isn't there?

-----Original Message-----
From: Wathen, Dorian, ThePeacocks
Sent: 14 May 2003 10:47
To: TheWhites, all 02/03 User group
Subject: RE: Wow man! like...Symmetry!

Many thanks to Dave for the hair-raising drive down there - "oh look there's a Leeds fan" he says taking his eyes off the road to check to see if he has that particular pennant/car sticker in his collection while driving 120mph and heading for a set of cones... thanks also to your mum for the sarnies and pies.

Good to see you all - hope we can all do more of that next season and thanks to Russ for the compliment - I have a picture of me in Barcelona too...in the attic. Don't look so young in that one ...look more like Shack.

-----Original Message-----
From: Andy@whitetoreply.co.uk
Sent: 12 May 2003 08:15
To: Dave.Shack@Ononon.co.uk
Subject: Aston Villa

Hi Dave

Cheers for the lunch yesterday. Very much appreciated and put me in the mood for dozing off after the first ten minutes. Lucky we picked up at the end and ever so glad Viduka popped one in as he looks a class apart from the rest. I think the second half was better as we stopped Gudjohnson having some very effective long range pots at goal.

Talk to you later. Andy

-----Original Message-----
From: Chris @ Noredscum.co.uk
Sent: 14 May 2003 10:41
To: TheWhites, all 02/03 user group
Subject: Re: Wow man! like...Symmetry!

Yeah - next season is going to be funny - I'll have to keep my inane ramblings pretty much to myself unless the sequels' already being planned?

-----Original Message-----
From: Shack, Dave, On on on
Sent: 14 May 2003 10:57

To: TheWhites, all 02/03 User group
Subject: RE: Wow man! like...Symmetry!

I can't stand another season - I'm gonna go to the games instead!!

-----Original Message-----
From: Shack, Dave, On on on
Sent: 15 May 2003 14:38
To: TheWhites, all 02/03 User group
Subject: Woooh, Eddie, Eddie - Eddie, Eddie, Eddie Eddie Gra-ay!
Ooh & the other bloke...

1. Bummer on Eddie. Top bloke - legend etc. But, Reid's the manager - so
we have to give him his chance. Baggage is a dangerous thing and these
guys have it - in huge Louis Vuitton sized suitcases! Revie had a clean out
when he came in - so did Wilko. Reid is what we've got and we just have
to accept that he is not a Martin O'Neil or a big manager - but we're not
the club we were that can attract that kind of big name either. There's no
point getting sentimental right now - maybe at Xmas if it's no better - but
not now.

2. Kidd - never liked that turkey really - seemed like a parasite to me.
Forget the scum thing, forget dismal failure at Blackburn, but a devout
christian seems likely to me to have a few problems with hedonistic young
men at a football club. Never a success at Leeds, so no tears from anyone
-especially after the picnic 'revelations' this weekend. Tosser - piss off to
England!

On the coaching side - a fresh approach is good for players that are stale
with a regime that's won fuck all. Fine if you're Arsenal or Scum - you
have evidence that the training works. What do the Leeds players think?
"I know better" probably & therefore they don't do it like they should. We
used to be the fittest team in the league under Wilko - now we chuck
games away in the last 10 minutes all the time.

What about discipline? Coaching should affect that - Mills, Smithy, Bakke?
C'mon we're awful.

Set -pieces? We're shite at them - that's trainers & coaches again.

Lads, it's awful for Eddie, but don't blame Reidy - respect his ambition to
make it work. You never know...

-----Original Message-----
From: Nelly @ Whitellie-phant.co.uk
Sent: 15 May 2003 12:36
To: TheWhites, all 02/03 User group
Subject: Woooh, Eddie, Eddie - Eddie, Eddie, Eddie Eddie Gra-ay! Ooh & the other bloke...

Eddie had, apparently, been expecting it and "already had his bags packed" some weeks ago. I'm gutted. He's the nicest footballer I've ever met, a terrific person to interview and a wonderful man. I've just sent him a message on behalf of you lot - my friends. A huge part of the heart of Leeds United has been cut away today. I'm gutted.

-----Original Message-----
From: Davidharveysmonkey@aol.com
Sent: 20 May 2003 20:35
To: TheWhites, all 02/03 User group
Subject: Re: Woooh, Eddie, Eddie - Eddie, Eddie, Eddie Eddie Gra-ay! Ooh & the other bloke...

Very optimistic and balanced Shacky. If you look at it from a financial perspectoive it's obvious Ridsdale had everyone on wapping big wages so no-one would complain about what he was on. Eddie is a legend and I think he's probably a better coach than Inchy Heath. The worrying thing is Reid's aken the opportunity to put together the partnership that failed him in the end at Sunderalnd. This might have been a good chance to get a good new partner in.
Funnily enough I always remember having doubles of Peter Reid in Football Cards when I was a kid. There were certain players that always came up in ever pack. I wonder if there was a kid in Bolton with hundreds of Tony Currie's?
Tomorrow I'm being filmed for Sky Soccer Years, championship season and O'Leary's first full, so that should be good. The thing is I get so tense during the games I often forget which match was which, what the score was who scored, what year it was.

-----Original Message-----
From: Wathen, Dorian, The Peacocks
Sent: 15 May 2003 12:26
To: TheWhites, all 02/03 User group
Subject: RE: Woooh, Eddie, Eddie - Eddie, Eddie, Eddie ,Eddie Gra-ay! Ooh & the other bloke...

am fucking depressed and pissed off that Eddie's got the sack - who the fuck is that wanker Adrian fucking Heath. (am competing with Tammsy and Russ...)

Courier New   10   B *I* U A   ≡ ≡ ≡ ≡   —

```
-----Original Message-----
From: Chris@Noredscum.co.uk
Sent: 15 May 2003 12:39
To: TheWhites, all 02/03 User group
Subject: Re: Woooh, Eddie, Eddie - Eddie, Edddie, Eddie Gra-
ay! Ooh & the other bloke...


I am also gutted - a true Gent in every meaning of the word -
I'm glad we managed a quick hello as he walked across the
carpark on Sunday - we now know why he was parked so far away
from the ground.

Every cloud has it's silver lining - that useless twat Brian
"11 men behind the ball at corners" Kidd is going too.
```

-----Original Message-----
From: Andy @ Whitetoreply.co.uk
Sent: 15 May 2003 12:53
To: TheWhites, all 02/03 User group
Subject: Re: Woooh, Eddie, Eddie - Eddie, Edddie, Eddie Gra-ay! Ooh & the
other bloke...

Un -bloody-believable. Why don't they just sell the team and the ground and go play
on Wortley wreck.

Good news about Brian Kidd though.

-----Original Message-----
From: Jeremy@Donsgloryears.co.uk
Sent: 15 May 2003 15:31
To: TheWhites, all 02/03 User group
Subject: Re: Woooh, Eddie, Eddie - Eddie, Edddie, Eddie Gra-ay! Ooh & the other
bloke...

I have been very fortunate to have got to know Eddie a little bit over the past few months,
and you would be hard pressed to find a nicer, more warm spirited man. He was totally
passionate and committed to the cause of Leeds United, and I feel a genuine sadness that he
will no longer be part of the club.

One interesting point - if it is a coach's role primarily to prepare footballers for football
matches, then what is one of the best perfromances in terms of attitude and commitment in
recent Leeds United times? Away to Charlton, 6-1. And who trained the players for the 10
days prior to that match? Eddie Gray, that's who. Brian Kidd was away with the England
team. Nuff said.

Times New Roman 10 B *I* U A

Thanks for everything, Eddie - you're a star and a gentleman, a true Leeds United legend.

```
-----Original Message-----
From: Chris Tams, No Red Scum
Sent: 23 May 2003 16:34
To: TheWhites, all 02/03 User group
Subject: A fitting start to the season
```

```
Apparently Leeds are playing in a tournament in Dublin 8-10th
August. Sounds like a decent weekend away to me - there's
already 12 of us going - anyone else fancy the trip?
```

-----Original Message-----
From: Shack, Dave, On on on
Sent: 25 May 2003 14:38
To: Chris @ Noredscum.co.uk
Cc: TheWhites, all 02/03 User group
Subject: A fitting start to the (next) season

Mate, sorry I can't make it - Nicky from Westlife's wedding that weekend!

Hey, I've got an idea! -

send us an email report will you....

Impact ∨ | 10 ∨ | ☰ **B** *I* U A | ☰ ☰ ⇥ ⇥ | ☰ ☰ ☰ ☰ | — 🌐 🖼

Appendix

Pre:dictions & Dreams: The Results

Back in August the e:malers made the following predictions. Here are the answers and the ones who got them right...or wrong.

1. Premiership Top 3
Answer: Man Utd, Arsenal, Liverpool
Correct: No-one. Firhad had Arsenal & Liverpool in the right positions, Russ, Jeremy & Andy had Liverpool. Prejudice had, as usual, precluded anyone from naming Man U champions.

2. FA Cup Winners
Answer: Arsenal
Correct: Nelly
Everyone else went for Leeds with only Liverpool & Newcastle mentioned.

3. Golden Boot
Answer: Ruud Van Nistelroy
Correct: Shack & Tamsy
The fact that I sold him from my The Times Fantasy League Team the day before he got his first hat-trick only makes me stronger in my resolve to not use Man U players next season. Most e:males went for Henry, but there were votes for Dubes(!) Dunno & Owen.

4. First Manager to go
Answer: Peter Reid (Sunderland - to be replaced by Wilco!)
Correct: Everyone except Jeremy, Tamsy & Dorian. Moylesy struggled with the question and asked Go where? On Holiday. Nil points!

5. First Leeds player to go
Answer: Robbie Keane (Tottenham, £7,000,000)
Correct: Only Jeremy. Nearly everyone plumped for Nigel Martyn after his public fall-out with El Tel & a large list of suitors...

6. Score vs Man City
Answer: 3-0 (Barmby, Viduka, Keane)
Correct: Everyone said we'd win, but only David Harvey's monkey got it bang on.

Elland Road E:males
Verdana   10   B *I* U A
  Appendix

7. Leeds Top Scorer for the Season
Answer: Viduka 21 (All comps)
Correct: Shack, Firhad, Dorian, DH'sM & Nelly. Alan Smith, Keane, Kewell & Fowler were the other contenders.

8. Leeds Player of the Season
Answer: Harry Kewell(not least for the winner against Man United!)
Correct: The same five as above!

9. I forgot to write one!!!
Answer: Err..there isn't one!

10. Team Vs Man City
Answer: Robinson, Mills, Radebe, Matteo, Harte, Barmby, Bakke, Bowyer, Kewell, Viduka, Smith.
Subs: Martyn, Keane, Kelly, Dacourt, Johnson.
Keane came on for Viduka, Johnson for Barmby
Correct: Nelly; 1 player wrong - Dorian, Jeremy, DH'sM & Andy; 2 players wrong, Tamsy & Russ; 3 players Shack & Moylesy; 4 Players: Firhad

Utilising a very simple points scheme of one for every correct answer & a minus for anything wrong in the team we see that the lads fared like this:

Firhad -	5 points,	minus 4	= 1
Moylesy -	0 points,	minus 3	= -1
Jeremy -	5 points,	minus 1	= 4
Tamsy -	1 point,	minus 2	= -1
DH'sM -	4 points,	minus 1	= 3
Andy -	2 points,	minus 1	= 1
Russ -	2 points,	minus 2	= 0
Dorian -	2 points,	minus 1	= 1
Nelly	4 points,	minus 0	= 4
Shack	4 points,	minus 3	= 1

So well done Nelly - as an 'insider' his team knowledge won him the accolade of e:male Know-it-all 02/03 Season, by virtue of having no minus points, over second place Jeremy & a cheque for bugger all .

Epilogue

They say that a week is a long time in politics; well, a close season is a lifetime in football!

The gap between this book finishing in May and the publication in December (wow! this even makes the record industry look quick!) has seen another book's worth of material metaphorically seeping out of the bottom of the now redundant Elland Road goldfish tank...

The Kewell saga - how to find, nurture & then throw away a world-class footballer - & his financial worth!; the invasion of the French Foreign legion (More Beau Geste & Laurel & Hardy's Sons of the Desert than an elite, international rapid reaction force!; Professor McKenzie's 'stand off' with Peter Reid - The 'Nutty' Professor takes a leaf out of his predecessor's book and goes for an 'open door' approach to running the club, unfortunately he was one side of it & the manager, the other! Finally, and far more importantly, another 'star' (sic) player arrested & detained upon allegations of (sexual) assault - or how not to learn lessons from the past Part II...

Suffice to say, if I had the stomach for it, there would be another Elland Road e:males for 2003-4, but as the stories above show, it would be the same old, same old.

2002-3 was not unique for Leeds United - we're not just another Premiership football team trying our luck at reaching for a European panacea; unfortunately we're a public domain brand that is as well known for scandal as for our raison d'être (which is playing football, by the way!) and so it's probably worth resting this format for a season or two for fear of multiple repetition: - namely, a brush (or worse) with relegation, cup failure, off-pitch scandal, management change, player departures yadda, yadda, yadda...

Yes, it's tough being a Leeds fan now. Never mind the old worries that were confined to the win, lose or draw result of a referee's final whistle; now it's as much about having acquired a worldwide reputation & association with a whole host of undesirable traits & events.

But no one element is bigger than this soon to be centurion of a club - although my heart trembles at how we might plan to celebrate that particular milestone! But, it's always about the future - it can never just be about the current squad, manager, board or striker, it has to be about the name, the place and the ethos.

To Yorkshire folk and beyond, Leeds United with all our help, guidance & support will be again at the vanguard of Yorkshire sport. After all, one of the greatest songs of all would be nowhere if we didn't have our Ups & Downs (Ups & Downs!) now would it?

On, on, on.
Dave Shack, London October 2003

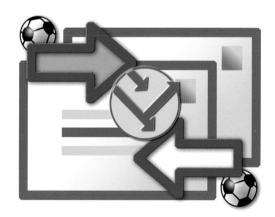